CATHERINE BRAMWELL-BOOTH

CATHERINE BRAMWELL-BOOTH

By Mary Batchelor

A LION BOOK

Tring · Batavia · Sydney

Copyright © 1986 Catherine Bramwell-Booth and Mary Batchelor

Published by
Lion Publishing plc
Icknield Way, Tring, Herts, England
ISBN 0 7459 1027 0
Lion Publishing Corporation
1705 Hubbard Avenue, Batavia, Illinois 60510, USA
ISBN 0 7459 1027 0
Albatross Books Pty Ltd
PO Box 320, Sutherland, NSW 2232, Australia
ISBN 0 86760 825 0

First edition 1986

All photographs by courtesy of The Salvation Army

British Library Cataloguing in Publication Data
Batchelor, Mary
  Catherine Bramwell-Booth.
  1. Bramwell-Booth, Catherine
  2. Salvationists—Great Britain—
  Biography
  I. Title
  267'.15'0924   BX9743.B84/
  ISBN 0 7459 1027 0

Printed in Great Britain
by Richard Clay (The Chaucer Press) Ltd, Bungay, Suffolk

CONTENTS

AUTHOR'S INTRODUCTION

This book tells the story of Catherine Bramwell-Booth, but it cannot claim to tell the whole story. In every human life there is much that remains personal and private. That is especially true of Catherine Bramwell-Booth. She always kept her deep feelings under firm control, and particularly so in the unhappy events which took place during the last painful months of her father's life. With the passage of time, more of her personality and circumstances may be made plain. There are also gaps in some of the details of her Salvation Army career: a number of records were destroyed when the International Headquarters of the Army was bombed during the Second World War.

The main sources for the material for this book have been Catherine Bramwell-Booth's own writings, and the memories of members of the family and of one-time Salvation Army colleagues. These reminiscences have been recorded in the informal conversational language in which they were given. I am deeply indebted to Colonel Olive Booth and Major Dora Booth, Commissioner Catherine's two remaining sisters, for the wealth of family background and incidents that they have provided. They have given unstinting help and kindness in entertaining me at their home at North Court and talking to me freely. They also answered numerous telephone queries and lent me precious letters and documents.

It was also a great pleasure to meet so many retired Salvation Army officers who had worked with and for the Commissioner and who shared with me vivid recollections of Army life at that time, as well as personal memories of Catherine herself. Their courtesy and kindness in talking to me has been unfailing.

At Salvation Army headquarters, Captain Rob Garrad, Director of Information Services, has been on hand from the outset to guide and help. From him I first learned to appreciate the Army's promptness, efficiency and humour, which has been shown to me throughout the project. I am equally indebted to Major Jenty Fairbank, The Salvation Army archivist, who not only gave me opportunity to research in her library but also generously offered me valuable material she herself had collected. Both Major Fairbank and Captain Garrad further helped by checking the manuscript for accuracy on Army matters.

I am also most grateful to those who have known and interviewed Catherine Bramwell-Booth on television and were willing to share their impressions of her with me by letter, on the telephone, or face to face. Malcolm Muggeridge also generously volunteered to contribute a foreword to this book.

Catherine Bramwell-Booth's wisdom, humour and joy in living have made an enormous impression on me as I have read her books and talked to her family and friends. I hope that some of this zest for life and love for God, which so characterize her life, break through the printed page to the reader.

Although I cannot mention each one by name, I am deeply grateful to all those who have helped in so many ways with this book, especially, from The Salvation Army, the late General Frederick Coutts, Commissioner Fred Hammond (R), Mrs Commissioner Olive Holbrook (R), Colonel Mabel Lindsay (R), Brigadier Minnie Zugg (R); and, from the media, Ted Harrison, Russell Harty, Malcolm Muggeridge, Michael Parkinson.

MARY BATCHELOR

THE FAMILY TREE*

WILLIAM BOOTH married **CATHERINE MUMFORD**
(1829–1912)   (1829–90)

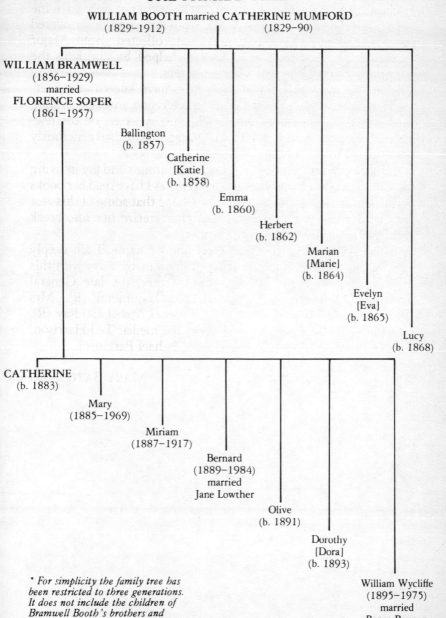

WILLIAM BRAMWELL
(1856–1929)
married
FLORENCE SOPER
(1861–1957)

Ballington
(b. 1857)

Catherine
[Katie]
(b. 1858)

Emma
(b. 1860)

Herbert
(b. 1862)

Marian
[Marie]
(b. 1864)

Evelyn
[Eva]
(b. 1865)

Lucy
(b. 1868)

CATHERINE
(b. 1883)

Mary
(1885–1969)

Miriam
(1887–1917)

Bernard
(1889–1984)
married
Jane Lowther

Olive
(b. 1891)

Dorothy
[Dora]
(b. 1893)

William Wycliffe
(1895–1975)
married
Renee Reynon

** For simplicity the family tree has
been restricted to three generations.
It does not include the children of
Bramwell Booth's brothers and
sisters, or of Catherine's brothers.*

FOREWORD

Anyone who has made the acquaintance of Commissioner Bramwell-Booth of The Salvation Army will assuredly remember the occasion. She is a truly remarkable lady.

I first met Commissioner Catherine in person when I was editor of *Punch*, years ago now. On that occasion she wore her smart uniform and bonnet. Born into The Salvation Army, she remained a faithful trooper. Subsequently, we exchanged an occasional letter; one of hers in her firm, clear handwriting I have treasured. It begins:

'In the hope that you enjoy some leisure and that you may care to dip into it, I send to you the book I have written about my grandmother. In a strangely vivid manner I believe that you may understand her and that perhaps she may have a word to say to you . . .'

Then came the Commissioner's 100th birthday, with congratulations from the Queen downwards; I had the honour of interviewing her for the BBC in the house where she and her two sisters resided. What struck me most forcibly in our dialogue was her wonderful candour. Thus, for instance, when I spoke of being well content to move on from my earthly existence to the heavenly future awaiting us she strongly disagreed, insisting that despite everything mortality was well worth while at any age, and she hoped to continue in that state for some time yet. Heaven no doubt has much to recommend it, but there was no need to expedite getting there.

So robust a view of life at her age and in her circumstances is quite remarkable, and her biographer, Mary Batchelor, does full justice to it. Thus she sees in her subject, Commissioner Catherine, a truly devout Christian, honest to the point of admitting contradictory stances.

For me the particular fascination of Mary Batchelor's biography of Commissioner Catherine is indeed her subject's poignant doubting. Mary Batchelor quotes her as saying that one way or another she has been tormented by doubt. For relief she turned to the Bible, thereby drawing close to Jesus whom she claims as her saviour.

Then from the Scripture she gets the answer to her agony of doubt. Thinking of her doubting anguish I recall some lines of John Donne which might have helped her at the time:

> Doubt wisely; in strange way
> To stand inquiring right is not to stray;
> To sleep or run wrong is. On a huge hill
> Cragged and steep, Truth stands, and he that will
> Reach her, about must and about must go,
> And what the hill's suddenness resists, win so.

She also recognized the reality of the Devil. Catherine wrote of her grandmother: 'From a child she had been as it were on speaking terms with the Devil. Strange as it may seem to some, I am convinced that her belief in the Devil, and familiarity with his ways, strengthened the loving, believing submission of her spirit to God as she went down to death.' Mary Batchelor adds this comment: 'Like her grandmother—and a long line of Christians stretching from the Desert Fathers, through Martin Luther, to C.S. Lewis in the twentieth century—Catherine believed firmly in the reality of the Devil and considered him a necessary adjunct to faith in God.'

Commissioner Catherine remains an inexhaustible subject—a great Christian on her own terms; a great pilgrim going through many of John Bunyan's hazards. Surely she will reach the Celestial City, with all the trumpets sounding for her.

MALCOLM MUGGERIDGE

PROLOGUE

'And Who are You?'

'Ladies and gentlemen,' Russell Harty announced with a flourish, 'will you please welcome in ascending order of both age and rank, Major Dora Booth, aged eighty-nine, Lt. Colonel Olive Booth, aged ninety-one, and Commissioner Catherine Bramwell-Booth CBE, who will be one hundred years old this July!'

To polite applause the diminutive and cheerful figure of Major Dora walked on. She waved, then made way for her sister to follow. Colonel Olive stood tall and dignified, waving gently to the unseen audience below. A pause—then Commissioner Catherine appeared. She moved to the front of the stage and, with a smile that seemed to embrace everyone in its warmth, waved enthusiastically with *both* hands.

Polite clapping gave way to rapturous applause. She had won the hearts of the television chat-show audience without speaking a word.

There was a little shuffling and shifting of chairs before the three sisters, correct in their poke bonnets and plain navy blue Salvation Army uniforms, were sitting upright, ready for their host's questions.

'Are you comfortable?' Russell Harty asked. 'Now then, you are . . .?' But he got no further. With an air of earnest but innocent curiosity Catherine leaned forward and asked, 'And who are you?'

It brought the house down. This rather formidable old lady, whose life, the audience assumed, had been spent in some pious backwater, had upstaged Harty as successfully as she had Michael Parkinson on *The Parkinson Show* a few years earlier.

When the interview ended, to the strains of a Salvation Army band, the Commissioner walked to the green room on Harty's arm.

'It worked, didn't it?' she asked in confidential tones but with evident satisfaction.

Catherine Bramwell-Booth was no beginner in the art of handling an audience. For eighty years she had been capturing the attention of passers-by at street corners, galvanizing a sleepy congregation into action, or quietening a rowdy one into attentiveness —making audiences eat out of her hand wherever she preached.

She was born in 1883, into a Victorian London of horse-drawn cabs, gas-lit streets and pea-soup fogs. In that year, Robert Louis Stevenson's *Treasure Island* was published, the first skyscraper in the world challenged the Chicago skyline, and the Orient Express made its first exotic journey.

Catherine was born a Booth, eldest grandchild of the fiery founder of The Salvation Army and eldest daughter of Bramwell Booth, the Army's second-in-command. These were days of adventure and danger for the Army, when members of the established church and unbelievers alike attacked the rapidly expanding mission with hard words—and sometimes with sticks and stones. But although her parents faced unceasing work and countless problems, Catherine's arrival was greeted with much joy. There was happiness, laughter and a great deal of love in the little house in London's Castlewood Road. In fact, it is doubtful if Catherine experienced a single dull moment in the whole of her life, from the day she was born until the nationwide celebration of her birthday one hundred years later.

CHAPTER 1

The New Baby

IT WAS SUMMER 1883 and Mrs Catherine Booth, wife of the founder of The Salvation Army, and a famous preacher and leader in her own right, was highly delighted. She had become a grandmama for the first time.

She was delighted but scarcely surprised. When her eldest son, Bramwell, had married Florence Soper ten months earlier, it was assumed that a family would soon follow. Mrs Booth had herself bought the young couple a mahogany dining-table with many leaves, to allow for a growing family, and with rounded ends, telling Florence—'no corners for the babies to knock their heads on.' The fact that the new arrival was a daughter, not a son and heir, caused surprisingly few regrets. The Salvation Army was unique in allowing a woman all the opportunities that a man enjoyed. She could preach, hold senior appointments and be in charge of a local corps, or church. The Booths had no doubt that the baby would grow up to devote herself to the Army, as the rest of the family had done.

Mrs Booth wrote posthaste to her daughter Catherine (Katie), who was leading Salvation Army work in France, and described the new baby:

'She seems to be the image of her father, of which Florence says she is very glad. It is a dear little duck, just a lovable baby, and is to be called Catherine.'

General Booth had chosen the name himself—and he retained the casting vote on the names of the six other children that followed in due course. When he had gazed at the baby in its muslin-covered cradle, he had pronounced a clear resemblance to his dear wife. The baby should be another Catherine.

Florence wrote later, 'We called her Catherine, after her grandmother—she thus became Catherine III of the Booth family.'

On 28 July, The Salvation Army publication, *The War Cry*,

carried the following notice in the column headed 'Coming Events':

'The Come Event: Mrs Bramwell Booth presented the Chief of Staff with a daughter on Friday, the 20th July. Mother and child are doing well.'

The Salvation Army does not practise baptism, either infant or adult, but a special service is arranged, normally at the local corps, when the baby is brought by his parents to be dedicated to God. Catherine's dedication service took place in October, when she was three months old. Since she was a Booth, and anything connected with the Booths was of absorbing interest to the whole Salvation Army, the chosen venue was large and central.

Exeter Hall, which belonged to the YMCA, held 4,000 people. The owners had not always been ready to let it to The Salvation Army, who had a dubious reputation in church circles. But Samuel Morley, a wealthy member of Parliament who was a trustee of the hall, was also a friend of The Salvation Army and had intervened on their behalf. The hall was hired for the whole day on Monday 22 October and three meetings were held. The programme was advertised to include a package of celebrations, as 'Coming Events' in *The War Cry* set out:

Great Thanksgiving

Exeter Hall — Monday 22 October 11.00, 2.30 and 6.30
Miss Booth will speak on The Army's Victories
and Prospects in Switzerland.
THE GENERAL will preside and
MRS BOOTH will speak during the day.
The Chief of Staff's child will be
Presented to the Lord on this occasion.
Admission by ticket only.

The Chief of Staff was the title given to Catherine's father, Bramwell, and Miss Booth was his sister, Katie. So when at the third and last of the day's meetings baby Catherine was carried to the front of the hall, all three Catherines of the Booth family were present. The youngest of them seemed to know even at this age how to respond to a large audience. *The War Cry* reported a week or two later:

'The infant daughter of the Chief of Staff was brought in its mother's arms to the platform for the purpose of being dedicated to God and the work of The Salvation Army.

'The bright little baby gazed around the strange scene with perfect composure and with an amusing air of interest in the whole proceedings. It never cried and even when the volleys[1] rose lustily from the cadets in the rear they awakened no distressful response from the infant, who at that time was pillowing its cheek in the General's beard. Mrs Booth, who appeared for the first time in public as a "grandmama" never rose to address an audience with greater self-command than her son's baby underwent the ordeal of its dedication service.'

Three days after the service, *The Daily Telegraph* carried a full report of the whole lengthy proceedings. The General began by saying:

'Now it is the principle of The Salvation Army that everything we have or possess belongs to God . . . This father and mother . . . bring the dearest, choicest treasure with which God has entrusted them, and offer this dear precious child up to him.'

Then the General asked his son:

' "Are you willing that this dear child of yours should be thus consecrated to God, and will you engage to train it for his service?"

'Mr Bramwell Booth replied:

' "My dear General and my dear friends, I am willing that my dear child should thus be given up to Him and His service, and I do this night desire to consecrate it to His Word and The Salvation Army . . ."

'General Booth, addressing himself to his daughter-in-law, then said:

' "Are you willing, my dear girl, that your child shall be consecrated to the service of the living God after the fashion I have described, and will you join with your dear husband in keeping from it everything in the shape of strong drink, or tobacco, or finery or wealth, or hurtful reading or dangerous acquaintance, or any other thing that would be likely to interfere with the effect of such training and such education?"

'The lady replied, "Yes, I promise with joy to train it for

[1] Of Hallelujahs!

17

The Salvation Army and God alone, and to do my very utmost to make her understand from the very commencement that that is the life she should share, and that that will be sufficient for her.''

'Upon this General Booth handed the infant back to its mother, and pronounced,

' ''Then, my dear children, in the name of The Salvation Army, in the name of the God of The Salvation Army, I take this child and present it to Him . . . I take the child for Him and I receive it for The Salvation Army; and I pray, and your comrades here, I am sure pray, that Catherine Booth Booth may be a true saint, a real servant and a bold and courageous soldier in The Salvation Army, having grace not only to make her own title and election sure, but to secure for a great number of other people rescue from misery and sorrow here and everlasting death hereafter.

' ''Take it, mother, take it. The father will help you to train it for God and The Salvation Army. Let us pray.'' '

But that was not the end. *The Daily Telegraph* informed its readers that Mrs Booth also offered prayers and that 'prayers, hymns and addresses followed, and the congregation, most of whom wore the badges of the Army, joined heartily in the proceedings'.

The child, so frequently referred to as 'it', was named Catherine *Booth* Booth out of deference to the General. His own daughters had been obliged to change their names—and those of the men they were to marry—by deed poll, in order to retain the name of Booth. Thus his daughter Emma, who married Frederick Tucker, became Mrs Booth-Tucker and Lucy, who married Emanuel Helberg, became Mrs Booth-Helberg. When Bramwell's daughters were born, William made provision for any future loss of Booth as a surname by expressing the view that 'for the interests of the Kingdom I should have Booth in'. It is ironic that none of them married, so none had occasion to use the additional 'Booth' in her name.

The birth of her first baby had a profoundly happy effect on Florence, who was not yet twenty-two. Later she wrote:

'When the eldest was born, I experienced something akin to a new birth myself. I became another woman. What a seal this little creature set upon our union, increasing our love for one another as our hearts were enlarged in love for her.'

She had admitted to the privacy of her diary that the months between her marriage and the birth of the baby had been the loneliest of her life. Almost every waking moment of her new husband's life was absorbed by Salvation Army business. More time was spent with the General and 'dear Mama' at their house at 114, Clapton Common, than in the new little home in Castlewood Road nearby.

Florence Soper was the eldest daughter of a West country doctor, whose practice was in the little Welsh mining village of Blaina, near Ebbw Vale. Their house was on the outskirts of the village and attached to its own home farm, with land which stretched across the hillside nearby. The children led a happy, carefree life. Even though at ten Florence was sent away to school when her mother died, she still ran wild during the holidays at home, where the four children rode their Welsh ponies and explored the countryside around.

Dr Soper had decided views as to how his daughters should be brought up as *The Deliverer*, a Salvation Army publication, described in May 1899:

'Her father, a medical man, brought up his children with the utmost disregard for the fanciful notions of present-day ladyism, and while insisting upon their education after the best models, included in it all that was needed to make a woman at home in her kitchen as well as at the piano, and in the sick-chamber as well as in the drawing-room.'

Her own daughter wrote, 'At eighteen she was beginning to be rather a rebel, looked scornfully out on women's life of that day, professed she disliked children, thought of taking to painting as a career.' (*Bramwell Booth*) But something happened to change the course of her life.

One day, as she came into a room, a friend hastily put down the magazine she was reading and surreptitiously put it out of sight. As soon as she had the chance, Florence retrieved the magazine to discover its guilty secret. The magazine itself, called *The Christian*, was certainly beyond reproach but she soon found the offending article. It was on the subject of that shameful new organization, The Salvation Army. The writer did praise the work that was being done but expressed grave concern over the methods used. As an example, the words of one of their unseemly songs was quoted:

The devil and me we can't agree
I hate him and he hates me.

Florence thought that this was by far the most sensible hymn that she had heard for a long time and determined to look into the whole matter further.

The Salvation Army had been formed barely two years before the appearance of this article, although its predecessor, The Christian Mission, had been founded in 1865 by William and Catherine Booth, when they broke away from the restrictions placed upon them by the Methodist New Connexion of which William was an ordained minister. Mrs Booth, as well as her husband, preached up and down the land and her meetings caused enough sensation to draw crowds from every social group to hear her. Florence, still at school, was taken with a group of older pupils to hear Mrs Booth preach in the West End of London. She wrote in her diary afterwards:

'As I took my seat at the back of the Hall I was conscious only of curiosity to hear a woman preach, and had no anticipation of anything that would specially interest me. Mrs Booth held my attention from the moment that she stepped on to the platform. The words of the hymn also struck me. They were quite new, and reading each verse arrested my thoughts. ''Lovers of pleasure more than God'' was the opening song, and the second, ''Time is earnest passing by'', which Mrs Booth herself gave out, made me feel she had specially intended me to hear it. The absurdity of thinking that she could know anything at all about me never occurred to me, for the feeling possessed me from that moment that she was addressing her words to me.

'As she spoke of Christ's last words to his followers, ''Ye shall be My witnesses'', a new vision of life came to me. Religion had always been impressed upon me as something of which I stood in need—a way of safety for which I must pay the price by renouncing the things that interested me most; but as a life of joyful service to someone we loved, as a vocation worthy of sacrifice and devotion it had never been presented . . .

'It did not seem long before she ceased speaking and asked that those who had received blessing during the series of meetings (it was the last) should give expression in testimony, urging those who had never so voiced their feelings to do so.

'From all parts members of the congregation rose, telling of their love of Christ and desire to serve Him better. I felt that if I remained silent I should pass under false colours. I found myself on my feet, saying with much trembling that I had never before understood what serving Christ meant, but that I wished to give myself to Jesus, and would Mrs Booth pray for me. She said some kind words in response, but our party immediately rose and we all left.

'I came home and at early morning, after thinking it all over, I knelt and gave myself to God; and rested for pardon and purity on the blood of Christ alone. I am His for ever. I felt I must serve God with all my powers—everything else seemed empty and cold, even my old idols, painting and music.'

She wrote to her father, telling him of her experience, and was met by a whirlwind of hostility. Dr Soper might be unconventional by some middle-class standards of the time, but he was horrified at the thought of his daughter taking up with those 'unspeakably vulgar' people in The Salvation Army, as he described them in an outburst to his sister-in-law. For it was not only in the pages of *The Christian* that the Army was criticized. Many churchgoers were shocked and angered by the new movement. Anglicans were accustomed to well-bred clergy who were Oxford or Cambridge educated but William recognized no requirements of education and allowed women as well as men to preach. Any Tom, Dick or Harry could stand up at the street corner and preach, provided he had experienced 'conversion', even though he might be—and sometimes was—a prize fighter or a chimney sweep.

The Army's methods grated on the well-brought-up churchgoer too. In the established church, good taste was the hallmark of worship and that was scarcely compatible with Army marches and bands and the new kind of informal hymn set to the rousing tune of a popular song. William Booth might encourage his officers to tell a man, once converted, to beat the drum and not his wife, but to many middle-class devout churchgoers, the whole noisy business was distasteful, even blasphemous. In 1882, it is true, there were some friendly overtures and 'talks about talks' between the

21

Church of England and The Salvation Army, but they quickly petered out and only a year later the Bishop of Oxford, speaking in Convocation, was hinting outrageously that he had reason to believe that 'this Salvation Army . . . promotes not holiness but immorality to a great degree'.

The fashionable world disapproved of The Salvation Army too. One magazine article in *Pick-Me-Up*, in 1895, complained:

'Last Sunday afternoon no less than six discordant bands brayed past my study window, some on their way, I presume, to a demonstration in Hyde Park, others to advertise The Salvation Army. It is bad enough that London on the Sabbath should be transformed into a wilderness. That it should be a howling wilderness is still worse.'

Punch fully agreed and, under the heading 'Bootheration' wrote:

'If the maxim of "Keep yourselves to yourselves, and don't say nothing to nobody," were accepted upon by all these so-called, or self-styled, Religious Bodies, how much happier we should all be . . . Don't let the different parties parade the streets, and come out and disturb good folks who, unable to forego their absolutely necessary work even on Sunday, are compelled to remain at home and to find their religious service in the practical maxim *Laborare est orare*; . . . Liberty for all, but don't make too free with Liberty.'

It is not surprising that Dr Soper was horrified by Florence's new enthusiasm but his storm of protest merely confirmed her determination to throw in her lot with the despised Army.

'The effect of his letter on my own mind,' Florence said, 'was to bring me the conviction that these people were to be my people and their God my God; that for me to be ashamed of them would be equivalent to being ashamed of my Saviour.

'A day or two later I saw in *The Christian* a notice from Mrs Booth that she sought as companion for her daughter a young lady who could speak French and was free to accompany her to France. I wrote to Mrs Booth telling her of her help to me in the Steinway Hall and that I longed to give up my life to God's service. A postcard came in reply asking me to call at 114, Clapton Common.'

As Florence arrived for the interview and was being ushered into the hall, a young man hurried past her on his way out. He was William Bramwell Booth, the eldest of William Booth's eight children. In spite of his haste he found time to glance back at the girl who was waiting to see his mother and to appreciate the way the blue cornflowers in her hat matched the deep blue of her eyes. The memory of her flashed through his mind during the day's hectic round of Army business—'unusual for me', he admitted. When he arrived home that evening he asked her name.

Meanwhile Florence Soper had made her mark on Mrs Booth too. She was duly appointed to accompany Katie and plans were set in motion for the expedition to France. But when Dr Soper was applied to he would not entertain the idea. As a churchgoer he disapproved of the Army, but he may have had other reasons for refusing permission. He probably feared for his daughter's safety. Wherever The Salvation Army went, at home and abroad, there was trouble. Their marches were peaceful—though noisy—but they attracted plenty of sticks and stones and on a number of occasions the Riot Act had to be read before order was restored. So-called skeleton armies were drummed up in many English towns to attack them and 'during 1882 alone six hundred and sixty-nine Salvation Army soldiers—two hundred and fifty-one of them women and twenty-three under fifteen years of age—were assaulted.' (*No Discharge in This War*) Some died from injuries received and others were sent to prison. Local magistrates were often also the local publicans whose pubs had been half-emptied when Salvation Army converts renounced drink, and they saw to it that Salvationists had a hard time of it when they appeared before the bench for marching through the town and causing 'obstruction'.

In February of 1881 a notice was put up in Salisbury to advertise the formation of a new society. It began:

'We have endured for a considerable time the noise and nuisance caused and created by the proceedings of The Salvation Army, through their perambulating the streets of our city . . . That patience has been exercised in vain.' The new society, they stated, would 'cause to be forcibly broken the ranks of The Salvation Army when in procession through the streets and they will use every means in their power TO STOP AND RESIST THOSE PROCESSIONS FROM DOING SO'. The implications of force and violence are scarcely veiled.

Dr Soper may have guessed that Paris would not be easier or safer to convert than the south of England.

'There seemed no hope of obtaining my father's consent to my going to Paris,' Florence wrote. 'In desperation I asked Miss Booth to come for a visit. We always had liberty to invite our friends, and my step-mother aided my plot. The impossible was accomplished and my father won over.' Florence was granted permission to go for a limited period but forbidden to preach. Her father hoped that one dose of this Army nonsense might cure her once and for all.

The four young girls who arrived in Paris to begin Salvation Army work were given a very bad time indeed. Florence and one of the other officers made sandwich boards advertising the meetings and walked up and down the boulevards 'causing immense astonishment among the passers-by'. Matters were not helped when Katie innocently named their broadsheet *Amour*. There were a good many ribald comments when the young English girls appeared on the streets shouting 'Amour! Un sou!' But the meetings were packed out, mostly with men. Florence described the scene:

'The disorder in the meetings increased. When we started singing, the crowd of hooligans—we had very few women in the meetings—would use their own words, laughing uproariously. The song for the prayer meeting with the chorus, ''Approchez-vous'' was turned by them into ''Embrassez-vous''.

'Samuel Stitt, a young lieutenant from England, was sent to help us keep order. His hair was red and caused much fun, our roughs pretending to light their cigars by it. He was terribly knocked about by them, but had wonderful patience.'

In July Florence returned home, in obedience to her father's orders, but asked his permission to go back to Paris and continue the work they had begun. Again the answer was no and again Katie intervened. On 12 September Florence wrote in her diary:

'My birthday. Miss Booth comes down to Blaina. I cannot express my thankfulness to God.'

The stratagem worked and two days later the diary stated:

'She has won and the poor dear father has given his consent until Christmas.'

Together Katie and Florence returned to France. It was here that Bramwell came to find them.

24

CHAPTER 2

'The Greatest Surprise'

WILLIAM BRAMWELL BOOTH was a child of nine when
William and Catherine Booth found their vocation in
London's East End. They had parted company with the Methodist
New Connexion at first in order to practise a travelling evangel-
ism, after the pattern of their hero and great forerunner, John
Wesley. But one night, after he had preached outside *The Blind
Beggar* public house in Whitechapel, William returned home and
told his wife:

'As I passed the flaming gin-palaces tonight, I seemed to hear a
voice sounding in my ears, ''Where can you go and find heathen
such as these?''... I feel I ought, at every cost, to stop and preach
to these East End multitudes.'

The label 'East End' was itself new and most middle-class
Victorian Londoners were scarcely aware that such an area
existed. But within a few years others were to expose its horrors. In
Mean Streets a contemporary, Arthur Morrison, described it as
'an evil plexus of slums that hide human creeping things; where
filthy men and women live on penn'orths of gin'. Another writer,
Will Crooks, commented bitterly that the same sun which never
set on the Empire never rose on the dark alleys of East London. But
most ordinary citizens neither knew nor cared about conditions in
the unending slums of East London, nor the catalogue of dirt,
disease, hunger, poverty, drunkenness and crime that plagued its
inhabitants.

These people never went inside a church, so Booth and his
helpers went to where they were, on the street corners and in the
public houses. All kinds of buildings were pressed into use for
services, among them a music hall, a skittle alley, a wool shed
and a dance hall. Booth recognized that 'no one gets a blessing
if they have cold feet and nobody ever got saved while they
had toothache,' and determined to meet physical as well as spiritual needs—although he rejected the completely free hand-out

wherever possible. Another Salvationist put it rather more pompously when she said, 'While the chief aim of The Christian Mission is to bring sinners to Jesus, we feel it a duty and a privilege to minister to the bodily wants of the necessitous.'

Catherine Booth needed great courage and faith to support her husband in his new venture. She had six small children and another soon to be born. There would be no regular income and little prospect of voluntary support in such work. But she embraced her husband's vocation wholeheartedly and so, before he was much older, did the eldest son, Bramwell. As he grew up his own deep desire was to study medicine, but his parents believed that God was calling him to the work of the Mission and Bramwell accepted their decision. He cared for his brothers and sisters while his parents were away preaching and became more and more involved in the day-to-day running of the work. He was entrusted with many of the business responsibilities of The Christian Mission when he was only sixteen and soon became answerable for providing the money for the ever-increasing number of new projects.

In 1878 The Christian Mission became The Salvation Army, with a simplified constitution and William Booth as its General with over-all power. Bramwell became his Chief of Staff. The uniform, the motto 'Blood and Fire' and the whole military concept of The Salvation Army do not match today's popular thinking but in 1878 the British fleet was lying in readiness to sail to Constantinople against the Turks. This was the year of the music hall song,

We don't want to fight, but by Jingo, if we do,
We've got the ships, we've got the men, we've got the
money too.

Great Britain was also still engaged in annexing territories overseas to add to the empire. A Christian movement dedicated to conquering the forces of evil and winning Satan's territories for Christ fired the enthusiasm of existing members and new converts alike.

The new Salvation Army grew by leaps and bounds. Army historian General Frederick Coutts writes:

'For every Christian Mission station in Britain in 1878, there were twenty Salvation Army corps in 1886. For every evangelist in 1878, there were twenty-five commissioned officers in 1886. For the year ended September 30th, 1878, the Mission's overall expenses came to £4,362. For the year ended September 30th, 1885, the audited balance sheet recorded an expenditure of £75,999 12s. 3½d. Half-pennies were still scrupulously counted!' (*No Discharge in This War*)

All this increase meant an increasing load of work for Bramwell. To make matters worse, his health was far from robust and he suffered from deafness.

His mother felt sure that marriage to the right woman would halve Bramwell's problems. In 1878 she wrote to him:

'All you want now is a wife, one with you in soul . . . God will find you one, and I shall help Him . . . I am praying for one for you.'

Three years later Bramwell was sure that he had found her. His first encounter with the young lady with cornflowers in her hat had developed into first-hand acquaintance. He was soon convinced that he loved Florence and wanted to marry her. He carefully weighed all the reasons why he should *not* ask her to marry him. But after six months of prayer and consideration, he crossed to Paris to try his suit.

'I plainly stated my feelings, carefully described something of my experiences during the previous six months, and asked her to be my wife. I felt bound to dwell rather fully on the probable hardships and uncertainties of my future, including the simple style of living I should have to adopt . . .'

Florence was flabbergasted by his proposal. She wrote:

'I had never looked upon Mr Bramwell Booth as an ordinary mortal, which indeed he was not. Such an idea as his ever wanting to marry had never occurred to me and no word or look from him had ever suggested to me anything of the kind in connection with me . . . When he made the revelation that he had chosen me . . . I had the greatest surprise of my life . . .

'I listened to him without making any remark. I remember my heart began to beat violently and I was conscious that my view of him had radically changed. He had always seemed to me to be on a platform of holiness . . . infinitely above me, like some angelic being, but in those few moments he became human . . .

'When at last I was compelled to speak I rose and went close to him and while speaking took hold of a button of his coat, which

27

button I found wrapped in white paper in his breast pocket some months after we were married.'

Without anything definite being said, it was clear to both that provided Dr Soper gave his consent she would become his wife. Not surprisingly, Dr Soper refused. Months of uncertainty followed with letters passing and visits made. Eventually Dr Soper agreed to Florence's marrying Bramwell once she was twenty-one. He could scarcely have stopped her doing so then, as he must have realized. But he positively refused to attend the wedding.

Bramwell still fretted over the future he was asking Florence to share. Only a month before the wedding he wrote to her:

'I have been very down the last day or two and am far from as well as usual. I had so hoped and wanted to be better when we were married . . . Just now we are very worried and very tired and I have only the prospect of beginning with you full of cares and anxieties . . . I have never fairly got over the feeling that I am not doing very kindly by you to bring you into such a whirl . . .

'All my love for you makes me long to make you happy and save you from the sort of worry and care which is so killing and in which more or less our lives are lived . . .'

Florence replied, urging the need to share their worries and commented:

'Your letter really sounds as if you did not expect me to be of the least help or even much comfort, but a sort of creature to be taken care of, looked at, wrapped up and put by in a glass case until you have leisure from business to play with it—whenever in the dim future that might be!

'I will not come at all to be such an one, indeed I am sure you could not make me such . . .'

The wedding date was fixed for 12 October 1882. Florence had hoped for a quiet ceremony but the General had other ideas and Florence conceded, not through lack of spirit but out of conviction that Bramwell's parents must be right. She wrote to Bramwell:

'My dear Love, I am very sorry we cannot be married quietly, but, of course, the General and Mrs Booth know best and I shall be best pleased if they are pleased.'

In spite of a packed programme of preaching, Mrs Booth found time to shop for the young couple. As well as purchasing the mahogany dining-table—which she bought at bargain price, because it had been rejected by the purchaser for whom it was custom-built—she advised on the buying of the matrimonial bed. It must be what would today be called 'kingsize'—long enough to accommodate Bramwell in comfort with room 'to stretch in'— and properly sprung on both sides in order to give each partner maximum comfort. She also gave orders for all mirrors to be removed from the wardrobes before they were taken to the new home. There must be nothing 'showy' in a Salvationist household.

Bramwell continued as busy as ever. The proposed month's honeymoon was to be reduced to a fortnight and even Florence's request for an hour with her future husband on the day before the wedding was met with the written response:

'Dearest, It is impossible. You can have no conception of the amount of work to be done . . . I am only a servant of servants and that means perpetual service. And yet I am conscious that it is not fair to you. Precious Creature, don't try to reckon how much I love you, you don't know.' And with that Florence had to be content.

Dr Soper's forebodings about the forthcoming link with The Salvation Army persisted. Florence described in a letter to Bramwell the kind of small incident that added fuel to the fire:

'I had just been chatting very happily with Papa when someone comes in with the June 28th number of *The World*, a horrid paper, and containing under the title of "Celebrities at Home" a page on the General. Papa read it, and then with a great sigh said, "Oh, dear! Well it is very unfortunate for me." I asked what? "Why, your connection with it"; and not another word could I get from him, and I suppose he will be melancholy for the rest of the day.' (*Bramwell Booth*)

Nonetheless, Dr Soper decided to change his mind and attend the wedding. What happened must have confirmed his worst fears.

A triumphantly noisy Salvation Army brass band marched down Linscott Road in Clapton, London, to meet the bridal couple, and led the wedding procession to the new Salvation Army Congress Hall. In 1881 the Army had purchased the London Orphanage Asylum in Clapton and by roofing over the huge open quadrangle, had provided a Congress Hall capable of seating 6,000. This was the venue for the wedding ceremony. Stewards were stationed at the doors, not to show visitors to their seats, but to collect admission money. The General was seizing the chance to pay off the debt owing on *The Eagle Tavern* in City Road, another purchase made that year. *The Eagle*—still remembered from the nursery rhyme, *Pop Goes the Weasel*—was described by Mrs Booth as 'that notorious hell-trap'. She rejoiced to see its whole complex of pleasure grounds, Moorish pavilion and 'commodious liquor shop', with six entrances and five compartments, claimed for Salvationist use.

The Daily Chronicle, reporting the wedding, commented:

'There are many ways, it is true, of raising money, and perhaps to General Booth is due the initiative in showing that even a marriage can be made profitable to the cause of religion. Excepting officers and leaders, nearly six thousand persons who filled the Congress Hall yesterday on the occasion of the marriage celebration, paid for admission, at the rate of a shilling a head. The funds so raised, together with the offertory, are destined to help in the liquidation of the balance of £8,000 that still remains unsettled in connection with the purchase for Salvation purposes of the Grecian Theatre and Eagle Tavern, in the City Road.'

Florence said afterwards that she remembered little of the service. She was conscious of seeing her father but of little else. Both she and Bramwell were plainly dressed in Salvation Army uniform. But one of her new sisters wrote afterwards, 'Both of you standing up on Thursday morning forms an unfading picture . . . You both looked so heavenly.'

The General spoke at length and so did Mrs Booth. Katie spoke too. The congregation had their moneysworth.

During the two-week honeymoon spent at Southborough, near Tunbridge Wells, urgent missives from the General, full of Army matters, kept arriving for Bramwell. They were no sooner installed in their home in Castlewood Road, not far from 114, Clapton Common, than he was in the thick of work and worry once again. An entry in Florence's diary for 3 November 1882, three weeks to the day after the wedding and a week after their arrival home from honeymoon, makes the picture plain:

'Tonight I am tired and melancholy. My love has gone to ''114'' to do business. He has to go every night, and will have, I expect. I see very little of him . . . though he is a greater darling than ever . . . I never mean to let him see that I am down or weary if I can possibly help it. I must be his sunbeam.'

More often than not, when Bramwell returned home, he would be burdened with Army worries, usually financial ones. He would often exclaim, 'Darling, I'm very burdened about money. I don't know where to turn, surely the Lord will help us!' It was to be a perennial problem. The children, in time, became aware of the need and used to add to their prayers, 'Let Papa not be worried about money!' or 'Dear Lord, send the Army a lot of money to make Papa happy!'

The last two years had been particularly heavy for expense. As well as buying the London Orphanage Asylum and the *Eagle Tavern*, the Army had purchased an ice-rink in Oxford Street— still, as Regent Hall, an important Salvationist centre, and still known affectionately, over a hundred years later, as 'The Rink'. Only the year before, new international headquarters had been purchased in the brand-new Queen Victoria Street. All these projects required enormous faith and vision. They also required large sums of money, which Bramwell was responsible for finding. A few years later, when William had crossed London Bridge on a bitterly cold night and seen the miserable human beings huddled in its alcoves in an attempt to keep warm, he had said to Bramwell, 'Go and do something!' When Bramwell remonstrated about the cost, his father replied, 'Well, that is your affair! Something must be done. Get hold of a warehouse and warm it and find something to cover them.'

Only a few weeks after the wedding Bramwell faced the prospect of signing cheques for wages, knowing that there was not enough money in the bank to honour them. Twice, in the nick of time, at four o'clock on a Saturday afternoon, an elderly lady had handed in a gift of £50 and Bramwell's cheques had been valid after all. But he was not suited by temperament for such stresses. A visionary by nature, he yet had to bear the daily wear and tear of making ends meet for the Army.

And that was not his only burden. Every day he would leave for the new headquarters at 101, Queen Victoria Street and arrive home in time to snatch a hasty meal before dashing off up the road to his parents' home to continue his work for the 'Concern', as the family termed it. It was their concern in every sense of the word, for The Salvation Army represented the whole preoccupation as well as the worry of the Booth family. And Florence was now a Booth.

But when summer 1883 arrived and her baby was born, Florence's days of loneliness were over. She was not aware of the work for the Army that lay ahead for her so soon. For the present she was wonderfully happy.

'What love and delight came with her,' she wrote of Catherine's birth, 'when they placed her in my arms!'

The following May, when Catherine was still less than a year old, Florence set off with her to France, scene of her early days with the Army, to visit Katie, nicknamed by Bramwell the 'Maréchale'. The baby was very sick on the crossing (Catherine was to be a bad traveller all her life) but she had recovered in time for the ordeal of a *second* dedication service in the packed Salvation Army hall at Quai Valmy in Paris. Opposition to the Army was still vociferous in France and *The War Cry* reported 'incredulity, amusement and derision' on the faces of the audience when the service began. But it assured readers that 'a blessed influence seemed to steal over the meeting' once the 'Maréchale' gave out a hymn of consecration.

Katie told her listeners how Florence had been her companion when she first began the work in France and went on to say how delighted she was that the baby was to be consecrated in particular to the work 'in this beautiful France'. She then questioned Florence, who replied, 'My only desire is to give her to God and to France.'

Catherine was then dedicated to the 'war in France' and to bring blessing 'to thousands of poor French men and French women who are plunged in darkness'. And there the matter rests. No one now seems to know why nothing ever came of this promise. Catherine herself was not even aware that such a service had taken place until she was told about it many years after her own retirement from active service. It seems that, in spite of the 'Maréchale's' intentions and Florence's desire, God and the Army thought otherwise.

CHAPTER 3

Florence and the Rescue Work

WHILE FLORENCE AND LITTLE CATHERINE were in Paris with Katie, letters arrived from Bramwell, full of the latest cares of the 'Concern'. One project in particular was on his mind, which, if carried through, would represent a new dimension in Army caring. It was also to affect Florence and her baby very closely.

The Pall Mall Gazette estimated that there were some 80,000 prostitutes in London alone at that time. They were very much a race apart, often having no home but the brothel from which they operated. Many of them were among the 'penitents' at Salvation Army meetings, both in London and the provinces. One Salvationist in Whitechapel who came into contact with these girls and women was a Mrs Elizabeth Cottrill, who had herself been converted when Mrs Booth preached near *The Blind Beggar* public house. She lived nearby with her baker husband and six children.

One snowy night a girl who had run away from home and 'got into trouble', asked her, 'How can I be a Christian—the life I'm living?'

Mrs Cottrill told her that she must give up her way of life and then took practical action to try to find her a home for the night. She told the story in her own words:

'It was very late that night, 10 to 11, when she gave her heart to God. I took her down to a home where they'd taken such girls before, but the matron looked out of the window and said,

' "I can't take girls in at this hour. We don't keep open all night."

'Then I went to a coffee-house. The charge was 2s 6d, and I only had 1s, and they would not trust me till the morning. I tried another and was told,

' "We don't take females."

'So I said, "*I'll* take her home."

'We lived at No. 1 Christian Street, Commercial Road, next

door to a pawnbroker's. It was nearly twelve, and my husband and six children were asleep. I gave her some supper—coffee and a little bit of cold meat and bread and butter. I didn't want any myself. I wanted to get to bed. I was full of prayer and thankfulness, thinking about her broken-hearted mother and how glad she'd be. I made her up a bed in the kitchen on some chairs with old coats and dresses—the best I could without waking the others. I couldn't undress her. She was a clean girl. She had run away from her home near Brighton with another girl, expecting to find London streets paved with gold. They went to the Tower Hill to see the soldiers, imagining they'd find a husband straight away, but only got into trouble. I took her home the next day.'

That story had a happy ending but Mrs Cottrill's rescue work had only just begun. Sometimes she would have four or even eight girls packed into her little front room. She began to pray for a bigger house, after asking 'Mr Bramwell's' advice. At first she hunted in vain, then with the characteristic Salvationist mixture of piety and practicality she prayed as she walked along Hanbury Street:

' "Lord, the earth is thine, and the fulness thereof. Oh, do let me have a house! You know these dear girls are thy children." Then, when I'd cast it on him, I thought: "I'll go home and have a cup of tea." But at that moment I lifted my eyes and saw an empty house, and a notice up, "This house to let." I forgot my tea and went to inquire.'

The landlord turned out to be the Congregational minister of the church next door who was willing to let Mrs Cottrill have the house for the twenty shillings she offered rather than the twenty-five shillings asked and already accepted by others.

'Let this woman have it for £1,' he had said. 'I wish there were a few more who had such a heart towards the poor girls.' But he added the proviso, 'Don't let there be any tambourines, because I may be preaching!' (*Booth's Boots*)

But even one pound a week was more money than Mrs Cottrill could afford and she went back to Bramwell for help. When he, in turn, consulted his mother, they recognized that the decision to be made was an important one. Up to this time, The Salvation Army had no centres other than local corps for worship, using other venues for larger meetings. There were no centres for social work. To rent this property would mark the beginning of a new kind of venture. The family came to a decision. Mrs Cottrill and her family should be found other accommodation and the house in Hanbury Street taken over as a refuge for 'fallen women', to be financed and run by The Salvation Army. But who was to run it?

'What about Florrie?' William asked. 'Let her have charge.'

Florence had returned from France but had gone off to Ireland on Army business, leaving little Catherine behind for the first time. She returned on 17 July, overjoyed to be reunited with her baby, and was met with a dictum from the General:

'Flo had better go down and see what she can do in her spare time. Let her superintend.'

Catherine herself told the story in her biography of her father. Her mother, she wrote, 'felt afraid to attempt a task of the nature of which she knew so little, but she was still more afraid to say "no"!'

The very next morning, clad in Army uniform, and carrying her baby in her arms, she left the leafy roads of Clapton Common and boarded a bus for Whitechapel. When she alighted she turned off the High Road with sinking heart, threading the maze of squalid side streets.

'I felt depressed and unhappy,' she admitted years later. 'Whitechapel seemed so far away from Castlewood Road for a work which I realized would need daily attention.'

Her uniform attracted the customary jeers and a few rotten cabbage stalks were thrown half-heartedly in her direction. Suddenly a potato, thrown with more determination by one of the costermongers, hit her smartly on the side of the head. Florence's spirits were instantly cheered. Catherine commented:

'This was interpreted by her as a seal to her venture. "God is going to make this work a blessing, and the Devil is stirred up in opposition," she said to herself. And she was right on both counts.'

A Salvation Army journal, *All the World*, published in 1888, wrote up the account of Florence's new venture in characteristically Victorian terms:

'The Chief (Bramwell, then Chief of Staff) wrote to her, telling her about those early beginnings of rescue work by a Whitechapel soldier (member of The Salvation Army) which someone was now wanted to oversee, reminding her that she had been longing of late for some definite work for God and saying that he felt convinced that *this* was her work. Her first feeling ''Oh no! The Lord can't mean that for me! The Chief doesn't know the limitations of a mother with a year old baby to look after.''

'But we rejoice to say that the visions of baby Catherine neglected, left to play with scissors or fall into fire by some careless nurse by day and feebly petted at night by a tired out mother who had brought home the seeds of some infection to her child, have never been realized, and only tempted her for a little while.'

At first the baby was not left behind with a possibly careless nurse, but taken to the scene of the 'seeds of infection' by her mother and laid in a clothes basket to sleep while her mother worked.

The front door of the little house in Hanbury Street opened straight onto the small parlour, which led into the only other room on the ground floor, a living-room cum kitchen. One very wet day, no more than a few weeks after Florence had begun her work there, she looked up to see a cab approaching. The horses were reined in outside the house and Mrs Booth and her daughter, Emma, climbed down. Florence's heart sank. She was diffident about her own capabilities and still very much in awe of the Booth gifts, and today was hardly a propitious one for an official visit. Wet washing was hanging from the airer attached to the kitchen ceiling. The place looked damp and depressing. But she bravely welcomed the visitors and led them through into the kitchen where the girls were gathered. Mrs Booth and Emma seemed perfectly at home and joined them round the kitchen table to talk and drink tea. After that first visit, Mrs Booth often spared time from a packed programme to hire a four-wheeled cab, known by the Victorians as a 'growler', and jolt across the cobbled streets to visit the little refuge in Whitechapel.

The house was soon overcrowded and it cannot have been long before the new work moved into bigger premises, for in a later account Florence wrote:

'Two years after my marriage, a derelict swimming-bath in Hanbury Street, Whitechapel, was fitted up to receive some 300 of the absolutely homeless women we had discovered.'

Florence's band of 'rescue officers' increased and she herself became immersed in the intricacies of running a rescue home successfully. Fortunately she found one helper who was also able to join the household at Castlewood Road and care for Catherine at home when Florence had to be away overnight. Marianne Asdell, a new young Salvationist, was asked to meet a girl at Waterloo station one day and conduct her across London to the Whitechapel refuge. She wondered innocently why the child needed protection and was horrified to hear of the incest which made it impossible for her to remain in her family. Marianne became one of Florence's officers as well as her home helper, as *The Deliverer* explained some years later:

'Mrs Booth is necessarily a good deal away from home. Nearly all her children have probably travelled more miles before they were weaned than any infants in the land! And as The Army grows and the responsibilities grow also, Mrs Booth must be ever on the move. Her ability to this end has been greatly increased by the help of her personal secretary, Major Asdell, who, while taking important responsibilities in the Women's Social Work, lives with Mrs Booth, and has been for years a great strength and comfort in the household, especially in making it possible for her to leave home for public work without undue anxiety.'

Unlike her contemporaries, but like many a working wife today, Florence Booth combined the role of homemaker and mother with an extremely exacting 'career' outside the home. Without Miss Asdell it would not have been possible. Her seven children were born at more or less two-year intervals, close enough to enjoy one another's companionship. All had their fair share of mothering too, because until each baby was weaned—at about ten or eleven months—Florence carried it to work each day and took it on her travels. She would carry a cushion with her, to use as a mattress, and ask her hostess for an empty drawer to serve as a cot for the night.

Mary, the second child, was born in the spring of 1885. Bramwell wrote to his father, 'I like her little head.' Probably the usual custom was followed of giving the General a list of names from which to choose the one he preferred. On this occasion he replied:

'Name for the new baby . . . I gave my opinion. But I have no particular feeling about it . . . I had my choice with Kittens (Catherine). I would not have any high-sounding name. God bless the dear child.'

The third child, Miriam, was born in June 1887 and made

up the trio of older daughters. In an interview with Michael Parkinson some ninety years later, Catherine described her first sight of this new sister:

'I can remember that I'd gone to dinner with my grandmother. My Aunt Emma was there and after dinner she knelt down in front of me and said:

'"Oh Cath darling, such a lovely thing has happened—God's sent you a baby sister and Mama wants me to take you to see her" . . . It didn't strike me as peculiar that my mother was in bed, and by her side was this beautiful cradle with pink muslin. I was lifted up and I burst into a howl of misery. I'd never seen anything so dreadful in all my life. It was like a red beetroot covered with hair, and I had to be taken into my mother's arms to be comforted. I think that's almost my earliest memory.'

In October 1889 there was rejoicing over the birth of the first son, Bernard. Bramwell wrote at once to his mother:

'The baby seems all right, though I can't say that I thought him at all handsome! He is dark and looks in splendid condition. Fat and round and comfortable and gazed at me in the most affectionate way twenty minutes after he was born—probably he has some wit therefore.'

Two girls followed—Olive, born in August 1891 and Dorothy, always known as Dora, in June 1893. The youngest, another boy, called Wycliffe, born in December 1895, completed the family— as well as the junior foursome of two boys and two girls.

Miss Asdell, known affectionately as Zazie, which was Mary's approximation to her name, stayed with the household throughout their childhood and growing years, holding the fort, with Catherine's help, whenever their mother was away.

In 1884 Florence was keen to visit other homes for 'fallen women' to study their methods. What she saw did not impress her favourably. She was convinced that harsh rules and a tough work regime was not the right treatment. The very nature of their previous way of life made it unlikely that these girls would be able to adapt to a repressive and monotonous lifestyle. She believed that they needed a 'real home'. Laundry work, usually considered the ideal work for 'that kind of woman', was to her way of thinking the least suitable.

She made up her mind to run her home with an absolute minimum of rules and regulations and to create an atmosphere of love and trust that would win their affection and restore their self-respect. She and her officers tramped miles looking for suitable work for the girls. This was usually domestic service in the right kind of homes. She did her utmost to persuade the girls to stay within the safety of the refuge until work was found, but if a girl was determined to leave, Florence saw no value in keeping her against her will.

Florence's trump card was her own attitude to the women, so unlike the usual Victorian self-righteous contempt. She did not feel superior or patronise them because she saw all men and women equally in need of God's grace and forgiveness. Quite un-Victorian was her ruling that:

'One of the first duties of a rescue officer is to take a stand firmly against the position that women guilty of immorality are *worse* than other transgressors. The Salvation Army has nothing but scorn for that code of morals which welcomes a repentant adulterer—if he happens to wear broadcloth—into the drawing room, and introduces him to the daughters of the house, while considering it the height of condescension to admit a repentant sinner of the other sex to be a kitchenmaid in the scullery.' (*Booth's Boots*)

Her mother-in-law held the same view. Twenty years earlier, when she had addressed a Ragged School, *The Wesleyan Times* had reported: 'She identified herself with them as a sinner, saying that if they supposed her better than they it was a mistake, as all sinners were sinners against God.' (*Booth's Boots*)

But in spite of her sympathy with the girls and her competence in running the home, Florence's introduction to the rescue work had come as an enormous shock. Incredible as it may seem today, she had not even known that prostitution existed before she began the work. She had only understood sex within the loving, tender relationship of her marriage. Now she was exposed to the results of the worst excesses of sexual lust and perversion. Many of the girls she was helping were not grown women at all, but children of ten or eleven. She would arrive home completely shattered. Catherine, years later, described her mother's reactions:

'There were often tears. Sometimes the young mother came home from that other Whitechapel home and its pitiful family and cried herself to sleep. Sometimes she talked to her husband all night, literally all night.' (*Bramwell Booth*)

At first Bramwell thought that Florence might be exaggerating conditions in her distress, so she implored him to investigate for himself, which he did, wandering the streets incognito. What he saw convinced him that the situation was every bit as bad as his wife had depicted. A letter to her at the time reveals his agony in trying to come to terms with a situation which seemed to sully the purity of the relationship that they had hitherto enjoyed. He sums up his resolution of it in a way that seems to indicate an acceptance of sex rarely reached by pre-Freudian Victorians and Christians at that time:

'I believe I can see in a way I have not seen it before, that a man and woman who love God and love each other, can and do glorify him in the happiness of that very closest union and oneness of flesh as well as spirit. I have sometimes had questionings I could not quite answer to myself and have left them: I think I see now . . .' (*Bramwell Booth*)

Perhaps Bramwell's and Florence's honesty and hard thinking about sexual love in marriage brought an honesty and freedom into the whole family relationship that was rare in a day when guilt and taboo often denied this aspect of married happiness.

'My faith was sorely tried,' Florence confessed later, 'and but for the opportunity of pouring out my grief at home to one so strong in faith and so full of compassion for the sinful, I wonder what might have become of me. How acute were the contrasts in my life at this time; such bliss at home, the purest love of husband and my darling baby in her cot, and then suddenly these terrible revelations. This underworld seemed indeed a scene of diabolic confusion and darkness.' (*Booth's Boots*)

One of the women sent to Florence's refuge turned out to be a very tough nut indeed. Rebecca Jarrett had graduated from child prostitute to madame of a brothel. She had first entered a Salvation Army meeting as an alcoholic in her thirties, wearing 'a large blue hat with great blue feathers'. When she was taken ill, the Captain of the corps cared for her and took Rebecca to her own home. She confessed later, 'It was not the preaching that done the work in my poor soul, it was the care and trouble they all took of me.'

Rebecca did not settle readily in the atmosphere of the rescue home and Florence used every possible stratagem to persuade her to stay. One day, when Rebecca announced that she was going to leave, Florence soothingly suggested a cup of tea first, then gave her baby Catherine to hold while she went to put the kettle on. She was certain that Rebecca would not walk out leaving the baby. And she was right. Years later, when Catherine was herself leader of the Women's Social Work which her mother had begun, she told the story in *The Deliverer*:

'Once, when she was in a difficult mood, she said to Mrs Booth: ' "You wouldn't let a woman like me hold your child, would you?" and my mother at once put me in her arms. Rebecca told me this herself, adding, "it went to my heart." '

The General and his wife agreed with Bramwell and Florence that every attempt must be made to change the law and raise the age of consent, as well as making it an offence to procure young people for immoral purposes. Mrs Booth preached extensively about the urgent need for reform. She also wrote to people of influence, including Queen Victoria, begging her for once 'to go off merely conventional lines in order to save the female children of your people from a fate worse than that of slaves and savages'. A reply assured Mrs Booth that Her Majesty fully sympathized with her on the 'painful subject', but nothing more. Mr Gladstone was appealed to, but merely passed the letter on to the Home Secretary. Nothing, it seemed, was to be gained on these fronts. Further publicity was essential, but The Salvation Army, as a movement, lacked credibility with the serious press. A champion arose in the person of W.T. Stead, editor of *The Pall Mall Gazette*. Bramwell invited him to his office to meet Rebecca Jarrett and three or four girls under sixteen who had all been procured and put 'on the game'. Stead was horrified and, Bramwell reported:

'Raising his fist, he brought it down on my table with a mighty bang, so that the very ink-pots shivered, and he uttered one word, the word "Damn!" This explosion over, I said, "Yes, that is all very well, but it will not help us. The first thing to do is to get the facts in such a form that we can publish them." '

Stead agreed and the two men prayed together and continued to meet to pray daily. Some days Stead was deeply distressed by the facts that were emerging but, as Bramwell sensibly commented, 'some earnest prayer, a cup of coffee, and he was braced for further efforts'.

Stead published a series of articles, entitled 'The Maiden Tribute of Modern Babylon'. The material was so hot to handle

41

that many newsvendors, including station bookstalls, refused to sell the paper. An eager public bought up single copies at half-a-crown a piece. William Booth opened up Salvation Army headquarters in Queen Victoria Street as a distribution centre and Bernard Shaw, among others, offered to sell as many copies as he could carry. But some Christians were up in arms at the publication of what they saw as filth. *The Times* complained that Stead was blackening the name of England before the world.

Josephine Butler, who had campaigned so long for the protection of women, added her support and now suggested that Stead should back up his printed statements by demonstrating the ease with which a girl could be bought. Rebecca Jarrett's aid was enlisted—against her better judgement—and with Bramwell's help a girl whose drunken mother willingly gave permission was bought and sent to Stead. When he had received a doctor's report that she was *virgo intacta*, he sent her to the continent for safety, in the care of a Swiss Salvation Army officer. As an added safety check, both the Archbishop of Canterbury and the Roman Catholic Cardinal Manning were apprised beforehand of the whole undertaking.

Meanwhile, a Salvation Army contingent, accompanied by brass bands, marched towards Westminster behind a dray drawn by white horses on which was a petition bearing 393,000 signatures. Uniformed Salvationists carried it into the House of Commons where members stood to peer at the monstrous petition as it was set down near the mace.

The campaign met with at least partial success. The Criminal Law Amendment Act was passed that summer, raising the age of consent to sixteen. The Salvation Army held a meeting for thanksgiving.

But all was not well. Stead's and Bramwell's experiment had backfired alarmingly. A rival paper to *The Pall Mall Gazette* published an interview with the girl's supposedly distraught mother and pointed to the fact that the girl's father had not been consulted before the money transaction took place. (Too late for The Salvation Army campaigners, it was found that the so-called father was not her father at all and had no rights over her. The child was illegitimate.) Bramwell Booth, Stead and Rebecca Jarrett were all three jointly charged at Bow Street with taking the girl from her parents without her father's permission and with indecent assault.

The public seemed glad to wreak vengeance on these moralizers who had dared to wash the nation's dirty linen in public. The Salvation Army uniform acted like a red rag to a bull and Bramwell was not only hissed but attacked physically. On 12 September Florence wrote in her diary, 'Darling one came home with bad blow on the nose. Been wretchedly mobbed coming out of Court by the Magistrates' door.' Catherine herself described the scene, perhaps with a mixture of memory and family folklore—for she was only just over two years old at the time, 'I remember the Black Maria calling and my father coming home bleeding, having been pelted with stones. He didn't really explain to me what was happening.' That is hardly surprising.

The hearing of the case at the Old Bailey began on 23 October and lasted twelve days. Florence went to court, taking six-month-old baby Mary with her. Bramwell's deafness prevented his hearing all the proceedings and it was a great comfort to him to look across to his wife. The judge insisted that no motive, however worthy, justified the abduction of a child without both parents' consent. The Archbishop of Canterbury and Cardinal Manning were given no opportunity to speak. In the event Bramwell was acquitted but Stead and Rebecca were sent to prison. Florence met Rebecca on her release and she lived happily for another forty years under a new name.

The Booths had done what they believed to be right and necessary, but they feared that the whole incident would bring even greater discredit on the Army. In fact it had the opposite effect. The movement increased at home and overseas at such a pace that it was difficult for the Booths to keep up with mounting costs and administration. In characteristic fashion the General wrote to his wife from Canada, 'We must have some more Divisional Officers here. Push it on Bramwell.'

'Push it on Bramwell' was to continue to be the order of the day.

CHAPTER 4

Childhood

STRAIN, STRESS, DANGER, ANXIETY, shortage of time and shortage of money—these do not seem likely ingredients for a happy home background for small children. Yet Catherine has repeatedly said that her childhood was so happy that she has never written about it because no one would believe that it could have been as perfect as she described. One of her first memories is of laughter—laughing with her father. She remembers the sheer bliss of toddling into her parents' room early in the morning and clambering into the big bed, to snuggle down between them.

Marianne Asdell remembers her first sight of what she described as 'the plump little babe' being danced up and down in her mother's arms in the small room at Castlewood Road. Florence was singing to her,

> *My baby is a soldier*
> *And growing up for God*

to the tune of 'I'd choose to be a daisy' (obviously well known in 1902, when Miss Asdell told the tale).

Music was certainly a delightful part of early years. Florence would play the piano while Catherine sat close by in her high chair. She remembers playing and singing a Victorian hymn, 'We'll cross the river of Jordan', and hearing Catherine, aged eighteen months, clap her small hands together and join in the chorus of ''appy, 'appy!' that followed.

Music was not merely sweet and sentimental, it was robust and noisy too. To a small child, the fun of banging a drum or playing a triangle and marching round the room to a lively tune must have been deeply satisfying. Words and music were lively and vigorous. One of Bramwell's favourites was 'Storm the forts of darkness, bring them down!' which went with a not surprising swing, since it was set to the rollicking tune of 'Here's to good old whisky, drink it down!' (As General Booth had said, 'Why should the Devil have all the best tunes?')

Family prayers were an occasion for happiness too. Today the phrase conjures up a picture of starched servants forced to assemble with the family in a dark, forbidding room to endure the hypocritical and lengthy orations of the head of the household. Cook, housemaid and nurserymaid did indeed join the family in Castlewood Road for prayers every morning, but the occasion was anything but dull and forbidding. Florence had a dread of children being forced to accept what she described as a 'parrot-like religion' which would put a 'gravestone . . . over the living development of their souls'. She firmly believed that 'all services and prayers for children should be as varied and unconventional as possible'.

She practised what she preached, for it was she who was usually in charge, Bramwell having already left for the office. There was plenty of variety, with singing and playing of musical instruments. As each child learned to play the piano, she or he took a turn at accompanying the singing. Then Florence would choose the same 'song' each day for the week, to give pianist and family the chance to learn it thoroughly. The little girls were allowed to bring a doll to prayers to hold on their laps, and when, on Saturdays, Bramwell was present, he usually nursed the youngest child himself.

One Saturday, when her father was taking prayers, Catherine felt compelled—with the inquiring mind that marked her whole life—to peep through the cracks in the small fingers that covered her face, to see what her father looked like when he was talking to God. She felt suitably guilty for such a breach of decorum.

In later life Catherine wrote:

'Everyone is born with a capacity for happiness. A baby can laugh before it can talk. Happiness can be developed so that it becomes an every day delight and when it springs from trusting in God's love, very young children can realize this comfort, and their happiness grows.

'Now I see that it was my mother who created for us the atmosphere in which our individual happiness flourished, chiefly by the way in which she showed us her love. None of us doubted *that*, at any stage of our lives. To remember the look on her face when she showed us the new baby, drawing our attention to some special feature—its hand and the perfection of the tiny fingers with their minute nails—while the baby was drinking at her breast, is happiness today! To recall how, as four or five of us stood watching, she explained the wonderful fact that you couldn't run short of love when God's love was mingled with ours. So she would love the new baby and that would not take away any of her love for us. Oh what happiness to know there would always be enough love!'

But a great part of Catherine's happiness was bound up with her father. She adored him and, all her life, considered him as near perfect as man could be. Soon after his death, she wrote of him in her biography:

'Children, I suppose, love their parents in varying degree; Bramwell Booth inspired in his children an affection which, looked at from the vantage of forty-five years, seems to me quite beyond the ordinary. To please him was for us all the most treasured happiness . . . When he talked to us about Christ, told us what He was and what He did, we understood. We felt, and in reverence I say it, that our father himself was like the Christ he loved!

'He was an adept at making himself seem on an equality with the companion of the hour. At every stage of my life he appears to me as understanding me, and understood by me. Though our time with him was so scanty, he never seemed out of touch with or in any degree distant from the interests of the moment. Books, dolls or red Indians were all well known to him! On the rare occasions, such as a birthday, when one might take breakfast with him, he could talk with them and about them with fullest comprehension and knowledge. In these questions he was one of the initiated . . .

'My earliest recollection of him was when I was, my mother tells me, about three years old. The picture my mind clearly sees, like a light patch in surrounding darkness, is myself holding my father's hand, to which mine reaches up, and we two walking down the passage into his ''office'' and across to the window. Here I am lifted up to peep into a nest of white mice. He talks to me of the ''dear little things'', and I have loved mice ever since.'

Miriam was born just before Catherine's fourth birthday, and Florence recorded the events of the new baby's dedication service in her journal:

'We started the three chicks in three perambulators . . . Baby was good all the time, but fidgety—my arms did ache—she would crow too. Mama spoke first and at length.' But this was by no means a criticism of Mrs Booth, for Florence continued with an enthusiastic account of her splendid 'message', fully appreciated in spite of the fidgety baby and aching arms. It was a happy family day and Florence felt optimistic about the future of her three 'chicks'.

'The children are a great joy,' she added in her journal, 'they will be good; the Holy Spirit is doing a work in Cath's heart already—she is God's.'

Meanwhile Cath was in the first perambulator to arrive home, where she gave her father an account of the service. 'Mama has given baby right back to God,' she told him, 'right back.' Then, in case he might take the words too literally—as *she* may have done before receiving adult reassurance—she added, 'Never mind, she's coming home in the perambulator just the same.'

Miriam was born on 18 June 1887. Three days later, on 21 June, the whole nation was celebrating the fiftieth anniversary of Queen Victoria's accession to the throne. Up and down the land foundation stones were laid and trees planted to commemorate the Golden Jubilee. It was a hot, dry summer and the streets of London were packed with thousands of cheering sightseers as the Queen made her way, in state procession, to Westminster Abbey, for the thanksgiving service.

The Salvation Army devised its own way of demonstrating loyalty to the Queen Empress by dedicating fifty officers to Army work in India. In July, when the Army held its twenty-second anniversary celebrations, these officers took their place in the march past, barefooted and in Indian dress. The venue for the Army celebrations was Alexandra Palace, the huge 'palace of the people' which had been opened to the public some twelve years previously.

The building itself was a great hall capable of seating 12,000 people, decorated in chocolate brown and lavender grey and furnished with a Willis organ. The grounds, which were extensive, were used for race meetings, marionette shows, balloon flights, performing elephants and any other kind of entertainment likely to amuse the crowds of ordinary people who arrived to enjoy a Bank holiday outing. But on the day that The Salvation Army took over, a news report stated that 'the ordinary amusements of the palace were suspended for the day, the supply of intoxicating liquors was stopped for the nonce and the utmost good order prevailed'.

More than 11,000 Salvation Army soldiers, accompanied by 100 drums and 1,000 brass instruments, marched past the General and Mrs Booth as they stood at attention to take the salute. The day lasted from ten o'clock in the morning till ten at night and went with a swing. A press reporter wrote:

'Such a genuine low-class mob can rarely be seen . . . yet the order and true courtesy that prevailed were astonishing. Very astonishing, too, was the general beaming happiness. Never have I seen such a mass of people more thoroughly enjoying themselves.'

Never before, perhaps, had any movement made religion such fun. 'Everyone saved and everyone at work to save others', was William Booth's aim for the Army, but that did not imply long faces, numerous prohibitions, or dreary good works. The only religion that the Booth family believed in had love as its source and end. They revelled in a personal experience of God's love and went on to lavish the same kind of free, undeserved love on others, irrespective of rank or worth.

William and Catherine Booth and their family were far more likely to talk about the need to be saved than the need to be religious. Words like salvation or conversion are not much used these days and, when they are, they are often misunderstood. Although The Salvation Army worked much of the time in the poorest and neediest parts of the land, in inner city areas, they certainly did not think that it was only thieves or 'fallen women' who stood in need of God's salvation. With complete sincerity they recognized their own need of God's forgiveness and salvation to be as great as that of a prison inmate or brothel keeper. Unlike many middle-class Victorians they did not look down on 'the criminal classes' but recognized sin in every man, woman and child, however respectable or well-bred. Everyone who had chosen to disobey God and go his own way—and that meant *everyone*— needed salvation.

To be saved meant to change over from being God's enemy to fighting on his side, whether in the ranks of The Salvation Army or not. In order to be saved a person must repent—or have a change of heart—confess his sin to God and willingly receive God's forgiveness, made possible through Jesus' death and resurrection. The Army definition of salvation is 'the work of grace which God accomplishes in a repentant person whose trust is in Christ as Saviour, forgiving sin, giving meaning and new direction to life and strength to live as God desires.' Salvation leads to 'sanctification' which is 'the outcome of wholehearted commitment to God, by his help living a Christlike life, in harmony with his love and holiness'.

In other words, converts were expected to change their life-style radically. They were expected to show by what they said and how they lived that God had saved them. A bad husband or father must be different at home and a harsh employer must be different at work. Thieves must stop stealing and prostitutes leave 'the game'. Converts were also expected to give up swearing and drinking. The Salvation Army gave practical help and support to converts and taught them that God's grace was available to help them make a fresh start. As soon as possible after conversion they were encouraged to 'give their testimony', which meant standing up in public, at a street corner or in a meeting, to tell others what God had done for them.

It is not surprising that The Salvation Army laid great stress on the actual moment of conversion. In many instances the decision to change the whole course of life by accepting God's free forgiveness was dramatic and emotional. At every Salvation Army meeting those who wanted to make this commitment would be invited to come to the front and kneel beside the drum, if it was an open-air meeting, or at the wooden bench at the front of the hall, if it was inside an Army citadel. The wooden form originated in the Methodist communion rail, but was now called either the 'mercy seat' or the 'penitent form'.

The Army believed that even a young child could make the decision to give his life to God and surrender his own will in order to accept God's way. They drove home the Bible teaching that 'all have sinned' to children and adults alike. But Florence and Bramwell wisely refrained, it seems, from expecting dramatic conversions for their children, although they recognized the need for every one of them to set out consciously on a path of obedience to God. But having grown up in an atmosphere where spectacular conversions must have been witnessed and discussed daily, it is not surprising that Catherine deeply regretted having had no dramatic conversion experience of her own. She said:

'I was four years old or thereabouts when I gave myself to Christ. I had been naughty. I had grieved my mother. I don't know now what it was . . . My mother was praying with me, and she prayed with me that the Lord Jesus would forgive me. I don't remember exactly what she said; I wish I could. Then she said to me, "Now, Cath, you pray, darling; tell Jesus you want to be good." Well, I prayed and did as she said—I promised ... I prayed and gave myself to Christ. That, I think, was my first step.' (*Commissioner Catherine*)

In 1902 Miss Asdell described the scene rather differently and in language more reminiscent of a Victorian Sunday School reward book:

'As a tiny child of four summers, Catherine became conscious of a real desire to have the "naughty" taken out of her heart. The circumstances come before me so vividly as I write. We were having a "little talk" in the twilight while Nurse was putting small Mary to bed. The dear Chief and Mrs Booth were away on a much-needed rest, and speaking of them and their love directed the talk to the love of Jesus, and their desire that their little girlie should give herself to God. And then the child's heart burst forth with a longing to be good, not only to please dear Mamma and Papa, but first of all to please Jesus. We prayed together, and with sobs and tears Catherine gave her heart to the Lord. She has never doubted that as a little child Jesus had saved her.' (*The Deliverer*)

Pressure to 'please Mamma and Papa', from without or within herself, was to influence Catherine's actions for many years to come.

CHAPTER 5

Grandmama

CATHERINE'S FIRST SIX YEARS were spent in a London of horse-drawn vehicles.

'What a joy to be on the top of a bus—they had no roofs then—and sit in the front next to the driver and talk to him about the horses,' she remembered at 100. (But there was also the horror of seeing an overworked, exhausted horse lying on its side.) She remembered the sound of the muffin man's bell on cold winter afternoons as he came down the street, balancing on his head his green baize tray with its load of crumpets and muffins for sale.

At Christmas time 1887 Florence took her three small daughters to spend the holiday with her father in Wales. Dr Soper had become reconciled to the 'unspeakably vulgar' Salvationists, which was as well, as his other daughter and one son also became Salvation Army officers. The weather was cold and snowy when the local Salvation Army band came to Blaina House and formed a large circle on the snow-covered lawn outside. There they played carols and delighted the visitors, as Salvation Army bandsmen have been delighting listeners-within-doors at Christmas time ever since.

As February 1888 drew to its close, temperatures remained at freezing-point. But a chill had struck the Booth family more bitter than any winter cold. Grandmama Booth had visited a London doctor who confirmed her worst fears. She was suffering from cancer. The first person she told was Bramwell. For both, the chief concern was to shield William from distress. But a further series of visits to specialists confirmed the diagnosis and the prognosis too. Although various types of treatment were tried, no hope of cure was offered. Bramwell and Florence both adored Mama and the long months of suffering she endured were hard to bear.

Mrs Catherine Booth was indeed a very remarkable woman. She

had grown up, a delicate girl, in a Methodist family but when she was seventeen she wept and prayed night and day until she possessed an assurance that she had received salvation. When she met William she found a man who combined all the qualities that she had listed as essential in a man she could marry. Their love was almost immediate—intense and lifelong. It was she who encouraged him towards spiritual excellence and she accepted every turn his vocation took, even though it resulted in no fixed income and a life of constant separations and incredibly hard work.

She was an idealist and put her whole being into everything that she thought and felt and believed. She had immense abilities—a fine mind and prodigious capacity for work. She was painfully sensitive to the suffering and emotions of others. Many of her beliefs have become cornerstones of Salvationist belief as well. She said of herself that, at seven years old, 'I had washed my hands of strong drink.' She was writing impassioned temperance tracts when she was scarcely more than a child. It was from her too that Bramwell learned his deep love and care for animals, which in turn he passed on to his own children.

Her most significant contribution to The Salvation Army movement must surely be her attitude to woman's status. When she was seventeen she wrote to her minister (anonymously, in case her youth should prejudice him):

'Excuse me, my dear sir, . . . in your discourse on Sunday morning . . . your remarks appeared to imply the doctrine of woman's intellectual and even moral inferiority to man . . . Permit me, my dear sir, to ask whether you have ever made the subject of woman's equality as a *being*, the matter of calm investigation and thought?' She went on to argue her case cogently, using both logic and Scripture.

Ten years later, married and with a young family, she wrote a pamphlet, called *Female Ministry*, in which she put forward the case for women preachers. She did not plead the cause from any desire to preach herself—nothing could be further from her wishes—and William agreed that 'you should preach if you felt moved thereto . . . although I should not like it'. Later she felt convinced that God *was* calling her to preach and after resisting the conviction for some months she stood up at the end of morning service in the Methodist chapel at Gateshead, where William was minister, and confessed her disobedience. William's immediate reaction was to announce her as the preacher for that very evening.

In spite of fears, shyness and reluctance to appear on the platform, Mrs Booth had great powers of preaching and persuasion and drew greater crowds than William himself. Her grand-daughter was to inherit both her fear of public preaching and her power to influence any audience she might address.

Catherine retained one vivid memory of her much-loved grand-mother before she was ill:

'I am nearly four years old. I am perched on a cushion to raise me high enough to sit at table. Grandmama is at its head, her back to the big bay window. I sit at her right hand. Uncle Herbert is on my right; there are aunts present too. Aunt Emma comes and, standing behind me, ties an enormous white napkin loosely round me and the folds touch my cheek at the sides as I feel her fingers fumbling at the nape of my neck. I am shy, silent, it seems difficult to raise my eyes *except to Grandmama*. I seem to know her quite well. I feel completely content because she is there. When she will not allow Uncle Herbert, who carves, to give me a piece of meat (my parents were vegetarians at the time, and all their children were brought up so except for occasional fish and poultry), I hear her speak distinctly, ''No, Herbert, she shall not have anything in this house that her mother would not wish her to have,'' and suddenly I have lifted my eyes to find her face turned to me and we smile at each other, as if we knew something nice that the others did not understand about. I feel a wave of happiness as if I had somehow escaped a danger. I like Uncle Herbert, though I am a little afraid of what he may do next, he teases sometimes; but I am sure that Grandmama knows *everything* and will let nothing harmful happen to me.'

The doctors prescribed sea air for Mrs Booth and she went to stay for a while at Clacton-on-Sea in Essex. The family realized that she would never be well enough to return to the home in Clapton Common. Somewhere quieter, removed from London noise and Army activity, was needed.

It was the period when Londoners were beginning to move out of London to the newly developing suburbs. A small new estate was being built at Hadley Wood, near Barnet, and the General bought a house for his wife to come home to, surrounded by green trees and countryside. Since Bramwell was constantly at his father's call and could not be far away, Bramwell and Florence bought a house nearby and moved there with their three daughters.

1889 was a difficult and demanding year for Florence. In the midst of the worry about her mother-in-law, she had to arrange the family move to 55 The Crescent. Once there, she had a longer journey to her Whitechapel office by train and bus. The new neighbours must have been surprised and perhaps a little shocked at the comings and goings of the family at 55. Middle-class wives and mothers did not go out to work at that time. The Sunday routine was most unconventional too. Florence herself wrote later:

'I know our neighbours when we first came to Hadley Wood were much amused as the party sallied forth from 55 The Crescent East: Catherine, Mary and Miriam, the three small children, wearing the poke bonnet. Later, a suitable hat carrying The Salvation Army ribbon was arranged for junior soldiers, so that our daughters did not wear the bonnet again until they were enrolled as senior soldiers.'

In the spring *The War Cry* reported that Mrs Booth had 'flu and added, 'Miss Booth, her eldest daughter, has been suffering with a slight attack of inflammation of the lungs but is better.'

A month or two later Mrs Booth was worse, following an unsuccessful course of treatment with electric needles. Emma, Bramwell's favourite sister, arrived home from her Salvation Army post in India and was 'such a strength of love and kindness', Florence wrote. She was the children's favourite aunt, too. The others inspired awe rather than affection.

Mrs Booth was ordered back to Clacton. She herself realized that she would never return home. Bramwell had now to snatch time from Army duties whenever possible to rush down to Clacton to visit her. He must have spent even less time with his family, in spite of the fact that Florence was again pregnant. He was away on Army business when Catherine celebrated her sixth birthday in July. Florence, who still seems mainly concerned with her daughter's spiritual progress, writes to tell him about the day:

'I called my loved one in to pray before coming down this morning. My heart was very full as I gave her again to the Lord. We mingled our tears and though Cath has much to struggle against, I am sure she is his.' Once downstairs: 'We had breakfast together, the chicks delighted with the parcels. A bassinette (wickerwork cradle or pram), drawing slate and book for the birth-day queen—Mary a dolly, and baby a basket carriage for the dolly.' Even then, consolation prizes were in order for younger children suffering from not being the 'birthday queen'.

Florence's high hopes for Catherine's character development were not fully satisfied. While Mrs Booth was at Clacton, the children were sent across to visit the General. On one such occasion his housekeeper's son accompanied them home and Florence noted in her diary—more in sorrow than anger:

'The dear chicks had been to see the General and come home romping with Tommy D. Had to be sent to bed in disgrace. I wish I could see more backbone in precious Cath on these occasions. She is perfectly obedient but not able to bear any responsibility alone.' 'Precious Cath' at six years old was soon to develop a great deal of backbone, enough to last her the rest of her life.

The very next month, after Catherine's birthday, Florence was plunged into emergency relief work during the London dock strike of August and September. The docks were often a centre of industrial unrest, as Asa Briggs explains in *Victorian Cities*:

'In good times they were crowded and prosperous. In times of bad trade they were idle and deserted, visible proof of the fluctu-ations of international commerce. In both good and bad times there was a tradition of industrial unrest.'

The Salvation Army has always refused to enter into politics or to take sides in any dispute but has concentrated energies on bringing relief to all who are in need. They cared deeply that '120,000 of the most poorly paid, and fed, and clad, and housed labourers in the world' were in extreme distress. During the strike Florence organized free teas for some 1,200 half-starved women and children. *The War Cry* of 14 September reported that 'in some cases the poor mothers had carried the pawning of their clothes so far that they could not come out, and had to arrange to send their children in charge of the eldest one'.

On 11 October Bramwell and Florence celebrated the birth of their fourth child and first son. Catherine, at six, was fast learn-ing Army ways. Her first question was, 'Mama, what shall we dedicate him to?'

Perhaps it was during Florence's confinement that Catherine was sent to stay at Clacton where her grandmother lay ill. She recollects the occasion:

'I am still shy, more shy than at three. I am not happy for I do not like being away from home. There seem to be many strangers in the big house. I feel safest in the garden to which I can go by the side door near the housekeeper's room where I have my meals. My Aunt Emma is in the house and always very kind when I see her, but I am silent, uncomfortable, wishing I were going home. But the moment I am beside Grandmama's bed, that feeling of being strange and shy is gone. She and I talk and talk. Would that I could remember anything she said! I have a small doll in a pale blue woollen frock. Grandmama talks to my doll and perches it on the bedclothes, and we keep on talking. I am completely comforted and happy, and there is still lots more to say when Captain Carr (nurse to Mrs Booth) or Auntie Emma comes to take me away saying, ''Grandmama is tired now.'' I am lifted up to kiss her as she lies propped up by pillows.'

Mrs Booth lingered, refusing drugs so that her mind should be clear. Catherine remembered how terribly her father suffered during that time. He visited his mother regularly and more than one special family gathering was called for when her death seemed to be at hand. Florence took her three little daughters for a last visit and Catherine burst into tears when her Grandmama asked, 'Darling, do you know that I am going to heaven?'

When W.T. Stead, editor of *The Pall Mall Gazette* and a great admirer of Mrs Booth, had visited her earlier, he had suggested to Bramwell that 'it is a sin not to have an intelligent and sympathetic stenographer or a person with a long memory constantly within call of your mother'. His advice was followed and later a screen was put up near the door, behind which a shorthand writer could sit and record Mrs Booth's last words. That presence may account for the lengthy report in *The War Cry* of the grandchildren's visit. It is headed, 'With Mrs Booth—Reminiscences of the Sick Chamber—Children Come to See her and Receive her Blessing' and begins:

'It is an impressive sight when the gaze of a child is fixed upon the features of someone dying . . . so gather the children round the bed. Let them put out their little lips to be kissed, and then bid them watch and listen . . .

'Catherine is the first. She is the Chief's oldest daughter, named after the woman whose voice was now speaking, but would soon be heard no more.'

The account ended with a picture of 'gold tresses' mingled with 'whitened locks' and the contrast between past and future, life and death, the beginning and the end.

That year, 1890, marked the Silver Jubilee of The Christian Mission that William and Catherine Booth had founded. Although it was only twelve years since The Salvation Army had been formed, it was twenty-five years since William had first preached in London's East End and The Christian Mission had been founded. The Central Great Hall at Alexandra Palace could seat only 12,000, so a larger venue must be found for these celebrations. The Crystal Palace was chosen.

Joseph Paxton's glittering dome of glass and iron had been built to house Great Britain's proud achievements in the realms of engineering and science. It was originally called the Palace of Industry and nicknamed the Crystal Palace by *Punch* when it was erected in London's Hyde Park for the duration of the Great Exhibition of 1851. The Victorians could not bear to part with such a monument to Britain's glory and although it was vastly expensive to run—there were fifty miles of hot water piping—it was removed bodily to Sydenham, in south London, where it remained until it was destroyed by fire in 1936.

Queen Victoria loved it—remembering, no doubt, that the Great Exhibition had been Prince Albert's brainchild—and often visited it along with other foreign royalty. The ordinary people loved it too, and flocked to watch the spectacular firework displays or to wonder at Blondin, who not only walked the tightrope there, but stopped midway to cook an omelette.

For the occasion of The Salvation Army Silver Jubilee the entire Crystal Palace was taken over and 50,000 people poured through the turnstiles to attend the meetings for thanksgiving. Catherine was among them:

'Few distinct impressions of it remain in the memory of a child then six years old, but those that do are clear, and here is one. She is seated towards the front of the huge central transept. It is gorged with people for "The Great Assembly", and a crowd, standing close packed, stretches away on either side of the enclosure which is filled with seats. The child remembers this crowd outside the partition, for she walked through a narrow lane in its midst on her way to the meeting, and she could hear the sound of its singing

57

joining in the mighty volume that rose through the echoing glass dome when the meeting began. She sees the mountain side of faces towering up behind the platform. The steep orchestra, including the space round the organ loft, is packed to its utmost limits with uniformed singers and bandsmen. The glitter of instruments and the kind of dull roar, as the movement of rising for singing spread about her, are a clear-cut memory. She remembers, too, that ''hugeous'' band, and what little sound it made. The sound of the brass was swallowed up by a different sound. A sound that seemed to fill the whole world, the sound of a vast sea of song. The child shivers and feels like crying. At the end of the verses the singing is still going on in the distant parts of the building, not quite in tune, and lagging behind in time. There are movements . . . kneeling, rising, but what form the service takes is quite lost to her. Until, in deep blue letters on a white background, words begin to creep across from one side of the orchestra front to the other: fixed high, and unrolling, a calico strip is drawn along, to be rolled up on the opposite side, so that a phrase is visible at one time. The silence is like cotton wool. Sharp sounds echo from far away in other parts of the Palace only to make the near stillness more still.

' ''My dear children and friends,'' the unrolling is stayed a moment, the little girl knows who the words are from, *she* is one of the ''children'' . . . and now the words are moving on; and there is another kind of movement; a dim rustling, an uncertain sorrowful sound; suddenly the great building is full of it, as it had been of the mighty sound of singing, only there are no verse ends. It goes on and on, it is not loud yet it fills every second with sound, it wavers, falls, rises. Someone *might* scream and be heard; the child feels anyone might scream . . . but no one does. Handkerchiefs fustle and flutter all over the mountain side of faces on the orchestra, *everyone* is weeping: all the people around her and the child too . . . and the words go on rolling; passing, pausing . . .

' ''My dear children and friends, my place is empty but my heart is with you. You are my joy and my crown . . . Go forward. Live holy lives. Be true to the Army. God is your strength. Love and seek the lost . . . I am dying under the Army flag. It is yours to live and fight under . . . I send you my love and blessing. Catherine Booth.'' '

It was October of that same year, 1890, when Catherine Booth was, in Army terms, 'promoted to Glory'. Florence recalled the events of that month, 'A coffin with a glass lid was taken to the Congress Hall, Clapton, where thousands passed by.'

It seemed that there was to be no end to the children's ordeal, for she goes on to say, 'Before the public was admitted on October 8th, I took Catherine and Mary and lifted them up to see the dear face once more. We talked about heaven and meeting Grandmama again.'

Florence pressed the matter further and asked five-year-old Mary if she was ready to go to heaven and the child burst into tears, admitting that she was not good enough. Her mother knelt with her beside the coffin and told her how to give her life to God and receive his forgiveness. Twelve years later Miss Asdell, companion help to Florence, wrote up the event for *The Deliverer*:

' "Is my little Mary ready, if Jesus should call her, as he has called precious Grandma?" asked Mrs Booth, as with her two elder children she was taking a last sorrowful look at the worn but peaceful face of the Warrior, who after years of suffering had laid down her cross to take up her crown.

' "Oh! No! Mamma," sobbed the child. Then, kneeling by the coffin at her dear Mother's side, Mary intelligently gave her heart to God. Her beautiful and consistent life should be a convincing answer to those who do not believe in child conversion.'

It is only possible to guess the feelings of Catherine—now a sensitive and imaginative seven-year-old, as she watched her mother and five-year-old sister and gazed through the glass lid at the dead face of her much-loved grandmother. Perhaps she later considered Mary's conversion, with its dramatic backcloth, altogether more suitable and satisfactory than her own uneventful experience.

For more than a week the body of Catherine Booth lay in state at the Congress Hall, while thousands of people passed by the coffin, many of them her converts or those she had helped personally.

Monday 13 October, the day of the funeral, was one of thick fog. The whole winter of 1890 to 1891 was the foggiest on record at a time of regular London pea-soupers. At Olympia, where the service was held and 36,000 passed through the turnstiles to attend, the fog drifted in from outside, blanketing the brightness that should have streamed from the new-fangled electric lighting.

The next day was foggy too. Salvation Army officers and bands began to assemble along the Embankment early in the morning for the 4,000-strong funeral procession that would march 'past the Royal Exchange, through Shoreditch, Dalston to Abney Park cemetery'. The watching crowds were greater than for any funeral since that of the Duke of Wellington, nearly forty years before, which had taken place on a day of torrential rain. Stands had been erected for the public and hundreds lined the rooftops along the route.

The procession of officers, carrying the Army flags, stopped at the International Headquarters of The Salvation Army in Queen Victoria Street to take in 'the high, flat, flag-draped dray on which the coffin rested'. William Booth stood on his own in a carriage behind the coffin and his two sons, Bramwell and Herbert, rode on horseback on either side of him. William's daughters followed in the next carriage and behind them came Bramwell's three small daughters, dressed in white, with a shoulder sash marked with a crimson cross and crown.

To the crowd, this absence of mourning clothes must have been one of the most surprising elements in the whole unusual proceedings. Queen Victoria had set the fashion for deepest mourning. All the family, small children included, would normally have been dressed in black from head to foot. The undertakers, their funeral carriages and the black horses that drew them, would all have been draped in black at every possible point. The Salvation Army Orders and Regulations strictly forbade mourning, for a number of reasons, both theological and practical. Mourning, it was argued, represented a 'worldly fashion'. It was a 'melancholy custom' which appeared to 'reflect on the providence of God' and which gave a false expression of the Army's feelings about death. Added to all that, it was a 'needless expense'. A white sash at the funeral and a black armband afterwards were the only concessions to dress.

The carriages were drawn slowly through the city streets to the accompaniment of singing and brass band music. Everywhere the shops were shut and even the gates of the Bank of England were closed while the funeral passed. Many years later Catherine wrote for *The War Cry*:

'The first clear memory I have of my Grandfather is at my Grandmother's funeral. From the carriage I was in with my sisters Mary and Miriam and Staff Captain Carr whom I knew was my Grandmother's nurse, I could see him standing some way in front

of us, bareheaded and alone. He turned from side to side in
response to the people, some of whom shouted, ''God bless you,
General.'' There were people all the way, pavements crowded,
windows and many rooftops filled with them. I was seven years
old.'

Ten thousand were allowed into Abney Park Cemetery where
William himself spoke.

'It was a most touching sight,' *The Daily Telegraph* reported,
'when the tall, upright General came forward in the gathering
darkness . . . He spoke manfully, resolutely and without the
slightest trace of affectation.'

What must have been the emotions of the seven-year-old child,
as she was driven home with her two young sisters through the fog
and darkness of that evening?

'I loved my grandmother,' she said in an interview in her own
old age. 'She was so busy, so important. I did not realize this at the
time, but looking back I know it now. In my infancy—at three,
four, six years of age—she was someone most beloved, who had
time to talk to me. I loved being with her.'

A month later Florence took her two eldest daughters to 'pour
tea' for her at a visitor's day in a newly-opened Home for women.
On their way they visited the cemetery, where all three knelt at
Mrs Booth's grave (in November!). Three women joined them,
who belonged, so *The War Cry* delicately reported, to 'the ''fringe
and feather'' make-up'. Florence listened sympathetically as they
told her how grateful they were for the help that the Army was
giving them. The Booths went on to the meeting, where Florence
served tea to the visitors while, again in the words of *The War Cry*,
'her little Cath and Mary performed the function of matrons most
gracefully'. After tea, Mrs Booth, addressing the meeting, told
them about the women who had approached them in the cemetery.

She told the audience, 'These are my girls, we will save them
. . . this Home will be one means to that end.'

At home in Hadley Wood, the three children included 'Mama's
other girls' in their bedtime prayers.

The following summer, on 14 August 1891, Olive was born.
Catherine, aged eight, wrote to 'darling Grandpa':

'I went to Ramsgate for three weeks with dear Aunty Emma.
Our little baby is a darling. She has a lot of dark hair. I love her very
much.'

CHAPTER 6

Home Management

W HEN BRAMWELL BOOTH wrote to tell his mother of their
son's birth, he added, 'We will try to train him as you would
wish and make him seek what you have sought.' Florence
thoroughly endorsed the sentiment and took Mrs Booth's advice
about bringing up the family very much to heart.

'The Army Mother warned me so earnestly against allowing
disobedience when the children were young, that I consider
my effort to carry out her advice contributed largely to our
success in training them,' she wrote in *The Sunday Circle*,
and went on to explain, 'They were all as strong-willed as
healthy and intelligent children should be, and but for my desire
to please Mrs Booth, it would have been easy to let them get
the upper hand.'

This resolve not to allow any disobedience ensured a speedy if
painful resolving of the toddler rebellion. With each child she faced
a clash of wills and 'the struggle for the mastery with each one
came upon me unexpectedly', she recalled. Mary, at nineteen
months, refused stubbornly to kiss anyone. Florence engaged in a
struggle for mastery which lasted two and a half hours. Mary
yielded.

Fortunately, as well as obeying her mother-in-law's precepts
scrupulously, Florence began to develop an altogether warmer
style of mothering all her own, firmly based on what is recognized
today as sound child psychology.

'Not one of them was ever punished in haste. When a battle
seemed inevitable I arranged the circumstances to make surrender
easy. As few commandments as possible but no transgression
excused from penalty, was the law of the nursery.'

Later, Florence wrote a publication called *The Care and
Training of Children* for the guidance of officers who ran the
children's homes set up by The Salvation Army Women's Social
Work, which was under her leadership. Her advice reflects much

of the accumulated wisdom gained from her own family, as she admits:

'Great care must be taken not to create forms and ceremonies of religion for children. I always felt with my own girls and boys, especially whilst they were young, that it was very necessary to keep them away from the large Meetings, and from too frequent public Meetings, so that nothing should become to them a mere form or ceremony. Children, being so quick to imitate, will pray as they hear grown-up people pray, using grown-up people's expressions. There is no reality to the child in such a prayer; it is a mere imitation.'

Florence emphasized, too, the need to provide variety for children and the danger of 'rigidly doing a thing in exactly the same way over and over again'. The dangers of monotony and a rigid regime were far greater in an institution, but many a well-ordered Victorian middle-class household must have suffered from the same deadening influences. The Booth children enjoyed freedom and adventure in abundance. Catherine remembered:

'We had a garden which ran down to the fields and I remember running barefoot in the dewy grass looking for mushrooms. In the autumn we would pick blackberries and make blackberry and apple jam.

'There were seven of us in the family and we had marvellous times. We were never scolded or smacked. The great power was our love for our parents and our desire to please them. The way Mother used to say, ''Oh, darling, don't do that. Papa would be grieved.'' That went to your heart.'

Olive remembers her mother coming in when they were eating breakfast one morning, and shooing them out into the garden with their half-eaten bread and butter, to pick an apple from the tree and finish their meal out of doors. Florence was far more relaxed and unworried about the children than her helper, Miss Asdell, as Olive explained:

'Zazie said to me one day, ''You see, your mother was young with you. I used to feel so nervous and say to her, 'Oh, do stop them! Look at them on the trapeze!' And she would say, 'Don't look at them! They're all right!' '' Mother was never a kill-joy. If we came in because we had cut our knee open, it was only a minor thing in Mother's eyes. She was sensible with us and it taught us not to make a fuss.'

Florence had her own ideas about diet too, far in advance of her time. The Booth family meals come closer to present-day recommendations for healthy eating than something out of Mrs Beeton, in whose *Book of Household Management* 'plain family dinners' often combine such courses as pea soup, stewed rump steak, cold beef, mashed potato and rolled jam pudding. Even in June one menu to be followed is asparagus soup, boiled beef, young carrots, new potatoes and suet dumplings, then college pudding.

The Booth diet was mainly vegetarian, with the exception of fish and chicken. There was plenty of milk, cheese and fruit and wholemeal bread, made to a recipe still followed in the Booth sisters' kitchen. Florence had a dislike of recipes which used boiled milk. She called it 'dead' milk, as she believed that all the beneficial organisms were killed in the heating process. Instead she daily prepared a soured milk sweet, still served at the Booth sisters' lunch table. (A few years ago, Catherine summoned their milk supplier and complained that his milk would not go sour, which made it impossible to make their regular milk dish. He commented that in all his experience he had never before had a complaint that his milk would *not* go sour and advised the use of Channel Island milk, which is not treated by the same process. The advice was followed and the glass dish of creamy sour milk continues to be served daily with accompanying prunes or brown sugar.)

Honey was bought in bulk and arrived in tall square tins. Olive remembers the pleasure of filling pots from the tins. Later, when they kept bees and made their own honey, Olive was in charge.

It was easier to increase their family of animals now that they lived in the country. Their father was an authority on them all. His mother had taught her children to love animals as intensely as she did and to feel as strongly about cruelty towards them. Catherine remembered Bramwell's concern for all their pets:

'As we grew older we kept all manner of pets and these were his special interest. What excitement when he brought home some new "person" from the city! A rat, a guinea-pig or a dog. He advised on all matters concerning them, and we were occasionally allowed to "sit up late" to show him fresh arrivals or to be comforted for some tragic loss. He inspired in each of us an intense devotion to dumb creatures. Cruelty in every shape, but under the guise of amusement most of all, was made hateful in our eyes. I do not remember hearing him say much about it, though what he did say was said in such fashion as to make an unforgettable impression. But his persistently expressed love for all living things, his reverence for their beauty (he could make us feel that even spiders and fleas had their good points) somehow linked all creatures with himself. If on our walks we met an overloaded horse, beaten by the hill (and by its driver!), it was for his, our father's sake as much as for the horse, that we persuaded the man to let us help unload some of the brick or swedes and push. Three or four of us at one wheel and the man at the other started many a load. There were ruts and mud in those days. ''Tell Papa!'' would be the cry when the adventure had been recounted to our mother, or to Miss Asdell, for he was seldom home before our bedtime.

'He came downstairs with me once in the middle of the night because I had heard a strange sound from the ''animal'' shed. We found the hedgehog had got in and was eating our favourite and oldest guinea-pig, queen of all the guinea-pigs! The queer part was that, although she paused to make, for a guinea-pig, horribly loud cries, she then resumed the eating of a lettuce leaf! How tenderly my father cared for the little creature, comforted me and gave me instructions how to nurse the invalid! She recovered.' (*Bramwell Booth*)

When Catherine was about ten years old she was given her first dog and called him Carlo. Bramwell used to pass a pet shop on his way to Salvation Army headquarters every day. Every day he saw the same sad little spaniel in the window and one day, unable to bear its misery any longer, he went inside and bought it. (From Carlo's time on, there has been a succession of dogs, up to the present day.) At eight years old, Catherine's letter to 'darling Grandpa' is full of news of the animals:

'The rat is all right. Mary calls it Scotty now after your ship. We have only one mouse; we sold the rest for Self-Denial. One rabbit is dead, the other is very big. Miriam had a hedgehog but it got lost. A lot of love and kisses from us all. Your loving Cath.'

Bramwell brought Catherine, Mary and a tame mouse into one of his sermons, to illustrate the practical implications of love. *The War Cry* for 10 May 1890 carried a report:

'One of my children has a tame mouse and she is very fond of it. The little animal is a real pet creature. Her little sister was talking to her one day and the conversation was overheard and reported to me. Catherine was telling Mary how much she loved her, embraced her and said she had never seen another little girl she loved so much and liked to play with so well . . . Mary looked at Cath with her great eyes and said, "Oh, Cath, do you say it or do you feel it, 'cos I want that mouse!"'

Florence's father, Dr Soper, had brought up his daughters 'to be at home in the sick-chamber', and Florence combined her own common sense with her mother-in-law's dicta when she had to nurse her children through the illnesses of childhood.

'Our seven children grew up without knowing the taste of any kind of physic,' she claimed, a most unusual relief from the customary Victorian dosing with purges. Mrs Beeton, writing about 'The Rearing and Management of Children', recommended giving an aperient for every kind of childish illness and still advocated the application of leeches as sometimes necessary in the early stages of measles. Nearly all Victorian homes kept a ready supply of 'black draught', to be administered to sick and healthy, old and young alike. A recipe of the time lists the ingredients:

'Infusion of senna, 10 drachms; Epsom salts, 10 drachms; tincture of senna, compound tincture of cardomoms, compound spirit of lavender, of each 1 drachm. Families who make black draught in quantity, and wish to preserve it for some time without spoiling, should add about 2 drachms of spirit of hartshorn to each pint of the strained mixture, the use of this drug being to prevent its becoming mouldy or decomposed.'

Happy the Booths, who were saved the horror of the black draught! Bramwell's mother had taken the advice of a homeopathic doctor not to take any laxative drug.

'He said, "Do as I advise and I will venture to say you will not need it."' His alternative was 'creed' wheat—grain that had been softened by gentle heating in the oven for fourteen or fifteen hours. Creed wheat became a regular part of the Booth diet for the next hundred years. During the Second World War, Lord Woolton, the Food Minister, arranged for special rations of it to be allowed to them.

As well as learning to use homeopathic medicine, Florence followed Mrs Booth's use of hydropathy. Hydropathy—practised today under the name of hydrotherapy—implies a cure by water, but is really a form of hot and cold treatment, using water as the medium. It was first introduced into England in about 1840, but the methods used were so drastic that they were suitable only for sturdy patients. Then Dr Smedley, a Derbyshire industrialist, introduced a gentler form of the treatment at his hydropathic establishment in Matlock. In 1860 William Booth had been suffering from a prolonged illness which began with a bad 'throat attack'. Mrs Booth had stepped into his shoes and taken all his meetings, but the strain was immense for the whole family. Then she wrote to her parents:

'Wm. is still very poorly, not able to work and so by the advice of many friends and two doctors he is going to Smedley's Hydro-pathic establishment at Matlock in Derbyshire. He thinks of staying three weeks or a month, the expense will be heavy unless he gets some favour, but he *must* get better . . . If you can borrow at one of the newspaper offices a book entitled *Smedley's Practical Hydropathy* it will give you an account of the institution and the treatment.' (*Catherine Booth*)

Simple forms of the treatment could be carried out in the home and Mrs Booth treated William herself when possible. On one occasion before her marriage to Bramwell, Florence had fallen ill and been treated by Mrs Booth. She described what happened:

'I was seated in a wooden box with a hole in the sloping lid which closed around the neck, leaving the head outside, a lighted spirit lamp under the chair, my feet in hot water. I felt cooked in it and made myself a little too much of a Spartan by enduring silently until I gave the attendant a fright by fainting . . . I had not before qualified in resemblance to the young women of the Victorian age as described in books of that time! Later I learned to enjoy this bath and other forms of the water treatment.' In fact, Florence went on, 'In serious illness I have several times seen hydropathy work a miracle and a life be spared when doctors had given up hope. Mrs Booth was very enthusiastic in her belief in the treatment of illness by water, externally and internally, and I became her docile follower.'

When Catherine had a feverish attack as a small child she was wrapped in a wet sheet, which in turn was covered tightly by blankets. When the sheet dried with the body's heat it was either rewetted, and the treatment repeated, or the patient was given a warm bath and put back to bed.

Not everyone approved. One Salvation Army officer, Commissioner Railton, wrote to Florence:

'I am so horrified at the idea of that precious little Catherine the third being put into packs that I cannot refrain from remonstrating . . . a cure by such a plan may be worse than most diseases . . . I know you will excuse my writing thus when I think of that lovely child.' The lovely child recovered and, with her brothers and sisters, continued to receive such treatment for all childish illnesses.

At first hydropathy was also taught to cadets at the Training Garrison and methods included in manuals for officers. In the days before both the 'panel' system of treating the poorly off and national health medicine, a simple and inexpensive form of home treatment was welcome. Florence, like her mother-in-law, used hydropathy in the course of her Army work too. Her daughters remember how, as leader of the Women's Social Work, she visited one of the Homes and found a girl in the laundry room who had suffered a bad accident. Olive explained:

This girl 'was standing up on the copper—she was very short —and she fell in. She had a most awful leg and the doctor had said, ''This young person must go and have her leg amputated.'' Mother said, ''No, let me first try the treatment I know, before you attempt that. If she's no better, all right.'' She soaked the leg, with the sore covered by a cloth, in hot soapy water, with pure soap, at least twice a day. The leg was covered with a clean rag before it came out of the water—that way it never came in contact with the air and no infection reached it. Then it was wrapped round. The leg was saved.'

As well as water, mustard was used for childish injuries and in the usual infectious diseases, as Florence recalled, 'Our seven children . . . were all nursed by me through the common ailments of childhood—scarlet fever, measles and whooping cough—with hot or cold mustard bran packs.'

Colman's were advertising their mustard bran and mustard plasters at this time as the ideal poultice for a wide variety of complaints. In the case of mustard plasters the instructions suggest that 'in the case of very young children, whose skins are delicate, interpose between the Plaster and the skin one or two folds (according to age) of cambric or fine linen, and afterwards secure with a bandage.'

No doubt all such precautions were taken in the Booth household.

Very little disturbed the happy security of the children's

carefree life at Hadley Wood. When Bramwell and Florence went away on 'furlough' they went alone. As Catherine explained, 'Except as infants and from necessity, the children did not accompany their parents on holiday; that would have made accommodation a prohibitive expenditure!'

But their home and garden, the surrounding countryside and one another's company seem to have been enough to satisfy them. Sometimes Bramwell would take some holiday at home and then, Catherine recalled, 'he and my mother went riding nearly every day. Oh! the delight of being hoisted on to the saddle and walked up and down, when they came home!'

Once she remembers the thrill of being allowed to stay up late so that she could go with her parents to hear the nightingales sing at Beech Hill. 'The only kind of musical entertainment to which he ever took us!' she adds, a little ruefully.

'I do not remember his going anywhere with us for an outing when we were small, but once or twice he came fishing for minnows and sticklebacks in the ponds by Harris' Wood at Hadley where we lived. Looking back on those rare hours, the sun seems to have been shining all the time, or was it just his presence? He made it all so exciting. I see him stooping over Miriam, a radiant child of five, steadying her hand, his smile in contrast to her deadly seriousness as he manoeuvres her net. There are dragon-flies about the pools, a lark is singing, the bullocks grazing have no disturbing influence. *He* is with us, we are safe and happy, perfectly, thrillingly happy. The homeward procession is as gleeful as was the outward. The small members of the party are perhaps somewhat dishevelled. The edge of the ponds are trodden by cattle, and zeal in pursuit generally means that mud is carried home as well as fish. On our return he helps to fix up a zinc bath, into which the garden tap drips. Instructions to take the fish back to the pond when they begin to get sickly do not cloud the joy of possession.' (*Bramwell Booth*)

Special events in The Salvation Army calendar provided opportunity for family outings too. The Christmas after Mrs Booth died, the vast Congress Hall, where her body had lain, was turned into a 'guestchamber' for the homeless encountered in the Army's rescue work. The General paid a visit to the centre and Florence took the three girls to a meeting there. In the train coming home, Florence asked them whether they understood the meeting and what they liked best. Catherine replied that her favourite bit was The Salvation Army lass who illustrated her remarks by singing:

> *I scrub the floors for Jesus,*
> *I turn the mangle for Jesus.*

She admired practical Christianity from an early age.

In 1893 when Florence was again pregnant, Catherine was invited to stay in Dartmoor, with the family of one of Florence's 'helpers'. Catherine was nine and it was her first experience of staying away from home with strangers. She wrote frequent letters home, one, Florence remembered, covering twenty pages. But her copperplate writing was flowing and large at that time. She told her mother about her visits to a twelve-year-old girl:

'She has hurt her knee badly and will have a stiff leg all her life. I go in and read to her.'

In another letter:

'I go and see the cows milked nearly every day and the calves fed, and, Mama, do moles spoil the ground in any way, darling, will you let me know? I was walking across a field. I saw an iron thing sticking up and went to see what it was and just underneath I saw the paw of a mole and knew it was a trap. I was so sorry for the mole and I saw the whole body. I covered it over and then picked up the trap and put it into the Leet where no one can see it.[1] It was a family of moles who lived there, for there were lots of little hills.'

Her hostess seems to have enjoyed the visit. She wrote:

'My dear Mrs Booth, we have this day parted with your dear little Catherine with great regret—she is a dear child and there is much in her that ought to delight any mother . . .' The rest of the letter is missing.

The longed-for baby arrived on 29 June. She was to be the youngest daughter and was named Dorothy, but affectionately called Dora.

Florence still felt concern about her eldest daughter's spiritual progress. When Catherine was eleven, Florence wrote in her diary:

'How my heart yearns over her! She is richly endowed in many ways but needs more grace. In our life of rush and worry I hardly

---

[1] The Leet ran through the grounds and conveyed water to Plymouth.

know how to foster in them the love of prayer and communion with God as I should wish.'

That birthday brought a special present for Catherine. In 1885 Mr Stanley of The Rover Cycle Company had first produced 'Stanley's Rover Safety Cycle' and, because he was a friend of The Salvation Army, Florence Booth had been one of the first women to own and ride one of them. Now Mr Stanley had made a bicycle specially for Catherine. Florence entered in her diary:

'The dear child was very delighted with her cycle and went out to ride on it.'

Thereafter mother and daughter rode together on the roads and lanes around Hadley Wood. In Catherine's words, they 'occasioned much fun to village boys and others'.

Although Catherine and her sisters and brother did not go away from home often, their parents did. But they seldom had the pleasure of going together. Their Army duties took them different ways. It may have been this same year that Catherine prepared a surprise birthday present for Miriam and wrote to tell her father all about it:

'Mimi's birthday went off well. I gave her a dress for her doll and a pair of shoes which I put in a tiny box which was half full of pink paper shavings; in each of the shoes I put a piece of light blue stuff and in one shoe I put one of my little black and white mice and in the other one of my white ones. She was very pleased. I wish you could have been with us; it would have been much more fun.

'We are all going to be very good while you are away. Dear Mamma has gone to Manchester, so we are all alone.'

It is to be hoped that Mama was there for 18 June—Miriam's birthday—and that the trip to Manchester followed. There is a little wistfulness in the comment: 'I wish you could have been with us; it would have been much more fun', and in the conclusion 'we are all alone.' No doubt there was Miss Asdell and of course nurse, cook and the rest of a necessary Victorian middle-class household. But without Papa and Mama, the children felt 'all alone'.

As an adult Catherine realized that it was his strong love for them that made Bramwell weigh up so seriously the words of his Master recorded in Matthew's Gospel, chapter 10: 'He who loves son or daughter more than me is not worthy of me.' But she also questions his almost total sacrifice of family to the Army:

'Did Christ require of him such an abandonment of the reasonable enjoyment of what were, after all, God-given opportunities for happiness? Did the Army usurp too large a share of what he was and what he possessed? He would have argued, ''Have not men given as much for their country, for science, even for mere gain?'' To which one might reply, ''Yes, but was it right?'' I never heard this discussed at home. I do not think he ever questioned himself about it. The Army came first and the position was accepted by us all as part of the existing order, and undoubtedly he was satisfied of the rightness of the course he took.' (*Bramwell Booth*)

CHAPTER 7

Broken Routines

W HEN DORA WAS STILL A BABY, William Booth moved
from number 19, The Crescent into a new, smaller house
built for him by The Salvation Army at the back of his old house.
The Bramwell Booths then moved across from number 55 to 19,
'The Homestead', which was a larger family house more suited to
their needs. They were able to cut across their own garden to visit
the General at 'Rookstone', his new home.

Perhaps it was during the upheaval of the house moves that
Catherine, Mary, Miriam and Olive were sent on a visit to their
Grandfather Soper. He had retired from medical practice in Blaina
in 1893 and returned to his native town of Plymouth, where he
and his second wife lived in Windsor Terrace.

When he retired 'he gave his daughter one of the Welsh ponies,
bred on the home farm at Blaina, whose mother, Little Dorrit, had
been a favourite mount. Panks lived and worked at Hadleigh
Colony and was available with a trap of the ''governess'' type to
accompany his owner for the holidays, adding much to their joys.
Swift enough to satisfy his mistress, he often rather startled
pedestrians in the Kentish lanes by the speed at which he travelled.
One day the closing of a gate behind him startled him, he bolted,
drove through the next five-barred gate, and a grave accident was
but narrowly averted. After this escapade he was not allowed his
part in the holidays, and for a time bicycles did duty in his stead.'
(*Bramwell Booth*)

At Windsor Terrace, Catherine, Mary and Miriam were put in
a room together at the top of the house. Bramwell wrote to
Catherine in serious vein:

> My daughter,
> Love to Mary and Mim and Olive. Pray with them. Tell
> Mary I want to hear from her. I was pleased with Mim's
> letter.

In speaking to friends do not forget your Lord and
Master. Put a word in for Him when you can, to both young
and old.

I pray for you all. My love to each and to the Aunties and
Grandpapa.

No doubt the words were taken to heart but the three older girls
also managed to have fun. Olive, who was only three years old,
probably slept nearer the adults, but she later recounted one of the
escapades that the older girls used to talk about.

'There was a big Victorian wash basin with a huge basin and jug
filled for you to wash every morning. One morning they were
having fun about cleaning their teeth and two of them pulled on
the legs of the washstand so that the whole lot came down with a
crash, smashing the basin and jug. Terrible sensation! Deathly
silence—they didn't know what to do, but Grandpapa Soper came
up the stairs like a tornado. Their absolute shock was to see him
with his little nightcap on!'

'He was a great tease, Catherine said. She was very sensitive,
you know, and one day he took her out and said, ''I want you to
look through the telescope.'' He put the telescope to her eye and
said, ''Can you see anything?'' She said, ''No''. So he told her to
shut one eye and then the other. Still she said, ''No, I can't see
anything, Grandpa.'' Then he'd roar with laughter. Every time
she looked he had put his newspaper in front—teasing her like
that. It made her feel such a fool. That's the sort of man he was. I
was terrified of him.'

In fact, Dr Soper was probably not very different from a large
number of Victorian adults who found amusement in making
children feel foolish and considered it harmless fun.

In 1895, when Catherine was nearly twelve, Florence was
expecting her seventh and last child. At that time it was normal for
all unmarried girls, let alone children, to be kept in complete ignor-
ance about a mother's or married sister's pregnancy. A younger
contemporary of Catherine's was in officer training when her
mother had a baby but was told little or nothing. As she said, 'You
knew that babies came, but not how. And you never asked
questions!'

But Florence told Catherine about the child that she was to have.
'My mother had shared with me the beautiful mystery of the

babe's advent. I learned then something new about love, that my mother's delight had taught me.'

The baby, a boy, was born on 7 December and was named William Wycliffe. But all was not well:

'After the child's birth she did not rally,' Catherine wrote, 'and though we children knew nothing of it there was much anxiety about her. On Christmas Eve she was taken suddenly worse. I clearly remember that evening. My father was at Headquarters. Since the baby's arrival we had hardly seen him; he had only returned home after we were in bed, and was gone before we were out of the nursery in the morning. I shall never forget going to meet him after he had been summoned by telegram—telephones were not in general use in those days. I see the cold, deserted station, I see him leap from the carriage, a look upon his face which makes him seem almost a stranger to me. He takes me by the hand and we run together up the station steps into the darkness of the winter night and home without word or pause. That night I learned something new about love, the marks of suffering on my father's face had taught me.

'Our mother's life was despaired of; for weeks she lay very near death. We were all packed off into the General's house near by; he was in India. Mercifully my Aunt Emma was within reach when this anguish came upon my father.' (*Bramwell Booth*)

Olive, who was four years old, remembers 'most distinctly' being carried across the road:

'Mother was so ill that we were moved into the Founder's house across the road. I *think* I'd been carried in to look at Wycliffe—I don't remember anything about the baby but I do remember going across late at night with the French maid and noticing the sky— never having noticed it in my life before—and looking up at the stars and thinking how wonderful they were.'

Miss Asdell was at hand to help, as ever, looking after Florence it seems, while Aunt Emma cared for the children. Bramwell wrote to the General, 'Miss Asdell has placed us under lifelong obligation by her toil and patience and skill', and Catherine commented:

'This was the only occasion since her childhood when my mother was seriously ill, and my father never ceased to look upon her recovery as a particular token of God's mercy to him and to us all, for she was our sun and his: what darkness for us had her light gone down!' (*Bramwell Booth*)

Florence gradually recovered but through her illness Catherine had learned another lesson about love. Suffering must always be an ingredient of loving others. At ten she had suffered when she found the mole cruelly caught in the trap and had hurled the iron snare into the water. Now that she was older she began to suffer with human beings throughout the world.

In autumn 1895 the first of a series of massacres of the Armenians by the Turks took place. In spite of warning moves by world powers, the massacres continued into 1896. Olive said:

'This was a great distress at home, with Catherine and Mary—they knew about it. I don't remember anything.[1] At home they were talking about it and Catherine felt dreadful about it—What could they do for the Armenians? Mary remembered how they were out for a walk by themselves in the country and Catherine covered all her hands with nettles and said, ''The Armenians are suffering and I'm going to suffer with them.'' Mary, being quite a different character—very practical—said, ''*I'm* not going to suffer! What's the good of my suffering with the Armenians?'' That showed her different character. I think it was rather unusual of Catherine and rather sweet. In a way it's almost the foundation of religion—you suffer with your Lord.'

Catherine was learning to forget her own problems and sorrows by entering into those of others. When she was a woman she wrote:

'I cannot explain *why* weeping with another dries my own tears, but it does; nor why sharing another's load should make me less conscious of my own, but it does; nor how putting out my hand to save some one else from stumbling in their sorrow keeps my foot from slipping, but it does . . . I long that you should prove it.' (*Letters*)

[1] Olive would have been four.

CHAPTER 8

The Old General

G ENERAL WILLIAM BOOTH, now living a stone's throw from
Bramwell and Florence and their young family, was a potent
force in their lives. Bramwell adored his father and whenever they
were apart wrote him 'a line' daily.

William was born in Nottingham in 1829 and retained his
Nottingham accent to the end of his days. His father made and
lost a fortune before the lad was twelve so when he left school
he had to be apprenticed to a pawnbroker, because his father
reckoned that 'there was money in it'.

His granddaughter, Catherine, wrote 100 years after his birth,
'At fifteen he was acquainted with slums and sinners, and had
already begun to speak of the beauty of Christ and to sing of
Heaven to the poor who gathered around to listen in the back
streets of the city'. When he moved to London he continued his
preaching in his few spare hours and was in time sponsored first as
an evangelist and then to train for the Methodist ministry.

When he met Catherine Mumford he found the woman he could
love with all his heart, who became his good angel for the rest of
her days. Together they worked heart and soul, first as Methodists
and then in the founding of The Christian Mission and, at last, The
Salvation Army. Their own lives and those of their children were
bound up with the Army and with one another in a peculiarly close
way.

In characteristic fashion, William channelled his energies,
during the long weary months of his wife's final illness, into
writing a book that would bring the terrible plight of London's
poor to the attention of the whole country. The book was actually
published a month after Mrs Booth's death and was called *In
Darkest England and the Way Out*. The title would ring a bell in all
ears, for the famous Henry Stanley, the journalist who 'discovered'
Livingstone after his long disappearance, had published a book
called *In Darkest Africa*. Booth's temerity in comparing

77

respectable 'Christian' London with the pagan African jungle shocked Victorian sensibilities. He focussed attention on what he described as 'the submerged tenth' and wrote, 'The lot of the Negress in the Equatorial Forest is not, perhaps, a very happy one, but is it so very much worse than that of many a pretty orphan girl in our Christian capital?'

William Booth's was not the only voice raised in protest. His contemporary and namesake, Charles Booth, a pioneer sociologist, reckoned that over thirty per cent of London's population lived in poverty and that those statistics were true for all the big cities.

T. H. Huxley, one of The Salvation Army's most scathing critics, wrote that the Polynesian savage 'in his most primitive condition' was 'not half so savage, so unclean, so irreclaimable as the tenant of a tenement in an East London slum.'

William Booth took action. Fast on the heels of the book came a scheme to alleviate the problem. It was known first as *The Darkest England Scheme* and later became the Army's Social Work. As part of the campaign, a large area of farmland was bought at Hadleigh, five miles from Southend. Those who wanted work but were unable to get it, for one reason or another, could live and work on the colony. There was arable farming, pigs, sheep and dairy farming and there were horses to be cared for in the stables. A mill and factories processed the produce and nearby road, rail and river transported the products to London for sale. The dining-room seated 300 and the colony provided work for men of many different trades—or none. Before long a refreshment-room was added to cater for visitors who arrived in hundreds, on special excursion trains. Queen Victoria herself came to inspect the colony. Major and Mrs Stitt were in charge—he known as Candle-ends Stitt because of his genius for economy.

The Booth children loved their visits to the Stitts and the chance to see the many animals on the farm. A 'thank you' letter from Catherine, dated 11 April 1894 when she was ten, and written to Mrs Stitt, hints at mutual affection and shared enthusiasms:

> Dear Mrs Sitt,[1]
> I don't know how to thank you for sending me such lovely flowers! It is so kind of you! Miriam and Mary both ask to

[1] Some problem with the name here.

have some put in their gardens; we shall go and plant them this morning when our lessons are over.

We are so fond of plants and animals, that we should like to live at the Farm Colony all together.

I hope your little baby is quite well! We were at the Two Days with God on Monday; we enjoyed it very much. I hear there were five hundred saved.

The dear General must be very tired.

Thanking you again,

Your loving little friend

Catherine Booth

It is good to know that the children visited the Farm as well as attending Two Days with God.[1]

Miss Asdell, writing about Florence's three eldest daughters in *The Deliverer* in 1902, assured readers that:

'Some of these young girls' most precious moments are spent with the dear General, when he is at home from his frequent tours. Advice and encouragement from him are greatly treasured by his three eldest grand-children; and it is a real joy to him and their dear parents that in a very decided way they give promise of following in the footsteps of their saintly grandmother.'

The reality may have been a little different. Catherine explained that it was love for her father that prompted her to care for her grandfather.

'He (Bramwell) taught us too that there was one person in the world to please above all others—''Grandpa'', or as we more often called him, the General. It was the rule that one of us should go over to see him every day when he was at home. In the latter years of his life he worked more at home than at Headquarters and there were often long periods of daily visits. I have more than once jumped out of a window to rush over to ''Rookstone'' as I heard my father coming into the house in the evening, for it was unbearable to hear him say, ''I think you might remember to go, for my sake.''' (*Bramwell Booth*)

When in 1976 Peter France asked Catherine in an interview for television, 'Were you in awe of your grandfather?' she answered:

[1] The title given first in 1887 to meetings held by the General in various cities.

'Yes. Definitely. Half frightened of him. He was very different from my father . . . He had a gruff manner and he had a dramatic personality—the way he spoke and even the way he stirred his tea and the way he could hold forth if the toast was not to his liking—and I was a horribly shy child. I remember going to see him and he'd say, ''Well, how did you get on at the corps?'' (That was our little post, where we went as soldiers.) So I was telling him something about it and he said, ''Did *you* do anything?'' ''Yes, Grandpa, I sang.'' ''How was it?'' ''Well,'' I said, ''I did my best.'' He turned round and I can see him now—he was sitting at his desk—''Did your best, Catherine? Anyone can do their best! You'll be no good if you can't do better than your best!''

'That was a very frightening response. I could have burst out crying, only I felt that I should have let them down at home if I had. Then he went on to say:

' ''Don't you see, dear child, that when you've got God to help you that's just what happens? Anyone can do their best but if God is helping you, you can do better than your best.'' '

Writing about him for *The War Cry* Catherine remembered another unhappy experience:

'I can recall now the horror that seized me when awakened one Christmas morning by hearing loud thumps of his walking-stick on the linoleum floor of our hall and my Grandfather's splendid voice ringing through the house as he sang, ''Christians awake, salute the happy morn''. It was our custom early on Christmas day to creep into our Grandfather's house and burst into song outside his bedroom door. He enjoyed teasing us about the way he had turned the tables on us!'

In the same article she recalled the happy times with her grandfather:

'I remember the wonderful parties he gave us when he was at home for Christmas. What feasts! We always sang grace with the chorus ''And above the rest this note shall swell my Jesus has done all things well'' with clapping of hands.

'After the feast (with 'every kind of cake' she says elsewhere) came the excitement of opening presents. My younger brother Wycliffe often talked of his joy at receiving his first Salvation Army uniform cap! And at another Christmas ''do'' my youngest sister had her first bonnet. Always there was singing before the party broke up. The General and all of us singing at the top of our voices. Someone at the piano, there was often some kind of drum "played" by one of my brothers. My Grandfather loved singing. His voice dominated the sound of song and always the last was "My Jesus I love Thee, I know Thou art mine" to the tune of "The Mistletoe Bough". The refrain, "Oh the mercy of God", was repeated again and again.

'As I write, I see like a coloured film, my Grandfather leaning back in his chair at the writing-table where sheets of paper he had scribbled on were scattered. I had come in to greet him as one of us did every day. He had a joyful look as he said, "Here Cath, what do you think of this?" Throwing back his head as he did when preaching, he recited the first two or three verses of "O boundless salvation". We had a happy time discussing and rejoicing together.'

Olive talked about the visits to the General when they were children:

'He lived alone—he had a secretary and he had a housekeeper and we used to go to see him often, dressed in our little uniforms— red blouses and blue skirts. We always lived in great awe of him. All of us in turn used to go to his house for tea, when he was at home. He didn't talk much but we went to pour tea for him, especially later on when he was nearly blind. But we went just to be a little bit of company for him. We were very meek. We used to listen to him talking. Sometimes he asked us questions—sometimes he was more silent than others. What we did like was when he and father were together. Then we would be frightfully quiet so that we should not be sent out. It was a lovely thing to listen to them talking. We had a world globe given to us so when they talked, say, about China, we went over and found China on our globe.'

Catherine wrote about those tea parties:

'There were often tea parties for the children at one or other of the two homes, to celebrate a birthday or the General's arrival from a journey. These functions nearly always ended in the complete absorption of father and son in each other. The elder young folk listened spell-bound, the smaller fry were kept from fidgeting by admonitory glances until the General would suddenly remember them with a laughing, "Here you children, be off!" and then fall to talking again. What a picture they made! All animation. The conversations strode over the universe. There was often laughter, always argument, sometimes invective, sudden gesture on the part of the General that put the cups and saucers in jeopardy, and now and then a shadow of inexpressible sadness. The miseries of the people, disappointments within the Army, were always with them. These two hardly ever met, and they met every day when they were within reach of each other, but there was some anxiety looming up, or some sorrow the wounds of which were not yet healed. And however widely the discussions might range, they always came back to the ''Concern'', the wholly-loved, the wholly-engrossing Army.' (*Bramwell Booth*)

Catherine grieved at never having had a good singing voice, but when she was young she used to sing for her grandfather when he was preaching. 'People like to hear a childish treble', she would explain. She used to sit behind him on the platform and watch, with a sensitivity unusual for a child: 'I can see him—head thrown back, hands behind him, and I could tell, from how he moved his fingers, whether he was feeling at home or not.'

Whenever the General returned from one of his frequent tours, the children would set out for the station to meet him, carrying drums and other brass instruments so that they could escort him home with a strictly family Salvation Army band. In 1895, when he was due to arrive home from a tour of Canada and the USA, they collected enough firewood to make a huge celebratory bonfire.

'He was a strongly affectionate man', Catherine wrote in 1929, 'and inspired us all with confidence in his love for us, which bred a desperate longing to do what he expected of us, and above all to help with the Army.' Perhaps for all his love for the children, the General aroused that 'desperate longing to please' rather than an affectionate response of childlike love from his small grandchildren across the way.

CHAPTER 9

'A Happy Discipline'

A S WITH MOST BIG FAMILIES, Bramwell's and Florence's
seven children seemed to divide naturally into two groups—
Catherine, Mary and Miriam in one, the four younger ones in the
other.

'I think we were a bit more rampagious than the older ones',
Olive remembered, 'because the boys were in our group. We used
to split into pairs for games—the older boy with the younger girl
and the older girl with the younger boy, to make it fair.

'We were never made to feel unhappy if we got dirty—even if we
were covered with mud from head to foot. We were told to come in
by the scullery and when we four were having a great time digging
a clay pit in the garden, we were told to go to the shed and take our
overalls off there. They used to stand up with the clay! But we
were never made to feel we weren't to do it. Mother was
wonderful.'

Florence allowed the four younger ones to sleep in an outside
shed all year round. She bought them bunks and before they went
off to bed for the night they would file into the kitchen where cook
would take a brick from the kitchen range, wrap it in a blanket, and
give it to them to keep them warm in their garden hideout.

But there were many times when Florence was not at home.
Catherine said in an interview for *The Sunday Times*:

'I used to look after all the others when we were small. Mother
went all over the country, and sometimes to France or Germany,
preaching. She took whichever baby she was feeding with her . . .

'When I was twelve, Mother took to going away without taking
the youngest with her. Then she left them to me. I loved it. I don't
think I could have loved children more if they had been my own.'

Florence wrote:

'I suppose that in every family the firstborn has a greater
influence for good or evil than the others. I have been fortunate
indeed in having as leader of my flock one who resembled her

father in heart and mind as well as likeness, and who even from her tenderest years has been my right hand. The depth of her affection was apparent as soon as she could make herself understood.'

Miss Asdell agreed:

'As for the manner in which Catherine has discharged her obligations as the eldest daughter and sister, it would be impossible to say too much. Affection and unselfishness are dominant in her, and she enjoys the unbounded love and confidence of those about her. To the younger children, ''Cath says'', is an unwritten law in both lessons and play. She is an ideal leader in romps and games, as well as in the daily duties, and nothing else is such a delight to the nursery party in winter evenings as when ''Catherine is coming up to play 'Bear' '' and the house rings with the shouts of those whom the ''Bear'' captures.'

As one of those younger children, Olive agreed:

'When we were children we used to fall out a bit, but we soon made it up. Of course, Catherine was almost a second mother to us because our mother was away a lot. To us younger ones, she was almost grown up. She entered into our fun though, and organized games for us.' And again: 'We all loved Catherine very much. I don't remember ever feeling any resentment because she was the eldest. She was someone to fly to for comfort, if you were in trouble or had had a terrible fall-out with your brother.'

How carefree a childhood did Catherine herself enjoy? Was she one of the little group that set off to walk barefoot to the sole shop in the village, where portly Mrs Brinklow dispensed sweets and other treasures in exchange for pocket-money? Or was she in charge of the expedition, seeing that the little ones were safe?

Probably she was in no way responsible for the nickname of 'the screaming Booths' by which the children were known in the neighbourhood. Their fun and freedom may have been acquired at the cost of Catherine's own. Yet her own memories show that there *were* carefree days:

'We had such wonderful times running through the country-side. We were never scolded or restricted and the only rule was that we had to clean our own boots.'

But life was not all freedom and running wild. The children had to be educated and on this matter, too, Florence and Bramwell had strong views of their own. They did not believe in sending the children to school and Florence taught them herself at home. This entry in Florence's diary in 1896 probably indicates the main reason for their decision:

'Pleasant walk in morning with Bramwell—talked over plans for future . . . he helped me to see that it was better to keep Catherine away even from classes (which she could have joined at the girls' school nearby). The influence of competition is not good. That a child should be led to think better of herself because she does better than another or worse because she does not do so well, is not helpful. So for the present I go on doing the best I can.'

Perhaps there could have been helpful lessons to be learned from the competition encountered at a school. But 'for the present' continued and, as Catherine later explained:

'None of us went to school, neither the boys nor the girls. My mother educated me. The younger girls had a governess because an old great-aunt, when she died, left her little bit all to my mother. It was almost nothing, £80 a year or something like that . . . But my mother's joy in spending that money! . . . One of the things my mother did with the money was to pay for a governess . . . so the younger girls had a governess who came once or twice a week . . .

'I distinctly remember the lessons with my mother. We had a schoolroom in the house. She came in at nine o'clock. We were supposed by then to have cleared everything and we sat there two of us on each side. She came in to take the lesson, whatever it might be, and she was a wonderful teacher. She made us enjoy all subjects, even arithmetic, which I was very weak on. She was keen on mental arithmetic. She used to give us sums on the spot. She taught us the rudiments of algebra. She also taught us German from Otto's Grammar. We had a French maid always so we got a good grounding in practical French.' (*Commissioner Catherine*)

The Deliverer for May 1899 described Florence's schedule of work:

'Sometimes in her public addresses Mrs Booth says that she is the mother of two families—her very large Salvation Army family and the smaller home circle in London . . . Mrs Booth, when at home starts her day by personally presiding at the breakfast, which is immediately followed by family prayers. These she leads when the Chief of Staff is absent from home.

'The mail next demands attention; and then Mrs Booth usually spends most of the morning in the schoolroom. She carefully supervises all of the children's studies; and having a talent for imparting instruction and inspiring industry, teaching is a delight to her. A lady in the neighbourhood comes three times a week for an hour with the older children.

'Timetables for the different days are carefully made out, and closely followed. They include lessons in music (Florence taught all seven to play the piano), French and German, as well as history, mathematics etc. Examinations are held at the end of each term.

'The children all speak French and already some have put their knowledge to some use for the Army. The little ones are not pressed very much. Both Mrs Booth and the Chief are rather opposed to early cramming of the children's brains, and there is evidence that their plan is working out well in the case of the elder members of their family.'

Mondays were sometimes interrupted if Florence had not returned from Sunday meetings the same day, so the children could only depend on four days of proper length teaching. Florence reckoned to spend two and a half hours in the schoolroom, setting homework to be done in the afternoon. Then 'she had a little drink of something warm, nursed the baby, got on her uniform and went to the station' to catch the 12.46 train. Sometimes her secretary would meet her on the train so that she could use the travelling time to dictate letters. Catherine, or one of the older ones, would carry the baby to the station for their mother. Sometimes the family would meet her on her return. Florence described the scene:

'The gift of a small governess cart gave them great pleasure. How delighted Bernard was to take his place as the pony between the shafts that I might drive to the station or be brought home in triumph when I returned in the evening. They galloped about the roads most happily, on one occasion frightening the horses of a carriage and pair and alarming the two lady occupants. But nothing untoward happened.'

The Deliverer informed its readers that Mrs Booth spent one day a week in the provinces, visiting some of the Homes for which she was responsible. On such days, no doubt, Catherine not only supervised afternoon homework but also helped put them to bed. Olive remembered:

'The older ones put us to bed, helped us to get up and that sort of thing. They kept us in order—we had to be punctual to meals because *they* would be. A sister can say things that you wouldn't accept from an outsider—love makes you accept what's said. The discipline was good and it was a happy discipline. Our one desire was not to grieve Mother or Father and we got that through the love of the older ones.'

Perhaps the most important part of the children's education was the love of books and reading that both parents gave to them. At ninety-six Catherine wrote:

'On one of the rare occasions when my Father had time from his Salvation Army work to be with us, he was reading to the upper end of the family from "Uncle Remus", when overcome by the fun of the tale he laid the book down on his knee, put back his head and shouted with laughter in which we all joined. A moment of pure happiness as clear to me today as eighty-five years ago!'

Olive and Dora recalled how their father encouraged them to build up their own library of books. Dora explained:

'In those days there was a series of books called Everyman. You paid a shilling for a hard back—there were no paperbacks in my childhood. They were all different colours—red was history, blue was fiction, I think. Father used to give Olive and me the catalogue—very small print—listing the books under headings of History, Science, Biography, Political Science. Then he'd say, "Now your birthday—or Christmas—is coming. Choose five books and I'll get them for you." And we'd all pore over the catalogue and choose. And I built up a childish library of history—they're in my book-case now—all bought in five-shilling blocks. He always ended up saying—"Mind, no fiction!"'

'Don't go away thinking fiction wasn't allowed. Fiction was for holidays and leisure time only.'

Certainly Florence read aloud to them all the standard works of fiction—Thackeray, Dickens, Trollope, George Eliot and the Brontës. The children lay on their backs or on their faces, which was 'good for the spine', while they listened. Reading aloud was a favourite Victorian occupation. Mrs Beeton, writing on 'The Manner of Passing Evenings at Home,' comments that 'there is none pleasanter than in such recreative enjoyments as those which relax the mind from its severer duties, whilst they stimulate it with a gentle delight . . . Nothing is more delightful . . . than the reading aloud of some good standard work or amusing publication.'

On a slightly higher moral note *The Deliverer* comments, 'When Mrs Booth has a free evening, she reads aloud to the children and shows them how to make their games instructive as well as interesting.'

More 'interesting' than 'instructive,' and certainly noisy, were the sessions of Snap and Pit where, no doubt, the 'screaming Booths' came into their own.

Music may have been part of Florence's educational programme, but it was also a source of much enjoyment to the whole family. Florence taught them all to play the piano and, as Olive remembers:

'At one time we had two pianos and it was great fun. Catherine and Mary would be playing one and Miriam and I the other. Wycliffe was the most musical of us all, he played the piano well enough by the time he was seven to play in family prayers—we each had our turn. Catherine used to play the 'cello and Miriam did too and Mary played the violin. Mother used to get various instruments and give them to us—"That's *your* violin—look after it." We formed a little orchestra, Catherine was great at that. The older ones helped the younger ones. But when we became officers we could hardly go on playing, there was no time at all. It's such a pity—in Salvation Army life you have no time.'

Catherine remembered using musical talents in the local Salvation Army band when she was young:

'I learned to play in the corps band at Barnet. I had a tenor horn and it felt wonderful. It was a wonderful feeling marching with the little band of ten or twelve. Then I was promoted to second cornet and then to first cornet. I became more and more important as a bandswoman.'

Life in the local Army corps was to become more and more important in the rest of Catherine's life too.

CHAPTER 10

Learning to be Good Soldiers

THE WORLDWIDE SALVATION ARMY was never far from the conversation at The Homestead, but the family was closely involved too with the local hub of the Army at the High Barnet corps. Barnet was three to four miles away and the normally barefooted Booths were required to wear sandals for the walk there and back three times on Sundays. Later, the children were allowed to go on their newly acquired bicycles.

They seem to have taken an active part in the services from an early age. Writing to her grandfather in 1891, at the age of eight, Catherine adds a postscript:

'The High Barnet corps went down a lot, but it is coming up now. It is very good on Sundays; on weeknights very few people. I think it was changing Officers. This one is married, his wife sings while we take up the collection.'

Olive came across that letter in 1929 and Catherine commented then, 'How vividly the faded ink revived the past! . . . The little Open-Air Meetings and Mary and I going for the collection!'

'They attended the meetings of the Barnet corps, going three times on Sunday, selling *War Crys*—the little ones taking delight in this and often succeeding because of their youth,' Florence wrote, and *The Deliverer* commented that they were 'good open-air soldiers, wet or dry'. Speaking after her sister Mary's death Catherine said, 'We three (Catherine, Mary and Miriam) began our Salvation Army warfare together, when Mary was ten or so, by singing in trios (accompanied by me on the guitar) in the Saturday evening open-air meeting on the square in Barnet.'

For *The War Cry* in 1973 she said:

'As we grew older we had our own corps interests and we became absorbed in that. As girls we were really active in our corps at Barnet. We were allowed to attend open-air meetings on Saturday nights. I played the guitar. These electric guitars that people play today are different, sophisticated, grand. But mine was just an ordinary guitar. My next two sisters, Mary and Miriam—charmers they were—joined me and we three used to sing a great deal in the open-air meetings.'

On Sunday afternoons, when the pubs closed, the 'roughs' would be rounded up for the so-called Free and Easy that took place at the Army corps. Catherine explained to Peter France:

'We had the Free and Easy in the afternoon. That was simply taking the title of what went on in the pubs—they had Free and Easys. It meant that anyone got up to give their testimony and we sang all sorts of choruses and when the pubs closed they poured into the Army hall. Oh, the thrill we had as children! They had to have a special sergeant on duty to close the door to the gallery otherwise the roughs, as we called them, from the pubs would fill the gallery and dominate the platform and that wasn't good. So we kept the gallery door closed until the hall was full, then the gallery door was opened and they went upstairs.'

They sang Army choruses—'they do sound a bit silly if you take them out of their context, but I do love them!' Choruses were sung over and over again, since many people could not read and it was important for them to learn the words instead. There were plenty of times when the 'congregation' sang their own version. 'We shall rest our weary feet by the crystal waters sweet', became 'We shall wash our dirty feet in the Jordan waters sweet', but, as Catherine remarked, 'It did nobody any harm—it was the Free and Easy!'

In contrast to the accepted image of the Victorian Sunday as utterly dull and boring to children and adults alike, the Booth children looked forward to a day of activity and enjoyment. As well as visits to the corps, there were special games to play at home. Olive remembers the Bible pictures they would paint:

'Catherine used to help us—we used to paint these special pictures and they were sent to the Indian children in the Homes (Aunt Emma worked in India). Then we had a Scripture game, answering questions. We each had a card with numbered answers which were Bible verses and Mother called out the questions. We used to shout out so terribly and Mother said that it wasn't nice to call out the Scriptures like that, so she would say, "Let's have the numbers you see on the card." So we shrieked the number to get in first. I can remember the answer to what is the shortest verse in the Bible—"Jesus wept"—it was number ten on the card. What happy days! Then we used to sing—we younger ones would walk round the table with our tambourines and sing and clap and we loved it!'

Catherine recalled her father's presence:

'He sometimes worked on Sundays with Grandfather, or was writing at home himself. On such days he would spend a little more time singing with us.

> *Where is now the good Elijah?*
> *Safe in the Promised Land*
> *By and by we hope to meet Him,*
> *Safe in the Promised Land*

was one song much in request. He improvised verses and led the clapping!

'"We'll roll the old chariot along", "We're marching through Emmanuel's land", and "Storm the forts of darkness, bring them down" were all favourites. He specially liked "Though I wandered far from Jesus"—a Salvation Army song written by a converted drunkard whom my father loved; this was always included. I can hear the tone of his voice now as he sang the chorus, "Yes, he gives me peace and pardon, Joy without alloy."' (*Bramwell Booth*)

Just before Catherine's fifteenth birthday, on 18 June 1898, *The War Cry* announced:

'An event of historical importance was the swearing-in as a soldier of the High Barnet corps of Catherine Booth, the eldest daughter of our beloved Chief of Staff.'

To 'become a soldier' is the Army term for church membership. There is no baptism or confirmation in The Salvation Army, but 'soldiers' to be enrolled are required to sign Articles of War. One such card, signed by a soldier in Pontefract in the same year, 1898, includes the following promises:

'I promise to be a true soldier of the Army till I die. I am thoroughly convinced of the Army's teaching' . . . (This was set out in full and included: repentance towards God, faith in our Lord Jesus Christ, salvation by grace through faith, inspiration of the Scriptures and the privilege of all God's people to be wholly sanctified.)

'Therefore I do renounce the world . . .

'I will abstain from the use of all intoxicating liquors and also from habitual use of opium, laudanum, morphia and all other baneful drugs, except when in illness such drugs shall be ordered for me by a doctor . . .

'I will abstain from the use of all low and profane language, from the taking of the name of God in vain . . . from impurity . . . reading of an obscene book or paper . . . any falsehood, deceit . . . fraudulent condition . . .

'I will never treat any woman, child or other person whose life, comfort or happiness may be placed within my power, in an oppressive, cruel or cowardly manner . . . I will protect such from evil and danger . . . promote their present welfare and eternal salvation . . .

'I will spend all the time, strength, money, influence in supporting and carrying on this war.

'I will obey my officers.'

Eighty or more years later, Catherine recorded a message for an anniversary service at Barnet corps and said:

'As I *picture* you there what memories come flooding into my mind. I was sworn in as a soldier with fourteen new converts at Barnet. We stood together on the platform under the flag and made our vows, we sang together, "I'll be true Lord to thee." And though it is more than eighty years ago I remember this step in my service to God as if it were today!'

Reports that Catherine was only a child of twelve when she was first 'out visiting the homes of the sick and drunk' are probably not strictly true. Catherine herself referred to running the Band of Love when she was twelve or fourteen, but Miss Asdell's account of her work in *The Deliverer* in 1902 would make her eighteen at the time it began. The Salvation Army had inaugurated the Band of Love, which was an early type of youth club, in 1892. Catherine's branch at Barnet seems to have been a thriving one. Olive remembers going along to help with the painting, cutting out and sewing. Miss Asdell describes it:

'In addition to their studies and home duties, Catherine, with the help of her sisters, during the past year started work among the children of High Barnet. They conduct a "Band of Love" at the corps and two nights weekly are gathered boys and girls who are taught to make frames ... and various other useful things; although the Band's primary object is to teach its members how to grow up ... useful. Each of those who join (the number is now about 100) promises to abstain from smoking, drinking and the use of bad language, and also to be kind to animals. This work is difficult, but the changed lives of some of the children are an encouragement to their young leader.'

The Band of Love certainly introduced Catherine to the seamy side of life and, in particular, gave her what she called a 'proper Salvation Army hatred' of drink. One of the boys in the group fell ill and Catherine went to visit him:

'I was very interested in a small boy who came to what was then the Band of Love, of which I had charge. I was twelve or fourteen at the time. He fell ill and I went to see him. He was all blown up with dropsy. And the landlady where he and his father lived (his mother was dead) said, ''You know, sister, it's his father's drinking that made the boy sick like he is.'' That was my first face-to-face encounter with the anguish of families where there is a drunkard.'

That other world sometimes penetrated the Booth household too, since Florence was leader of the Women's Social Work, with its rescue Homes for prostitutes and alcoholics. Sometimes she tried to give one of her 'other girls' a new start on her own domestic staff. Olive still remembers Ellie:

'Sometimes there would be a woman who had been a drunkard and was cured and who wanted to go out to work and in those days women went into domestic work. So Mother would bring a woman like that to be our cook. And she'd say to us—''Be specially kind to so-and-so.'' So we learned that there were those people that you helped. Of course some of them failed.

'I remember one dear woman we had—Ellie—she was ever so good to us. We always went to Ellie when we lost things and that kind of thing. It was a terrible shock to me when I found Ellie drunk. I couldn't believe it. I was about eighteen, I think, and I thought she was ill. I rushed in to one of my sisters who was older —Mary—and said, ''Mary, come quickly, Ellie's ill!'' And very gently and kindly Mary went in and found Ellie drunk. A great calamity because she had been with us many years. Mary came out afterwards and told me. I said ''Drunk? She can't be!'' I couldn't believe it. I can remember that it made a mark on me. And then

Mary said, ''Yes, darling, she is'' and so on. Then, of course, Mother had her back in the Home.'

When she was a few years older, Catherine was made Publications Sergeant at the High Barnet corps. Miss Asdell explained: 'That is, she is responsible for the proper distribution of *The War Cry*, *Young Soldier*, *Deliverer* and other Army publications,' and, she adds loyally, 'nearly every week new customers are being made.'

Salvation Army duties were carried on in the home too. *The Deliverer* of 1899 reported that 'the three elder girls carry on a most interesting correspondence with Soldiers and Sailors of the Naval and Military league, sending weekly *The War Cry* and showing the deepest concern in what affects the spiritual welfare of the services.'

It was in 1899, at the outbreak of the Boer War, that the Salvation Army work among members of the services had begun. The daughter of a British Army general (who had become a Colonel in The *Salvation* Army) went to South Africa in charge of the work. They set up tea and rest-rooms for the forces. Florence and her children paid for three dozen copies of *The War Cry*, which they despatched to Salvationists who were out there fighting.

Olive, a child of eight, remembers the scene in the schoolroom:

'They used to clear the classroom table and put the pile of *War Cry*s on it—I can see it now. Then they would address them, roll them up in their covers and we used to put them in our aprons. Then we'd run to the post, barefoot. As we took each paper from our apron and put it into the box we'd say, ''God bless you!'' Years later, when I was an officer, I was in charge of our work among the troops. I was talking to a small meeting of soldiers and sailors down at Portsmouth, and one of the retired men, sitting at the back, called out, ''I got a 'God bless you!' '' Wasn't it lovely?'

The family continued to take part in special functions connected with Florence's Women's Social Work. *The Deliverer*—magazine of the Women's Social Work—gave suitably sentimentalized accounts:

The Deliverer, March 1901: 'At small tables in our New Hall, about 125 officers of the Women's Social Work sat down to their ''Annual Tea-Party'' as Mrs Booth called it . . . the singing and playing of Mrs Booth's children added much to the brightness of

the meeting, which followed the tea. As five-years-old Wycliffe—
in his simple white frock and bare feet—stood alone at the piano
and sang to his own accompaniment ''We have no other
argument'', someone whispered softly, ''A little child shall lead
them.'' '

The Deliverer, February 1902: 'On the evening of the last
Saturday in the old year, Mrs Booth's annual Christmas gathering
of the London Officers of the Women's Social Work took place in
the beautiful hall attached to the Nursing Home, Laura Place,
Clapton. The building was prettily decorated with flags, holly and
evergreens.

'A large company welcomed by Mrs Booth, Commissioner
Cox, and Mrs Colonel Barker, sat down at five o'clock to a bounti-
ful tea, during which a homely little entertainment was given by
the children of the Chief of Staff (Bramwell). Master Bernard
indulged his love for Zulus by imitating one of the war-dances,
assisted by his brother Wickliffe (*sic*) and his sister Dora. The
entrance of The Salvation Army (in the form of Miss Catherine,
Miss Mary and Miss Miriam Booth) singing and preparing to hold
an open-air, attracted the attention of the small Zulus and ended in
their expressing a desire to ''join 'em''! This little reminiscence
of the great Exhibition was heartily enjoyed and applauded by the
guests, as were the songs, piano, and violin solos, and the recita-
tion which followed.'

The Deliverer, February 1903: 'A great privilege was accorded
to the editor on Christmas Eve. She received a special invitation to
''The Nest''! Everybody knows that ''The Nest'' is our Army
Babies' Home at Springfield, Clapton, and that Major Asdell is the
mother of a most interesting family there. On Christmas Eve
Misses Catherine and Miriam Booth and their brother Bernard,
took their lantern and showed a variety of slides to the Home
children and their young mothers.'

Later, Catherine wrote:

'Everything at home was subordinate to the Army's interests.
How easily we might have come to hate it! It robbed us of so much,
especially of those two beloved ones, and there were many things
we must not do, nor have: ''it would not be Army.'' But instead
we loved it, and first at the corps . . . and later as officers, we
learned to regard it as our chief love. And it was he, our father,
who inspired that love . . .

'He entered into all our little attempts at work. The library for the children in the neighbourhood; the care of converts at the corps; the children's meetings we held there. He made us understand his joy in our efforts, and he had a wonderful way of encouraging the timid, whilst at the same time showing it was not anything we could do but only what God would do through us that was of any use.' (*Bramwell Booth*)

*The Rev. William and Mrs Catherine Booth, grandparents
of Catherine Bramwell-Booth and founders of
The Salvation Army*

Bramwell and Florence Booth with their family, 9 June 1890: Mary, standing; Catherine, seated; with Miriam, standing behind.

Florence Booth, Christmas 1891, with the five eldest children. From left to right: Mary and Catherine, standing; Miriam, baby Olive and Bernard in front.

Mary, Catherine and Miriam mail copies of The War Cry *for March 1899 (see page 98).*

A photograph of the Chief of Staff's three eldest daughters from The Deliverer, *1902: Miriam, left; nineteen-year-old Catherine, centre; and Mary, right (see page 101).*

Cadet Catherine Booth in 1902, aged nineteen.

Catherine's grandfather, General William Booth, Founder of The Salvation Army.

General Booth visits Hitchin on one of his motor tours, July 1908.

Commissioner Catherine Bramwell-Booth with three little girls from The Nest, one of The Salvation Army's Homes for which she was responsible as leader of the Women's Social Work.

*General Booth's funeral cortège passes the Mansion
House, London, 1912 (see page 144).*

CHAPTER 11

Doubts and Questions

IN 1902, when Catherine was nineteen, a photograph of the three eldest daughters of the Chief of Staff (Bramwell) and the leader of the Women's Social Work (Florence) appeared in *The Deliverer*. Florence wrote:

'It is only after several requests, and with some reluctance on my husband's part, that we have allowed the portraits of our three eldest daughters to appear in this issue of *The Deliverer*. I have asked my dear friend and faithful helper, Major Asdell, to tell our readers something about them; and I trust that what she has written will lead our friends to praise God for my own and the Chief's happiness in possessing these dear girls, and to pray that they may be ordered and blessed in the more responsible work for Him which they are now longing to take up as Officers in The Salvation Army—a work to which we consecrated them as soon as they were born . . . It has been an inexpressible joy to give my one life to Salvation Army warfare; but it is a still greater joy to see the children growing up, preparing to take their place in the ranks, and to uphold and carry forward the work begun by their grandparents, and which is more than life to father and mother alike.'

Miss Asdell painted a glowing picture, in words, of three virtuous sisters:

'They are hard workers, and from their earliest years have been taught both by precept and example that it is a sin to waste precious moments. They put their whole hearts into whatever they have at hand, whether it be work or play. The chief recreation they now allow themselves is a change of occupation and they are as much at home in household matters as in swimming, cycling etc.

'Each has her own particular little hobby. With Catherine it is gardening, and while tending the plants she is laying in store for the future valuable knowledge and vigour. All are musical; and while Mary excels at clay modelling, the violin is likewise her especial delight; it is no hardship for her to rise at six and get a good practice before breakfast. Miriam's forte is her aptitude for and great patience with little children.

'A daily share of housework and responsibility for the practice and lessons of the younger children is apportioned to each of these three sisters. They are thus being fitted—I might say intelligently fitting themselves—for careers of usefulness in their chosen life-work as officers in The Salvation Army.'

Beneath the outward order described by Miss Asdell, Catherine had been experiencing years of intense turmoil. The great cause of distress was doubt.

'I wanted to be good,' she explained in old age. 'I wanted to please my parents. I don't think I was consciously disobedient, but I was condemned to doubt. I questioned so much. That was my agony.

'I had got an unbelieving heart. God has been very patient with me. I talked freely with my parents, especially my mother, but I never told them that I was really tempted to doubt the whole thing. It would have broken their hearts, you see. I knew they were so set upon our being good.' (*Commissioner Catherine*)

She did not realize that it was natural and healthy that her childish acceptance of all that she had been taught should give place to questions and independent thinking.

In a centenary interview for the American *War Cry* Catherine said:

'I was brought up from the beginning to love God, and I remember, as a small child, never questioning anything . . . I drank it in at home, from my father and mother, from their example. It was when I grew older that Satan attacked me. It was then I had my secret trials. I spoke of everything to my mother, but not that. I felt she would be shocked to think that she had such a wicked child who doubted after all. But that was my difficulty.'

'Broken-hearted'—'shocked'—those were the reactions she expected from her parents had she confided in them. Perhaps they would have understood, but she would not take the risk and share her burden of doubt, compounded with guilt. She could not talk to her sisters either until she had resolved her problem:

'They all looked to me to be their guide. They used to come and tell me things . . . They all came to me in one way or another and that compelled me to settle the question for myself.'

She must know the answers not only to satisfy herself but also to lead and counsel her sisters as she had always done. Later:

'I remember having a talk with my sister Miriam. She said, ''Oh, I feel so wrong because I doubt.'' I thought to myself that I had had to come through my own doubts to understand what she was feeling.' (*Commissioner Catherine*)

Catherine's own problem was probably aggravated by what she considered her lack of an adequate conversion experience:

'As I grew older and heard other people testifying, I used to grieve that I hadn't got the sudden change in me, so I thought it might have been better if I had been a drunkard or a real low-down.'

Surrounded by 'testimonies' to conversion accompanied by strong emotion, Catherine had to grapple with establishing a faith founded on decisions of mind and will rather than feelings. Later she wrote to a young officer, 'As I have said to you before, feelings have not helped me much with my religion.'

How then, she was once asked, *did* she deal with her doubts?

'Well, I went to the Bible. My mother was a great lover of the Bible and she encouraged us in reading it even when we were very small . . . so I would go to the Bible because it is so full of exhortations about trusting God. It was as though unbelief in Jesus was the sin of sins. That's how I felt. I grew up then to know and be interested in everything that the Lord said and did on earth. He became very near to me as a Person—as well as the Saviour of the world. He was *my* Saviour. From Scripture I got the answer for my doubts—I learned to recognize the devil.'

Catherine's solution, then, was along two lines. First she resolved to obey the instruction of Scripture to trust God. Secondly she discovered that Christianity is a personal relationship with Jesus Christ. The more he became part of everyday life, the easier it became to trust in spite of unsolved questions.

Nine or ten years later, writing to a young officer, she describes a watershed in her spiritual experience which must surely have taken place during these teenage years of private agony and decision making:

'I remembered the months of controversy and anguish of spirit leading to those moments of action. I saw myself on my knees by the hour, yet defeated again and again, until I began to wonder what good was praying.

'Then came this place of uttermost surrender. It was, after all, so simple. I see now, looking back, how I had stumbled at its simplicity; and yet, it is not only a difficulty to understand that makes things hard to do.

'I had consecrated all to God. I had ceased to consider myself. I did long to be used for souls; but there were still two things that had barred the way to perfect victory and made my prayers of little use—unbelief and self-will. The first, and perhaps greater step, brought me to the place of the absolute committal of my faith to God. I chose Him as God. I said, "I will, I do trust Thee"; and from that moment I knew that to allow a doubt would mean a going back from my side of the contract. Whether or not He would ever vouchsafe me any feelings, signs, or other manifestations, I was from that moment pledged to believe God, and to act as though I believed.

'The next step meant the renouncing then and for always my right to choose. I said, "Thy will be done now in what I know, and in the things that are still hidden, and for always."' (*Letters*)

Two generations before, the first Catherine Booth, also in her teens, had worked out her own salvation in deep distress and anguish. Her granddaughter, with equal honesty, hard thinking and agony of mind and soul, had found her own way through the doubts and the differences of temperament that cut her off from the expected patterns of Salvation Army response to God. She seems never to have had to fight that battle again.

Catherine had solved her personal problem of dealing with doubt in God, but she did not pretend that life's questions had any easy answer. When she was 100 she said:

'You can pray till you're black in the face asking "why?" about anything—a grief or anything. "Why?" But there's no answer. I've never had an answer. I've been asking why all my life —I can't help it.'

But she did offer guidelines that helped her own questioning mind. Asked to write on the mystery of prayer, she said:

'Prayer is . . . part of the mystery of life and death, of time . . . and of everlastingness . . . Does not the growing sum of man's knowledge serve to multiply the mysteries by which he is encompassed? . . . The man-in-the-street used to be content to call a spade a spade. Now, even he, or anyway his son . . . knows that a spade is composed of infinitesimal particles so small that no microscope can make them visible to the human eye; that these particles are each an ordered universe of "bodies" revolving in space . . . in familiar everyday things we are faced with mysteries; . . . the mystery, though real, has no power to prevent our enjoyment of it. The atomic mystery of the spade may be a mystery "too wonderful for me", but that does not prevent me from using it to dig with!' The spade—a mystery—can still be put to practical use. It may be impossible to understand God and his ways but 'God can draw near to man and we need not *bar*, but receive with joy God's promise, "I am with you always." '

During these months or years of wrestling, Catherine recognized a further ingredient in the spiritual conflict: 'I learned to recognize the devil.'

She wrote about her grandmother:

'From a child she had been, as it were, on speaking terms with the devil. Strange as it may seem to some, I am convinced that her belief in the devil, and familiarity with his ways, strengthened the loving, believing submission of her spirit to God as she went down to death.'

Like her grandmother—and a long line of Christians stretching from the Desert Fathers, through Martin Luther, to C.S. Lewis in the twentieth century—Catherine believed firmly in the reality of the devil and considered it a necessary adjunct to faith in God.

The second burden that had to be shouldered during the years of growing up was the increasing awareness that she should become an officer in The Salvation Army.

'I had become a soldier—a member—but my parents never said anything to me about being an officer—a leader—in the Army. But I knew they'd be pleased and it gradually encroached on me until I had to give in . . . and I was so unhappy. I wept oceans in private, losing the children, my parents, the home circle, everything that had made life precious.' Elsewhere she said, 'I had a sense of *oughtness* about being an officer.'

The Salvation Army officer is the equivalent of the ordained minister, in charge of a local corps and responsible for taking regular services, marriages, funerals and dedications as well as for administration and pastoral care. Under Army regulations, an officer could be posted, without prior knowledge, anywhere in the world. Before becoming an officer, Catherine would have to leave home and go into training.

Her reluctance to become an officer in the teeth of growing conviction that she *ought* sprang mainly from her feeling that it would be entirely against her nature and temperament. 'I felt that my nature was against what the Army was asking me to do', she told a much later generation of officers. 'My life,' she concluded, 'has been in contradiction to my nature.'

'I was a horribly shy child,' she told an interviewer when she was 100. 'I was one of those stupidly shy children.' Her shyness had been a cause of torment when, as a small girl, she had been summoned from the nursery to appear with her sisters in the drawing-room to greet visiting Salvationists. She confessed to Olive that she often used to burst into tears. Adults, including her two grandfathers and Uncle Herbert, were not always reassuring. She suffered as only a shy child does and, as a sensitive adolescent, the thought of a life in the public eye, holding forth in the open air, as every good Salvation Army officer must, and leading out front, seemed more than she could bear. Above all she dreaded leaving the home and family which meant everything to her.

'How did you force yourself out of your shyness?' Russell Harty asked.

'Once you feel you've got a duty,' she replied, 'it's wonderful how duty makes you do things you wouldn't.' She strongly believed, too, that there was a power beyond her own to enable her to do her duty. She often repeated the story of the General roaring at her when she claimed to have done her best in singing a solo. *Her* best, he had thundered, was not good enough. He had explained to her that there was a power beyond herself on which to draw if her work was to be good enough for the Army—the power of God the Holy Spirit with her.

Looking back on life she saw that God *had* enabled her:

'It's no good your saying, ''Oh, Lord, I can't do this or that''— I know that experience, I had it at one time in my life . . . But when I look back now, I feel, ''Oh thank you, Lord!'' for the miracles he's worked in my own life.'

Although Catherine insisted that her parents said nothing to her about being an officer, she must have been aware both of what was said at her dedication and of their burning desire that their children should give their lives to the 'Concern'. It is plain to see why she had such a burning conviction that it was her duty to become an officer. She was too closely bound by ties of family and intense loyalty to do otherwise. For father and grandfather, the Army was their whole life:

'My father . . . was devoted to his father, and to please my father was the highest joy you could aim at at home. And to please my father we had to be in touch with my grandfather as much as possible.' It was a close, strong link, which it would be unthinkable to break.

Since Catherine's skills and enormous ability have come to wider public notice through television appearances, those who spoke to her have speculated on what she might have otherwise achieved in life. Perhaps an academic, Malcolm Muggeridge suggested, a professor of history. Ted Harrison envisaged university—as an early woman entrant—followed by pioneering work on behalf of women in some chosen sphere. Russell Harty commented, 'What might she *not* have become? Prime Minister?'

Born a Booth, she had no practical alternative to the Army. Yet being a Booth compounded her problem. 'The Booths were our royal family,' a contemporary Salvation Army officer commented. Certainly everything that happened to them came under public scrutiny especially where Bramwell, the General's eldest son, and Catherine, Bramwell's eldest daughter, were concerned. Bramwell and Florence's wedding was reported in the secular as well as the Army press and Catherine's dedication service was reported at length in *The Daily Telegraph* as well as *The War Cry*. Appearances at Christmas gatherings, childish illnesses of the Booth children—all were recorded in Army journals. Salvationists took an interest in their everyday lives and felt a thrill at meeting one of the Booths. They had few friends and intimates outside their own family and were apart, as royal children once were. The fact of being a Booth must have made meeting others more of an ordeal, arousing interest and raising expectations of how good and capable she was likely to be. And Catherine and her sisters and brothers moved in no circles other than Army ones.

Even on snatched holidays, they ran the risk of being recognized. George Cadbury, cocoa and chocolate manufacturer, generously lent his house, Wynd Point in the Malvern Hills, for family holidays and sometimes Bramwell would join them for a few brief days. Catherine described a rare day out together:

'There is one ever-to-be-remembered day there, when all things smiled. The sun shone as the "cavalcade" of bicycles and pony trap defiled merrily down that straight stretch of road which takes you to Upton and the Severn. It was one of those rare occasions when mother and father and the seven were together. The boat selected, the party and accessories, including the dog, safely aboard, the pull down-stream began, father at the tiller, elder youngsters in turn at the oars. He was a keen critic of rowing, and it was a proud day to take him down and up without mishap, "feathering" as was the fashion then. Lunch was eaten on board, in friendly shade, tea at Tewkesbury, after an inspection of the Abbey. Towns were seldom visited when he was on a holiday because of the risk of being recognized, to which he greatly objected. Re-embarkation was in progress, everyone in high spirits and the young people congratulating themselves that the incursion into the haunts of men had been satisfactorily manoeuvred without recognition, when the chatter of the party was drowned by a stentorian voice, "God bless the Chief. Hallelujah! God bless Mr Bramwell!" The voice belonged to the driver of an empty four-wheeler, who in his excitement was standing on the box, waving his whip overhead and shouting at the top of his voice. There was nothing for it but to wave and shout back, but the party shot upstream for the moment rather crestfallen.'

Catherine's teen years were marked by bouts of physical illness too. It would be interesting to know how far these coincided with her mental and spiritual struggles. There are only the brief and cryptic comments in the Salvationist press to go by. *The War Cry* for 2 April 1898 reported Florence Booth as saying, when Catherine was fifteen: 'I am much better . . . my eldest daughter is also better, although her complete restoration will probably take some time.'

In May 1899, when Catherine was sixteen, *The Deliverer* carried this news in Mrs Booth's 'Personal Notes': 'It has been a great pleasure to receive for a few days in our own home at Hadley Wood, my dear sister, Miss Eva Booth, the Field Commissioner. Great excitement prevailed among members of the "small family" when her visit was announced, clouded, I am sorry to say, at the time of her arrival, by the serious illness of dear Catherine, who was, however, sufficiently recovered to enjoy some talks with her auntie before Canada claimed her again.'

In her article about the three sisters in *The Deliverer*, 'Zazie' (not unlike 'Crawfie' describing her royal charges for readers of a woman's magazine some forty years later) summed up Catherine in these words:

'With a strong will and lively imagination, combined with high spirits, Catherine has had many battles and struggles with herself; but her determined nature, inherited from her father and mother, has come to her aid, and with the grace of God has helped her through.

'Diffidence has been one of her great difficulties, and still has to be battled against when outside her own family circle. This and extreme nervousness are possibly increased by her not over strong health.'

Miss Asdell seems to have got it about right.

CHAPTER 12

In Training

IN 1880 a lively group of seven Salvation Army lasses had sailed from the Victoria docks, London, under their leader Commissioner Railton, to establish the Army in the United States of America. *The War Cry* had stated that 'New York and the United States must, throughout their length and breadth, be overrun by salvation desperadoes.'

The 'desperadoes' were extremely enthusiastic but only one was over the age of twenty and none of them had received any training whatsoever. Bramwell was seriously concerned. 'I only hope we shall not live to repent,' he had written about the expedition.

A year earlier he had written to his mother:

'If this ship is to live out the storms, ought not the whole strength and skill of everyone aboard be concentrated on the one great want, organisation of the rank and file, and training of the officers? . . . I beg you to consider this. Here is no plan for training these women. After all we have said and seen and suffered, we are daily taking out girls without any previous training or education whatever.' (*Bramwell Booth*)

Money was the usual problem but Bramwell pushed ahead and in 1880 a Training Home for women was founded, under the leadership of his sister Emma. A year later Ballington, his brother, opened a men's section of the college.

As soon as the London Orphanage was purchased and the huge Congress Hall provided in 1882, the building was adapted to receive a batch of thirty women students, or 'cadets'. The long corridors were converted into tiny cubicles, on two levels. Her father, Catherine wrote, 'guided and watched over it (the training work) in every land, not excluding such mundane matters as the quality and variety of diet. By his arrangement a vegetarian "bill of fare" was provided at Clapton for those who wished to do without meat. He often called for the menu and discussed with officers responsible the importance of a balanced diet for young people, the majority of whom were for the first time living a sedentary life.' (*Bramwell Booth*)

Bramwell chose Principals, often selected suitable teaching staff and laid down guidelines for the kind of training provided. Cadets were not selected for officer training on the basis of mental ability. The emphasis was on spiritual rather than academic potential.

'I am far from depreciating the value of the book-teaching which goes on there,' he wrote. 'It is all good, and so also is the instruction in the great facts and doctrines of the Bible, the public-house visiting, the dealing with the sick, the fighting in the streets, the praying with people in the dark, dark slums and homes of filth and vice—it is all good—it is all proper to equip the men and women of God for their great work in the future, and without it they would often be of very little use. But it is not what I am thinking of just now as being the *great* work accomplished in the training of our officers . . . That work is rather the work done in the very warp and woof of their nature . . . *in the training of the heart.*' (*Bramwell Booth*)

Bramwell saw no reason why his own children should be exempt from training, should they wish to become officers. William Booth had appointed his own children as officers and the notion of his grandchildren coming up through the ranks was, he told Catherine, laughing, 'your father's nonsense'.

'The feeling that I ought to become an officer grew stronger and stronger from when I was about fourteen,' Catherine said later. 'It grew on me until I said, ''I feel I ought to go.'' And at nineteen I left home to go to the training college.'

In her 'Personal Notes' for the May issue of *The Deliverer* in 1903, Florence wrote:

'It is a very deep and true joy, both to me and the Chief, that our eldest daughter, Catherine, will be among the number of Candidates who enter training during the next Session at the Congress Hall. The losing her from home cannot be other than very painful to us, and, for my own part, I wonder how I can manage without her, and whether I shall not be compelled to relax in some measure my outside work. Catherine has now, for years, been a very real right hand in the home, and yet this step which she is taking is, after all, the flowering of all our hopes and desires for her, as it will be also for each of the precious seven that God has entrusted to our care, if they follow in her footsteps. May I ask, on Catherine's behalf, the prayers of our readers, that she in spirit may tread in the footsteps of her sainted Grandmother, whose name she bears.'

The next session began on 19 May. Catherine remembered:

'We all went for a walk together with the dog along a favourite road—my mother was at home because she was going to travel up with me. I thought that I had turned my back on everything that was joyful and precious and beautiful to me—that I'd lost it all. I was put in a cubicle to sleep—no top to it. My cubicle looked over the window and occasionally the moon came and looked at me. That was my link with home. I'd only the moon left. And I used to shed tears of longing to be back with those I loved.'

During the thirties, Florence Booth contributed a series of articles to a non-Salvation Army magazine, called *Sunday Circle*. Under the title, 'The Joys of Motherhood', the editor informed readers that 'Mrs Bramwell Booth lays bare the secrets of her home life, and tells of the joys and cares of motherhood.' Florence wrote:

'My letters to Catherine and hers to me are very intimate, and first thoughts would lead me to refrain from making any of them public, but realisation of the blessing brought by the harmony of love that reigned in our home makes me hope that some of the mothers among my readers may share our joy and be encouraged to cultivate a closer fellowship with their children. Below is part of my letter the day she left us.

> My precious girl,
> This house seems very desolate to me, as you will know, but I will be brave and do my part. I am going to try to send you some letters which will be really like a diary of the home doings.
> Olive is very tearful. She wept on the sofa all the while I was giving Mimi (Miriam) news of you and some time in my arms afterwards, and when Mimi went to tuck up Bernard she found her still in tears—hers is a very tender little heart! You must have her to stay with you if you go to the Field. She is going to be 'very good'. Bernard, too, has been most sweet. When I kissed him goodnight and said, 'you must comfort me a little extra', he gave me such a hug and said, 'you will see, darling'. He came over from Mr Waight (our

opposite neighbour) with a basket of six young rabbits. He
can have four if I approve! They don't know what to do with
them evidently, and we should soon be in the same
condition. I hope Papa will say 'no' this time. (Subsequent
letters show Papa said 'yes'.)

Mary and Zazie (Miss Asdell) have arrived, and we have
been listening to all the news of you. So glad you have to
speak tomorrow. Mary says she saw by the look on your face
you had an idea. 10 p.m. Goodnight, my firstborn.

Thursday. Gregg, just arrived, brings word that you talked
well last night; that you and the saved policeman's son did
best! So we say three cheers . . .

I am feeling your miss very much today, and quite broke
down at prayers. We have a lovely day. It is really hot. The
petunias are out and look quite handsome. Olive is working
steadily at the garden.

Olive confirms her deep distress at Catherine's departure, in spite
of the fact that almost daily messages and messengers seem to have
flown from Clapton to 'The Homestead'.

'Catherine left home when I was between eleven and twelve and
you might say I came out of childhood that year, because of that
happening. It nearly broke my heart. Dreadful! I couldn't sleep. I
can remember it well. I had a special relationship with her, I think.
She used to talk to me about looking after Mama. It's a time that
stands out in my life.' Perhaps Olive found some relief in 'working
steadily in the garden'—as Catherine would have been doing had
she been at home.

Florence included Catherine's first letter home, dated 20 May
1903, in her *Sunday Circle* article. It is noteworthy that in spite of
her record in later years that she 'wept oceans' every night, she is
the only member of the family who says nothing about her grief!

My own darlings,
I have just a few moments before I go down for my first
exam.

I am all right and very comfy, except that they will make
such a fuss. Mama will tell you how I arrived. At the
meeting in the evening it was too funny. One cadet came up
to me while we were waiting and said, 'Come along, Cadet,

how are you?' Then someone whispered, 'It's Miss B.' and they all shrank away as though I might be a leper. But I think that will all wear off . . .

The exam is all over. I could not remember how to spell 'heaven' so you can all guess my feelings. There is inspiration in thinking of all the battles won here. The Lord has kept me wonderfully comforted. The flowers . . . look so fresh.

A week or two later, on 7 June 1903:

My own darlings,
My last letter was such a muddle that I hardly know what I told you . . .

First I must send ever such a big thank you for all the letters. They come as such surprises. When I am coming downstairs or doing something, I meet a cadet who says, 'There's a letter for you on the dining-room table!' Sometimes two or three will tell me before I can get to it. Then the flowers—they make me and so many happy . . .

Yesterday I was at office work again directly after breakfast, and colonel sent for me—had a little word and made me an Orderly. So now you can imagine me with my stripe on. There are many others also made so. We are all having quite a bit of fun over it. Some of the girls were so amazed. One (a good little soul) pulls a long face and says, 'Oh, colonel, what have you done!' They all feel it such an honour. So do I.

Olive explained the organization of the Training College—or Garrison, as it was called, at the time when Catherine was a cadet:
'When Catherine went, the training of cadets was for six months. There were two intakes a year. Later it changed to a ten-month course. After the first six months, some cadets were chosen to become sergeants. This meant that they stayed on for further training and with responsibility for the new intake of cadets. It also meant that when they were commissioned (at the end of this further period of training and responsibility) they would be made captain in charge of a corps. Those who left after six months would be lieutenant, second in command at the corps.

'Cadets were put into brigades. The Colonel and her officers carefully selected which brigade the girls should be put in. A good mix was necessary, as some cadets would have much more mental ability and education than others. Half-way through the training the brigades were reshuffled so that the girls had a new group to be with. Every brigade had a sergeant in charge and every officer was responsible for four or five brigades. Every brigade was assigned practical work to do—serving meals, laying tables, cleaning bathrooms etc.'

The course was part academic, part practical and cadets were taken to neighbouring corps for training in corps duties. Bramwell insisted too on half an hour of quiet every day, during which each cadet had opportunity for prayer and Bible reading and meditation.

Catherine's brigade was on dining-room duty. The scrubbing-brush she used was kept to decorate her office in later years, as she reminded a young officer:

'Certainly it is not a thing of beauty, nor of use, yet it is dear to me. I do rather like a tangible reminder of the unseen, and the old thing represents much. I remember the day I sorted it out from among many brethren in the old bucket room. I was ''on the dining-room'' then, and we scrubbed it every day when I was a cadet. I'm afraid we were inordinately proud of the colour of the boards. This particular brush was selected because of two qualifications—it was light, having lost the top half of its wooden back; and its bristles were short and stiff. It did good service, being carefully hidden away after use; and when I left the Training College I took it with me, and have had it within view ever since . . .

'When I look at the (brush), the actual companion of the first duties that entering the work entailed, I am glad it means to me now, as it meant then, the work of the hands as well as of the heart and mind. ''Body, soul, and spirit, Jesus, I give to Thee.''

'If I were ever in danger of getting above scrubbology, I hope the sight of the old original would make me ashamed . . . It has always been an easier thing for me to serve others in *doing* something for them than by merely talking to them, especially when they seldom really want to hear what you have to say. How strangely, truly grateful people seem for some service to the body, and how slow to value a service to the spirit; though the latter costs the giver beyond all comparison more than the former. If the practical had been hardest to me, probably the Lord would have given me that to do, for He knows there is ever the greatest blessing in the service that costs most.' (*Letters*)

Probably the hardest part of the training for Catherine was the open-air work. She described the methods used to Peter France:

'You had an officer in charge of about ten or twelve of you and you would be taken out into a street and one of you would be dropped here and another there—not within hearing of each other —and then the officer went from one to another and you had to hold forth. How to start? Well, one of the griefs of my life was that I couldn't sing solo, but if you were a soloist you could begin by singing a solo. I might have a tambourine and I was great on playing that—that might help to draw attention. I'd see some-body's face at the window or two or three small boys might appear and then you had to talk. You had to make your voice heard. I shouted—I had to, that was the order—that was why you went. You were left in the street alone and you had to make your voice heard. You might give your testimony. Then, hopefully, someone might come to the door and you could go and have a private conversation. That was one of the things all the cadets had to learn. We were taught how to sing solos, too, in the Army way, not with the music before your eyes so that no one could see you. You had to know your solo by heart and you just stood up and sang.'

The tambourine seems to have been Catherine's chief remedy for nervousness. As well as the old scrubbing-brush, she kept her Training College tambourine:

'When I first used it I was a fearing, feeble creature. The tam-bourine often helped me to hide that fact, and perhaps I began to learn what it meant to offer the sacrifice of praise in those first days of playing—how to praise when it would have been easier to grumble! The cheerful sound of jingles is symbolical of that brave spirit that helps me to smile in the face of failure—anyway, in face of aggravations.

'I wish I had a more naturally smiling face and a less worrying spirit; because I do believe in the ''Happy Sally'' religion. That's one of the things that the tambourine stands for to me—so I still play one as well as listen respectfully to what my pensioned one says.

'We do need a bit more of the pluck that first made the tambourine a part of the armour of a Hallelujah lassie. It seems to me it was like cheeking the devil—shaking it in defiance of every preconceived notion—bringing it in to add to the joyful noise in the very heart of the devil's strongholds. So they played them down in the slum alleys and in the courts, making music of a special sort. You cannot play a tambourine without feeling, or at least showing a bold front to the foe.' (*Letters*)

'Feeling, or at least showing' a bold front—Catherine seemed to be learning how to subjugate the 'fearing, feeble creature' and to present the outward behaviour of the happy extrovert 'Hallelujah lass' that she would never by nature be.

Nearly three weeks after her arrival, she described a Sunday at College in a letter home dated 8 June 1903:

> We have had a lovely day to-day—did not get up till 7.00—just a little dusting before breakfast and then breakfast and prayer, led by Sergeant-Major in the dining-room. After that washing up, etc. Then just a breath of air before Colonel's meeting at 9.20. We did have a melting time—really wonderful—the nearest to Papa's meetings I have ever been in—and all the more wonderful because so short . . .
>
> Later. I and about twenty others went with the Sergeant-Major to have a prayer meeting before going to open-air bombardment. We had the open-air meeting in that space near the swan's pond. First we all marched round and round single file quite solemnly—such a crowd of people—about eighty or ninety of us. Then we stopped in a double ring. Mrs Major Blundell had me to speak, which was too bad. The people listened. They announced who I was. We then came into supper after the open-air meeting. I had a nice little talk to Sergeant-Major.

'They announced who I was'—there was no getting away from it. From the very first evening, when the nudging and whispering had spread the news that she was 'Miss B', Catherine had no relief from being treated as a member of the 'royal' family.

William Booth was in Switzerland when Catherine entered Training College but he wrote to her from Berne a few days later, 23 May 1903:

My dear Cath,

I have thought no little about you since saying 'good-bye' at
Hadley Wood Station. You will by this have entered your
position and had a taste of the duties. I hope you feel happy
and contented with it as far as you have gone.

Don't judge of things too quickly; give yourself time to
take in the new order of things; make allowances for what
appear to you mistaken ways of doing things. There will be
many reasons for usages that seem strange to you, and where
everything is not all it should be remember that perfection is
not found in this world, and therefore not to be expected at
Clapton.

Try to begin as you hope to go on by being thorough in
what you learn and what you do. Never forget that a little
new ground every day will make a good total by the end of
the term.

Your error will be, I fancy, trying to do too much. I beg of
you to beware of it; make a classification of your duties.
What is of most importance must be attended to first, then
that which comes after.

Don't trouble to write me in reply to this. If you do I shall
not feel so free to write you again, because I shall think I am
putting an extra and needless tax upon your time, and I shall
hear through Papa how you are getting on.

God bless and keep you, my dear girl. I shall pray for you
and hope in you, and believe that God will make you a great
power for good in the world . . .

I am just off to Zurich. Aunt Lucy is only middling, the
baby is a dear little creature.

Your affectionate Grandpa
(Signed) W.B.
General

P.S. Aunt Lucy sends her love.

Later, William visited the College while Catherine was a cadet. It is
a little difficult to believe that she did in fact achieve the anonymity
that the article in *The Deliverer* in 1905 portrays:

'As a cadet, Catherine Booth made herself so absolutely one
with her comrades, that, when the General, on passing through
the schoolroom one day, stopped to take the face of a tall girl-Cadet

who was black-leading the stove, between his hands and kiss it, the
Officers who accompanied him enquired of one another, ''Who is
that girl?'' Her hands and apron were dirty, but the stove was
resplendent with the results of her vigorous application of the
brushes.'

It made a good story. Catherine certainly enjoyed the fact that
no one knew her identity when, with other cadets, she visited the
pubs, as she described in a one-hundredth birthday interview:

'I was stationed as a cadet on the Whitechapel round, so I visited
all the Whitechapel pubs and they used to say, ''Oh, you poor
girls, you're took in by the old blackguard'' . . . I'd let them run
him down for a good while, then say, ''You're wrong—I'm his
granddaughter'' and put them down with a bump.'

The Deliverer had another version of the story:

'We can only briefly refer to one charming story we have heard
about her Cadet field days. It concerns her visit to a cross woman,
and sending ''you poor girls'' to do the work. ''Why didn't he
send his own family?'' the old complainer asked. Cadet Booth felt
it necessary on this occasion to reveal the identity about which she
was generally silent, and then the scene changed!'

The rest of the Booth family visited Clapton too. Olive
remembers:

'After a few weeks, when she left home, they took me up to see
her. I wouldn't have quite reached my twelfth birthday. Of course
I took my little rabbit to show her (was this one of Mr Waight's
kind offers?). We just wanted to show her and she helped us
with our pets—taught us how to look after them and that sort
of thing.'

Perhaps this was the occasion when her pet mouse arrived:

'On certain days visitors could come up and one day the
children came to see me. I call them the children, the youngest
end of the family. Thinking it would cheer me up they brought
with them my pet mouse. It was so lovely, a darling little thing,
that I said I would keep it for a few days. I had a cubicle to live in
and I used to let it sleep in the hollow of my collarbone. We didn't
have such tight collars as you see now. And once it woke up in
class. It crawled up and looked round the corner. But the terror on
the faces of the other people! Oh, how I did enjoy frightening them
with this mouse. We were all sitting in a solemn class and then
suddenly the others couldn't contain themselves either with

horror or with laughter, when they saw the mouse looking round and then going back. I didn't get into trouble. Perhaps I got away with it being the General's granddaughter; I don't know.' (*Commissioner Catherine*)

The training course included Bible lessons, doctrine lessons, practical advice on how to lead a meeting, including how to stop someone whose testimony was too long without giving offence. Cadets were taught to shout—in the open air—and even to walk backwards, as Catherine explained to Michael Parkinson:

'You see, in those days the Salvation Army procession wasn't always a very large one and in any case, large or small, we were liable to be attacked by ruffians and the Captain had to learn to walk backwards to see what was happening to the march behind, because it might have been, say, cut in half by a set of hooligans who then pretended to be in the march—and the flag might be going away!'

Cadets at the Training College were allocated to local Salvation Army corps, to take part in the activities there, as part of their training. Catherine's brigade was assigned to Limehouse corps, where Captain Mercy Ellen Souter was in charge. In 1981 her daughter recalled her mother's experiences in a letter:

'My mother . . . grew up in Brading, on the Isle of Wight, towards the end of the nineteenth century. Brading was a quiet peaceful village but after the family moved to Gosport, my mother became converted and entered The Salvation Army Training Home, as it was then known, at the turn of the century. After a period of training as a Cadet, and then a Sergeant, she was appointed to Limehouse Corps, still under the auspices of the Training Home, as part of her duties was to train cadets. The little country girl grew up to be working in a strange part of London where ships from the Far East docked and sailors, with wages recently paid, would toss a few coins into the Salvation Army Open-Air ring. In those days it was not safe even for a policeman to go about on his own, but the Salvation Army lassies used to walk some very shady streets, but they always went in twos and they remained unmolested.

'One of the Cadets sent to Limehouse Corps for training was Catherine Booth, a young sensitive girl who worked hard and took her place alongside the other Cadets and Officers. At that time there was a great deal of unemployment, food was scarce and special meetings would be held for men only. Afterwards they would be served with a cup of cocoa and a hunk of bread—the cocoa they drank, but the bread they nearly always wrapped up and took home for 'the children' . . . The Officers had to rely mostly on what the soldiery could give them but the Cadets always brought a basket of rations with them from the Training Home, carrying it between them on the long march.'

A favourite story of Catherine's, which she recounted to Michael Parkinson, concerned the one occasion on which she was physically assaulted, and belongs to this time:

'I was thrown out once—but it was my fault. I was in a pub in Haggerston and we were visiting as the cadets were taught to do in the afternoon—not selling *War Crys*—but getting into conversation with somebody sitting about. I'd been talking to a man and he said, "Oh sister, would you pray—would you pray with me now?" "Yes, of course"—and I went to go down on my knees, and that was my mistake—I like going on my knees to pray, though now I don't do it so often because I can't get up so easily—because I could have prayed with him where I was. The barman leapt over the counter (he must have been in very good form to do it) came over and took me by the shoulder, flung me out. It took me all my time to stagger across the pavement, but I didn't fall. But it taught me a lesson. There was no need to go down on my knees, make a display of it. I could see it from *his* side. He couldn't have me starting a meeting.'

There is no record of Catherine being ill at this period, but there must have been some indication of the weakness that led to prolonged sick leave the following year:

'At that time, Cadet Catherine Booth was not particularly strong and she was excused from attending Open-Air duties. Nevertheless she always had a bowl of hot water ready for the Captain (my mother) to warm her hands in, when she came in from the Open-Air, thus ensuring that she would be comfortable to conduct the meeting to follow . . . In the twilight of her years, when my mother could no longer get to meetings, she often used to recount at great length about her days as a Training Officer at Limehouse corps and of Cadet Catherine Booth, of her sweet influence towards her fellow Cadets, and her kindness to her immediate Officers.'

In October 1903 Catherine was made sergeant. Not surprisingly, she was considered to show sufficient officer potential to remain for a further period before being commissioned as captain in due course. But by June 1904 she was on sick leave at St Ives. It all seems to have happened rather suddenly, as a letter she wrote to 'Captain'[1] implies:

My dear Captain,
I am still 'on rest', finding that patience is a long lesson and very hard to learn.

I do hope you had a good time and feel really better. I do wish it were possible to have you with me today. I am writing this high up on some cliffs overlooking the sea. The sun is pouring down. The sea foaming and splashing below and all the fishing fleet just passing slowly by on their way home. It seems so selfish to be having all this—and I cannot enjoy it as I would because I do so long to be back, especially when I find that the sergeants have not yet been moved!

I am so sorry to find that in the hurry getting away sooner than I expected I did not tell Davey about the map.

Would you let me know what it comes to and I will send the money for it at once.

I know you will not mind a few extra pence.

I was so pleased to hear the lassies did a good meeting on Wednesday. I heard that you were pleased. You cannot think how I wish I was back—it is three weeks now since I was in a meeting!!

Please remember me to Lieutenant. I hope she is keeping well and 'preaching' as well as ever!!

I do not forget to pray for you—I know you must feel tired and disappointed sometimes, but if we only keep close to God and go on fighting victory is sure to come.

When you see her—would you remember me to Captain Saunders? I hope she is keeping well and not too late in her office.

May God bless you
Yours in the Army
Catherine B. Booth

[1] Possibly Captain Souter, who was only a few years her senior.

In the summer of 1904 the third International Congress of The Salvation Army was held in London, lasting from 24 June to 8 July. On 22 June William Booth was received by His Majesty King Edward VII. Salvation Army historian, General Frederick Coutts, described the event:

'The Court Circular announced that an audience had been granted to "the Rev. Wm. Booth, Commander-in-Chief of The Salvation Army by His Majesty King Edward VII" . . . As the *St James Gazette*—with a sly dig at *The Times*—remarked: "No inverted commas around the General now." But *The Times* went on using them just the same.

'It was on this occasion that the King asked William Booth how he got on with the churches. "What is their attitude to you now?"

' "Sir, they imitate me," he replied—whereat the King gave an understanding chuckle.' (*No Discharge in This War*)

Since the second International Congress, held in 1894, the work of the Army had spread to Java, Guyana, Iceland, Bermuda, Alaska and Barbados, increasing the number of delegates from all over the world who arrived in London that summer.

As Professor Cronfelt of Odense said, the 'ugly duckling' of the youthful Salvation Army had become 'the beautiful swan, the beating of whose wings can be heard over the whole world'.

Catherine had been three years old when the very first Congress was held in 1886 and now she was fit enough to be back at work and taking her share of duties. In 1978 she told a *War Cry* reporter her memories of the occasion:

'We had a lot of delegates billeted in the Training Home. We squashed up to make room for them.

'I think it was very good for us all to realize that the Army belonged to all nations or that all nations belonged to the Army . . .

'I was a cadet-sergeant that year and spent most of the time washing up. The cadets were mostly at work behind the scenes.

'We marched from Clapton Congress Hall to Hackney station and from there we travelled to the hall the Army put up in the Strand.'

The cadets may have been confined to kitchen quarters for the Congress, but they were able to get out and about in Edwardian

London during the rest of their college days. A former cadet, who trained a few years later, remembers that they walked regularly from Clapton to their corps training appointments, which might be in Limehouse, Stratford or Islington, over three miles distant, along hard London roads.

On Sundays they bought fresh watercress for tea. Catherine remembers the sellers who used to push their barrows along the street crying, 'Fresh watercress. Tuppence a bunch!'

Even while she was herself a cadet Catherine felt concern for her colleagues, especially those who were finding the course hard. Some were unable to read or write, not through lack of ability, but because they had missed any chance to be educated. She helped them to learn. When she was off sick she managed to send a gift of twenty shillings, out of an unexpected windfall she had received, to help some cadet who 'has worked well but who has not been very successful'.

The Deliverer summed up her year as a cadet sergeant with these words:

'When she became a Sergeant, and was responsible for a company of younger Cadets, no trouble was too great to help a trembling girl through her struggles. She was specially patient with those who were slow or dull, and her happiest moments came when some Cadet over whom she had thus laboured emerged into full liberty.'

Catherine's time at the Training College came to an end in November 1904. Every cadet who had completed training then, as now, signed a solemn covenant at a service led by the General. Sometimes it would be signed at the 'mercy seat' in the Congress Hall, or it might be done in the privacy of the cadet's own cubicle. It read:

'I GIVE myself to GOD, and here and now, bind myself to HIM in a solemn Covenant.

'I will love and trust and serve Him supremely so long as I live.

'I will live to win souls, and I will not allow anything to turn me aside from making their Salvation as the first great purpose of my life.

'I will be true to The Salvation Army and the principles represented by its Flag, under which I stand to make this Life Covenant.

'DONE in the strength of my dear Saviour at Clapton in the presence of my beloved General and of my leaders and Comrade-Cadets . . .'

In Catherine's day, an officer could be posted anywhere in the world without prior notice. (Today, first posting is almost always to a corps in the home country.) It is only at the ceremony on Commissioning Day, when the Principal reads out the posting and hands the new officer a completed card, that the Lieutenant or Captain knows where that corps will be.

Captain Catherine Booth was posted to Bath, but it was to be another six months before she took up her duties. Again she fell ill.

CHAPTER 13

On Active Service

'I DIDN'T COME into physical contact with misery,' Catherine confessed at 100, 'until I trained to be a cadet in The Salvation Army Training College and left home and worked in the East End.' She went on to say, 'My first post was in Bath, a very respectable city, but we had enough poverty and wickedness to keep the Army busy.'

When Catherine was fit enough to take up her first appointment, in May 1905, as Captain of Bath II corps, she was still only twenty-one. With a girl lieutenant to help her, she was responsible for the running of the local Salvation Army corps, helped of course by local Salvationists.

Nearly eighty years later she admitted in an interview for *The War Cry*:

'I think the public work was the most difficult. I shrank from it. I felt my own nature was opposed to it. All the things I loved were private things, and I used to pray, ''O Lord, you know I'm no good at public work, but I can love the people.'' So I felt that I made up for what I couldn't do on the platform by loving individuals— loving them into the kingdom.' Bramwell would have been reassured, for he had said, 'The Salvation Army is love for souls.'

When the two young officers arrived at Bath they found the corps in debt to the amount of fifty pounds. Catherine set about raising the money needed in a characteristically Booth fashion. Her twenty-second birthday was at hand, so, *The Deliverer* reported, she 'pocketed her modesty, and arranged a birthday tea, to the soldiers' delight, actually encouraging them to bring her birthday presents in little red, yellow or blue bags (the colours representing different amounts). Colonel Whatmore received these on the happy evening, and there was great rejoicing over a debt burden rolled away.'

But money was not at the top of Catherine's list of priorities. She was later to advise another field officer:

'Better finish up on Sunday night with prayer and words of encouragement, sending the soldiers and converts away inspired by the influences of the last fifteen minutes, even if you *are* five shillings and elevenpence halfpenny short in collections for the day. Better a loss financially than a "wind up" that helps the finances up, but brings the spiritual temperature down.' (*Letters*)

Her own pay was seven shillings and sixpence (37½p) a week. *The Deliverer* described how she and the lieutenant lived on that amount in their shared 'quarters' and detailed their 'bill of fare':

'They have a housekeeping purse, into which each puts a certain sum for the week, and this is made to last. A good breakfast of porridge or boiled eggs, fruit and coffee (milky and not strong); a light and cold luncheon at midday (perhaps brown bread and butter, cheese or nuts, fruit and milk); a cooked meal at six (prepared in the morning); a glass of lemonade and a biscuit before retiring and *tea* on Sundays as a special treat. This is the sensible bill of fare which takes very little time to prepare and keeps both Officers well and fit.'

In old age Catherine recalled her day beginning at 6 a.m. but *The Deliverer*, describing the officers' routine, says:

'They rise at seven and retire as soon as they can at night, have separate rooms and both sleep soundly and restfully. Their private half hour for Bible study and prayer is religiously secured every day—this is a much valued Training Home habit—a timetable for daily work hangs in the Quarters, which are kept clean and orderly all through: housework is done before breakfast, and cleaning on Saturday morning; the washing (except heaviest things) on Monday morning, and considerably more than regulation hours of visiting are fitted in. "Even so, there isn't time to do all we want to," sighs the Captain.'

Catherine herself described the routine some fifteen years afterwards to an officer in the field:

'I think I told you once . . . that if your heart were in your work as an Army officer, you would always have more to do than you could do; and I quite agree with you that to have a plan does help you to do the very most, which is what we are aiming at all the time. On the other hand, I found that hard-and-fast rules as to the day's or week's work are not practicable in an FO's (field officer's) life. So many things that go to make up an average week are not the things we reckon for, and often the unexpected opportunity is far more urgent and important than the duty for which we had planned.

'Therefore I should advise you to have a general idea as to the sharing up of your time, but not to attempt to tie yourself to details. Even a general idea has to be modified according to the special circumstances of the locality. Hours of visitation, for instance: these should be regulated by the hours of work in the neighbourhood. In some parts you can put in the most productive visiting of the whole day after tea, making it often worthwhile for one of you to miss the open-air in order to visit.

'In our first corps I found this a good working basis for a week. To begin with the question of the housework: this can be made good fun and a real relaxation if you both take an interest in it. My lieutenant was best at the house, and I at the cooking; so she did upstairs and laid breakfast, while I did downstairs, got the breakfast, and started preparing dinner.

'After breakfast we finished dinner preparations (it was often partly cooked while we had breakfast), and, with the help of a gas stove, we could leave puddings, soups, pies, etc. to cook in the oven while we were out. The fact that the food was prepared and cooking always provided us with a common-sense reason for declining when we were asked to stay out to dinner. In this way we had a properly cooked meal every day without robbing ourselves of too much time. The half hour for prayer was fitted in for one of us after breakfast and for one after dinner, while the other washed up, etc. These plans applied every morning.

'Monday morning, the lieutenant did the washing, and I did all the business outstanding. If I finished in time I helped with the washing, but always cooked the dinner. Afternoon and sometimes part evening, visiting of converts. Of course, there were times when we were off first thing on Monday morning to follow up a special case. Tuesday, Wednesday and Thursday we reckoned to be out visiting by between 9.30 and 10 a.m. . . . Afternoon and evening, visiting—according to the time of the meeting. Friday morning was spent by us both in prayer and preparation for the week-end meetings; then an early dinner, followed by a long afternoon's visitation. Saturday morning, cleaning and mending; afternoon, visiting; and, of course, always booming the pubs at night.

'Occasionally we spent a free evening each; and if I were starting in the field now I should take this regularly for health of body, mind and soul. If you have no evening free from meetings, plan it so that one can carry through the work while the other rests. You can always leave something in the way of supper handy, and the on-duty one can come in without disturbing the off-duty one. I think you will find this workable with variations.' (*Letters*)

Catherine would have been specially grateful for that separate room, in which she slept 'soundly and restfully'. She explains the importance of 'a corner of your own' with great insight:

'How fortunate that you have a second bedroom! because however jolly you are together, I do feel that a little corner of your own is essential. If it is only an attic, and a mattress on the floor, to *yourself*, you are better off than if you shared the best furnished room with some one else. It may be bare enough, but to you it can be a sanctuary—a holy spot, where you meet God alone, and talk to Him face to face. Besides which, it is a sort of harbour into which you can sail for a few minutes' peace in the time of storm; and where, too, you can have a fit of the blues on your own without running the risk of infecting your comrade—for the blues are catching! There are times for every soul when to be alone is a necessity.' (*Letters*)

Somehow the public work had to be faced and 'I was such a wobbler!' Catherine told young officers many years later. 'Only the Lord knows what a weak creature I was—how fearful . . . how helpless I felt in facing the opportunities . . . but I was made to feel that . . . my Saviour understood me.' She discovered her own way of dealing with her problem, as she explained to a *War Cry* reporter in 1983:

'I cared about people and that helped me to overcome my fear of the platform. Generally, there was in my first corps, Bath II, someone in the congregation, a man or woman, backslider or newcomer, for whom we were praying. Well, I would talk to that one, and that helped me to forget that I was sermonizing. Even if you have 5,000 people, you still talk to one person. (Radio and television presenting techniques are surely based on the same principle.)

'So I say to anyone who has this fear of doing things in public: "Be in touch with people, and then whether your congregation is large or small won't matter." It's when you are really interested in people that you have your heart full of something you want to say to them.'

Catherine was responsible for special occasions as well as ordinary services and *The Deliverer* reported that 'Captain Booth ''suffered agonies'' before conducting the first Dedication service which fell to her lot.' There were funerals to conduct too, and one elderly lady remembered Captain Booth walking three hilly miles to visit her mother when her Salvation Army bandsman father died. She took his funeral afterwards.

Catherine developed her own methods of dealing with the ones and twos that she wished to speak to during meetings. She described her methods to students at an International Training College 'Spiritual Day' long after she had retired from active service:

'I often used to leave (the platform)—no one took any notice of me. I used to creep down the stairs and go down the aisle and no one turned a hair—they were used to it. And then I went out of the door at the back, and then came back in, so that I could creep up behind the person I was going to tackle!'

Her first question to those she 'tackled' was likely to be, 'Are you saved?' but she insisted that she was never impatient with people if she made no headway. She let them pour out their heart to her and felt compassion rather than impatience for them.

The Deliverer noted that 'many souls have found salvation, though in this respect she (Catherine) is far from satisfied as yet', and Catherine saw to it that her new converts had an early opportunity of giving their 'testimony'. That meant saying in public what God had done for them and how he had changed their lives. She recalled one specially moving testimony at Bath, of a man 'who drove a coal-cart with a pair of horses. They went round the streets with coal in sacks. It was a Monday night and he had been saved on the Sunday or Saturday night. . . . I called him forward: ''Come and give your first testimony.'' ''How have you got on?'' I asked. And he said, ''Well, no smoking, no drinking, nor swearing''—pause—''and the 'orses know the difference'', and he sat down. I like to remember that . . . It's wonderful, the work of the Holy Spirit. Changing people in the twinkling of an eye.' (*Commissioner Catherine*)

As their weekly timetable shows, visiting occupied much of the Captain's and Lieutenant's time. In November 1905 *The*

Deliverer carried a photograph of Catherine, with the caption, 'Captain Catherine Booth, the General's first Grandchild-Officer'. The accompanying article began:

'Many young people will this year be spending Christmas away from home, or in positions of new responsibility. Among them will be the General's first Officer grandchild, Captain Catherine Booth, who, after six months as a Cadet and a year as a Cadet-Sergeant in the International Training Homes, proceeded last May to take command of her first Corps, Bath II.

'We are sure that readers of this—the organ of the work superintended by Mrs Bramwell Booth—will be specially interested to possess a picture of the Chief and Mrs Booth's eldest daughter, and to read some little account of her experiences since she stepped out from the shelter of her loved home into the battlefield for which her whole life has been a preparation . . .

'Bath is very hilly, and some of the Soldiers dwell at such distances that the Officers, even though they use bicycles, will sometimes spend one or two hours en route to get half an hour in one house. But the country is beautiful, and they enjoy it all, even when, as is not infrequent, they lose themselves! One entry in their visiting-book reads, "5¾ hours, 1 house." "That breaks the record!" remarks the Captain.

'It is interesting to learn that the Captain and her Lieutenant took their aprons, and arriving at 9.30 at the home of a new and out-of-work convert with a sick wife, sent him off to look for work, and his wife to hospital to get treatment for the gathering in her ear, while Captain Booth washed the baby and Lieutenant fetched the coal, lit the copper fire, and the two then did a fortnight's washing for the little woman, incidentally losing some of the skin on their fingers. Surely 5¾ hours well spent! . . .

'Her soldiers love and are proud of her because she is so intensely practical, and such a Salvationist. They like to meet her coming up a street with a bundle on one arm and a big baby on the other, helping a poor woman, who, with two children, has toiled many miles to seek work. In such a case they know she will carry the matter through, and not rest until the woman is employed and the children provided for.

'Nor are they ashamed when they meet the Captain and Lieutenant carrying buckets and soap, or brooms and dusters, to clean out some sick woman's room. Cadet Booth wore out three coarse aprons in the Training Home and mentioned a new supply as one of her needs before coming to Bath.'

In vain for Catherine was the Bible's injunction to 'beware of practising your piety before men.' She could scarcely avoid publicity. She was especially in need of the 'inner chamber' into which she could go to pray with the door shut.

Soon the 'old General' himself descended on Bath and carried Catherine off on one of his newly arranged motor tours. The first of these had taken place in the previous year, 1904, the same year in which Rolls Royce was founded and only eleven years since Karl Benz's first four-wheel car. As usual, The Salvation Army was in the vanguard of progress. Catherine told the story:

'My grandfather visited Bath for a Sunday's meeting, held in the theatre, when on one of his motor tours. I was Captain of the Corps. He arranged that I should accompany him for two days. It was a thrilling moment for me on the Monday morning when the great open car moved off and I was sitting beside him. We travelled by roundabout ways to Clevedon where we stayed with a relative of Commissioner Theodore Kitching and on to Bristol. Each day the General gave a luncheon lecture, but what I remember is the groups of people, often with children, waiting to see the General pass by. It was a most moving sight. Sometimes as we neared a group waiting ahead he shouted ''Stop!'' and in spite of protests from the officer in charge of the tour, the General stood in the car talking to the little company. At some he put his hand on the head of a little child held up by father or mother who called out, ''Bless him (or her) General, bless him.'' The loving eager look on their faces, the smiles and tears as we slowed down to pass them made an ineffable impression on me. I realized how the people loved the General and understood something of the strongest traits in his character. My grandfather, William Booth, cared for people.' (*Salvation Army Archives*)

As well as visiting members and new converts and conducting services at the corps, Captain and Lieutenant did the usual round of the public houses of Bath. In conversation with Anthony Gordon in 1983 Catherine said:

'With my lieutenant I completed the round of pubs every Saturday night. She was a jolly girl with a beautiful soprano voice and the happy knack of always knowing the right reply. When the men

were impudent or rude she could answer back. I used to take my
guitar and they would ask us to sing. I couldn't do a solo but I
could put in a bit of 'alto. At that time the most popular Army
instrument was the concertina. These are now very rare and cost
around £1,000 each. I used to have my tambourine too. I enjoyed
playing that. It gives a cheerful, lively background and attracts
people's attention.'

The Deliverer contained an account of this side of the work too:

'On Saturday night, after the meeting, they go *War Cry* selling,
sometimes selling 84 between them, which helps to account for
the doubled literature sales of which we have heard. In several
public houses they are welcomed and asked to sing. A piano
in one is opened as they enter and salvation invitations and warnings thus reach people who otherwise would perhaps never hear
them. It is not an unknown thing for Captain Booth to stop a
street fight. It *is* unknown for her to receive any hurt while thus
engaged.'

Every Monday morning Catherine sat at the desk that she had
made for herself out of an old washstand and dealt scrupulously
with any 'business outstanding'. She considered it an extremely
important part of an officer's duties to be punctilious about money
matters and every other aspect of the administration of an Army
corps. She advised other young officers:

'Promptness and accuracy does mean a saving of time for you
and for others, to say nothing of other things. Get a few good
strong clips, so that you can always have your papers sorted and in
order. Never toss them down anywhere, but clip them up immediately with the bundle to which they belong. Keep all matters still
requiring attention in a prominent place, making it a rule to go
through every paper each Monday; filing away or destroying those
that are finished with, and dealing with everything as far as
possible up to date.'

There seems to have been little or no free time, except for an
occasional free evening, in their seven-day working week. Reading
was important so 'I learned when I was in the field to read in
snatches and I have been thankful ever since.' She recommended
having one meal a day set aside for reading and reserving a chapter
last thing at night to help 'to drive out the petty worries of the day,
besides sending you to sleep with a helpful thought.' The 'mind,
no fiction' rule of Bramwell's still seemed to prevail, 'except when

on furlough'. A letter from him at the time gives some indication of the reading matter Catherine enjoyed:

> My dear Kath
> I am pleased that you like the books. You will find the volume of Froude's *Essays* very good in parts. I think the one on Teresa is suggestive. I quite agree with your view of Caesar. It is valuable.
>
> I think Mama better than she was—distinctly so. Mary seems to be settling in and coming out of her shell . . . I want to see you some day soon . . .
>
> God keep you. Live in tomorrow as well as today. He is leading you and you are learning how to deal with men and things for the future.
>
> I send you my tenderest greetings and assurance of my highest trust.
> Yours with all a father's love.

After eighteen months at Bath, Catherine was moved to Walthamstow, in North London, to take charge of the corps there. Public relations seem to have been rather more flamboyant here, as suited the new neighbourhood:

'As a young officer she led "pub raids" round drinking establishments at closing time.' As she told Rowanne Pascoe for *The Sunday Times* in 1978, she would call out:

' "Come and sober up at the Army with coffee and buns!" She took up the concertina and even played a hurdy gurdy complete with monkey on street corners in Walthamstow to raise funds.'

Catherine entered into the sorrows and troubles of the soldiers in her care. One serving officer said, 'My mother remembers Catherine Bramwell-Booth when she was corps officer at Walthamstow. My grandparents had eight or nine children and one of them, a little boy called George, died when he was about a year old. My mother remembers her coming to the house at just about the time that the baby died and my grandmother placing the dead little baby in the arms of Catherine.'

Another Salvationist of ninety-one wrote to Catherine saying:

'I will never forget what a Christian you were . . . It must have been about 1906. Our Salvationist who carried the Flag with the band (in which my sweetheart was then a bandsman) had some family trouble and he and his wife broke away from God's teaching and took to drinking . . . You took over the shop, a greengrocer's . . . to help them get on the right road again. I can see you now, with a black apron on serving up the vegetables—it struck me then what a real Christian you were.'

Christmas 1906 was cold and frosty. The General was at Hadley Wood and Florence remembered that 'Our elder children sang carols to their grandfather early on Christmas morning at Rookstone and he came over to The Homestead in the evening.' There was also 'splendid snow'. 'Tobogganing was fast and furious for three days on the slopes at Hadley Wood and at Hampstead Heath. Occasionally I had to brave my nerves and take a place on the sledge, accepting Bernard's assurances of safety.'

It is to be hoped—though it seems doubtful—that Catherine had time off from Walthamstow to join in the fun.

Catherine's time as a field officer was soon to come to an end. The *Deliverer* article sums up her transition from eldest daughter to Salvation Army officer with a mixture of unalloyed admiration and shrewd perception which brings Miss Asdell to mind. She had been trained for 'hardihood', the writer insists and not 'on the hothouse plan'.

'Captain Catherine Booth is a woman of distinct personality. Already she would, in a company of women, be marked out as such, and the first impression would be more than sustained . . . She was the faithful confidante, guide and mother-interpreter to sisters and brothers. Her judgement, expanding and ripening with experience, is remarkable. Heredity has naturally dealt with her generously, but if not well-disciplined and harnessed to high and noble objects, abnormal possessions—whether mental or material —are apt to be troublesome. Captain Catherine, however, has a well-poised brain and the grace of God in her heart. She has her gifts under wise control. Her inner life—the struggles of her soul —is sacred to herself, except in so far as its lessons help others . . .

'She has fought for all her spiritual possessions. Like the great woman whose name she bears, mind and heart have to be blended together before she is convinced of the rightness or otherwise of a step . . .

'When you talk to the Captain, however, you forget altogether that she is either the General's granddaughter or the eldest child of the Chief of Staff . . . She stands to God for herself. She needs no props; and although one of her highest ambitions—as laudable as it is Scriptural and rational—is never to disappoint her General or her parents, Captain Booth is an officer by choice, conviction and experience.'

CHAPTER 14

Family Matters

I N OCTOBER 1907, Bramwell and Florence Booth celebrated their silver wedding anniversary. Catherine wrote later:

'The celebration of their silver wedding in 1907 was a time of exceptional happiness to Bramwell Booth and his wife. He instinctively discouraged words of personal appreciation: knowing well how to give them, he was an adept at warding off attempts to express them toward himself; his natural reserve prevailed, and he would silence the half-spoken word of gratitude by a little fun. Few men succeeded in *saying* much to him on those lines: what was said had to be by letter, and such letters he generally destroyed. But the silver wedding gave many their opportunity. There were a week's meetings.' (*Bramwell Booth*)

Not surprisingly, the Booth family event became a pretext for furthering Army matters, both spiritual and material. The General was in America, so Bramwell wrote giving him details. One comment, 'I had a most kind note from Miss Emery sending £50, which I think she intended for ourselves, but which I am using to help a few officers', tells its own story. About the meetings Bramwell wrote on 14 October:

'Clapton. The congregations were enormous. The children's meeting in the afternoon turned out a great success in every way. By common consent they all did well, especially Catherine and Miriam and Wycliffe. At night we had a remarkable meeting; 140 people at the penitent form, the great feature of which was the large number of *married couples* and *family groups*.'

Catherine explained that the meeting on that Sunday afternoon was conducted by the Booth children, 'who formed a little musical combination of two cornets, two violins, 'cello, drum and piano for the occasion. The family was complete at this anniversary, the eldest a Captain in charge of a corps, the second a cadet in training for officership, the third a candidate, the three younger children corps cadets, and the youngest, not old enough for corps cadetship, was active as a Junior Soldier.'

Wilfrid Kitching (General of the Army from 1954 to 1963) described a meeting at the Congress Hall specially for young people, where 4,000 were present:

'The Chief's address was on his boyhood days. He spoke of the need there was that young people should endure hardness, if they wished to win souls for God. He showed how the fair-weather soldier acted. ''He would so like to be a soul-winner, but he does not understand that he must suffer if need be,'' said the Chief in effect, ''and the moment hardship comes along away he runs, so'' —and gathering up his coat-tails the Chief fairly fled the platform, leaping over the steps two at a time and hiding at last behind a curtain in a corner of the Hall, whence he peeped out like a fugitive rabbit!

'A perfect hurricane of applause greeted this most forcible illustration, but though the young people laughed they knew that what the Chief had said was true.' (*Bramwell Booth*) 'It was often said that our father should have been an actor,' Olive remarked, and Catherine certainly inherited his ability to hold the stage.

One month later, three years after she had completed her time as a cadet sergeant, Catherine was posted back to the Training College as a member of the staff, under the leadership of Colonel Harriet Lawrance, who had been Principal during her own student days. Harriet Lawrance was a Yorkshire girl, one of the first intake of cadets at Clapton. She was almost illiterate when she arrived and learned to write during her cadetship. But Mrs Booth, 'the Army Mother', recognized her potential. 'God's gifts are far more generously and impartially distributed than we are apt to imagine', she had once said. 'Polish is not power; education is not intellect.'

Catherine sketches Harriet's history:

'Whilst she was a cadet Lawrance had been badly injured in an open-air meeting when she was knocked down by roughs and her knee jumped on. The Army Mother visited her in the Training Home ''cubicle'' and found her in great pain . . . Not satisfied with the cadet's condition she arranged to meet the doctor attending, and insisted that a specialist should be called. The report was serious. Eventually three doctors came and the Army Mother with them. After they had examined the injured knee, they retired down the corridor, but Lawrance overheard them say that the leg must come off, above the knee, without delay; and they enquired for the young woman's parents.

' "Then they walked away, but Mrs Booth came back and said to me, 'Now Lawrance, the doctors think your leg ought to come off, but I don't believe in the knife, will you leave your leg to me?' When Mrs Booth looked at you, you felt you could trust her with your life, with everything, so I said 'yes'." The Army Mother gave orders that Lawrance was to be carried at once to sit in a hot bath, this treatment to be continued at intervals daily, with cold water packs between whiles. Catherine (Mrs Booth) often applied these herself. The leg was saved and Lawrance lived to give brilliant and fruitful service as a Training Officer, and for many years as Head of the Women's Side of the International Training College. She recalled being sent for by the Army Mother and told, ' "Lawrance, you've a brain like Railton.[1] I want to send you to Switzerland for two years to be educated.' 'Oh, no, Mrs Booth. If God had wanted that he'd have done it before I began my work.' Then she looked at me a moment with her wonderful eyes, 'Very well, Lawrance, if you feel like that you shall go on with the Training Work.' Not long afterwards Mrs Booth spoke to me again, 'Lawrance, I'm giving you someone to help you to do the things you can't do, and you will help her to do the things *she* can't do.' " Aggie Jones, an educated young Quaker lady, was appointed as secretary to help Lawrance with all that side of things.'

Catherine must have made a similarly suitable colleague when, in 1914, she became Harriet Lawrance's second-in-command. It is from that period that most of the memories from her one-time cadets are drawn. But family griefs and illnesses were to cloud these years between.

Miriam, the third sister in the family, had completed her training at Clapton but became ill before she could take up her first post. Catherine talked about her in an interview for *The Sunday Times* in 1983:

'She was the cleverest, the most beautiful of all of us. And she was the only one to become engaged to be married. She went into a nursing home to have the appendix operation, then coming into

[1] Commissioner Railton, an early leading light in the Army.

fashion, in her early twenties. Not a serious thing. Then she got a streptococcal infection. Antibiotics hadn't been discovered. Penicillin would have saved her life. It was an awful experience—we were all so devoted to her. And she was so charming and so courageous. One operation after another. Every time your hopes would rise that it would be a success. But each time the infection came back. Seven years dying. It was very harrowing.'

Olive, a younger sister, recalled the details:

'She had what they thought was probably an appendicitis. Mother had the most eminent *woman* surgeon to operate. They found a huge abscess—not the appendix. Miriam was in the nursing home doing quite well and then the surgeon suggested to my mother that while she was there it would be wise—and a very simple thing—to have her appendix out as it was quite likely to go wrong in future. As a result she had the horrible streptococcal germ and she never got well. She had abscess after abscess.'

Later, Olive took Miriam to Switzerland for a year, hoping that treatment at a clinic, and the mountain air, might prove beneficial. But it did little good. First of all she went to a little Salvation Army rest home for officers at the small Suffolk resort of Southwold.

'Mother had a secretary with a friend in Southwold and that is how we were introduced to the place. The Army rented a home first—both Catherine and Miriam went there. Later, when the Army gave up their home, we bought a cottage with some money that an aunt had left to us. It was quite near the sea. We bought two plots, so that it wouldn't be built on next to us and Catherine made a lovely garden there. It was ideal as Father could go down the road to our little house without even going through the town (where he might be recognized). The military took it for the war, of course, and it was an officers' mess. But we kept the little house at Southwold until we retired.'

In 1912 General Booth was eighty-three. His eyesight was badly affected by cataracts and although he had undergone a successful operation on one eye, inflammation caused, it was thought, by grit on a motor tour meant that the eye had to be removed.

General Coutts describes his last public appearance, at the birthday meeting held on 9 May at the Royal Albert Hall:

'His peroration will never be forgotten by those who heard it. "While women weep as they do now, I'll fight; while children go hungry as they do now, I'll fight; while men go to prison, in and out, in and out, I'll fight; while there is a drunkard left, while there is a poor lost girl upon the streets, while there remains one dark soul without the light of God, I'll fight—I'll fight to the very end!"

'This was the end.' (*No Discharge in This War*)

But in that same month of May, Mary was taken seriously ill with pneumonia at Hastings, where she was stationed as a field officer. Meanwhile Miriam lay ill at home and Bramwell was at his father's bedside. It was one of those periods of trouble upon trouble, which every family experiences at one time or another.

The General's remaining eye had been operated on for cataract but without success, for a few days later the specialist 'pronounced him blind'. Catherine described what followed:

'Bramwell is once again the bearer of ill tidings to the man whom above all others he would shield. Who shall say which of them suffers more? They are alone together. The General is in bed; after the truth has been told his first words are, "I shall never see your face again?" . . . and after a moment, calmly, very calmly the General says, "God must know best", and after a pause, "Bramwell, I have done what I could for God and the people with my eyes. Now I shall do what I can for God and the people without my eyes."' (*Bramwell Booth*)

Catherine went down to Hastings to nurse Mary. She was so ill that the doctor had given up hope. Hydropathic treatment was tried and mustard packs applied to her legs. Catherine was not satisfied. On 24 May Florence wrote in her diary:

'Found Catherine very concerned because of pleurisy and of pus found in the fluid. Doctor asks to see me. Find him very perturbed —must be an operation and he fears Mary may not live.'

The rickety staircase in Mary's little 'quarters' was too narrow for a stretcher, so the patient was wrapped in blankets and carefully carried down to the waiting ambulance. Bramwell arrived from his father's bedside at Hadley Wood and the two parents waited outside the operating theatre. Mary's life was saved and at length she was well enough, one beautiful June day, to be brought back to Hadley Wood.

But the General was growing weaker. In August Florence wrote in her diary:

'Dr S says no hope of his ever doing anything more. Catherine and I went in and looked upon him asleep—such a wreck.'

On the twentieth of that month he was 'promoted to Glory'. Newspaper placards carried the headline, 'BOOTH DEAD: End of Salvation Army in sight.'

General Coutts wrote:

'His body rested for three days in the Clapton Congress Hall where some 65,000 people paid homage to his memory, and where wreaths were received from King George V and Queen Mary, Queen Alexandra, the German Kaiser and the American ambassador. Among many others was one from the Costers' Union.

'An estimated 35,000 people attended the memorial service at Olympia on Wednesday, August 28th and next day the traffic in the City of London was halted as the funeral procession, marching six abreast, took sixty-five minutes to pass the Mansion House where the acting Lord Mayor, with other city notables, saluted the coffin. It was half-past twelve when the last section of the long column entered Queen Victoria Street and three o'clock in the afternoon when the head of the procession entered Abney Park where William was finally laid to rest beside his beloved Catherine.' (*No Discharge in This War*)

Catherine remembered the vast crowd and the 'mighty sound of the singing multitude'. In those days before amplifiers or loud-speaker equipment, the people were controlled and guided by instructions displayed at the appropriate moment. For her, the most moving moment of all came when her father broke free from his 'rather strained attitude of manifest sorrow' and, raising his right hand, led the crowd in singing over and over again the refrain to the verse of a hymn that spoke of a coming day when 'we shall with Jesus reign, and never, never part again.'

Twenty-two years before his death, William had handed a sealed envelope to the Army's solicitor. In it was a paper bearing the name of his chosen successor. When the envelope was opened at headquarters, in the presence of all the commissioners in London as well as Bramwell and Florence, there was no surprise. Bramwell, the first General's eldest son and right-hand man, was to be the next General. He was formally asked if he accepted the position and in his speech of acceptance Bramwell said, 'I have no interests but Army interests. I take you to witness that my wife and children are yours in a sense that they are not my own. We want to serve you and the world.'

Bramwell's duties now included a great deal of overseas travel and in 1913 Catherine accompanied her parents to Scandinavia, going on into Russia with Commissioner Kitching. 'He (Commissioner Kitching) went to Moscow and she went to Petrograd— she was mad that she didn't go with him to Moscow too,' Dora remembers.

The Salvation Army had not then been established in Russia but there was danger for those attending these preliminary meetings. When Catherine preached, huge shutters were put up at the windows and thick curtains drawn to prevent the sound of singing escaping to the streets below. She remembered the suffocating atmosphere and the eager faces turned toward her at the secret meetings.

A Finnish officer, Helmy Boije, who was also in Russia, became a close friend of Catherine from that time. She remained in Russia and was largely responsible for the setting up of the first Salvation Army corps in Petrograd in 1914. Later, Helmy was arrested and finally left the country on a stretcher, ill from starvation. She went to Hadley Wood and often visited the Training College—'a quiet heroine'—as a cadet of that period recalled her.

Foreign travel came to an end with the outbreak of war in 1914. Catherine was promoted to major and became second side officer, or second in command to Colonel Lawrance, on the women's side of the College. But by 1915 the men's side closed. The women of The Salvation Army were left to carry on their Army's war, and Catherine was equal to the task.

CHAPTER 15

Teaching

T HE MEN WERE AWAY AT THE WAR but 330 women
Salvation Army cadets arrived for the intake in 1915, from all
parts of the country. The course that they followed was varied,
ranging from physical exercise to such examination subjects as
Old and New Testament studies and the doctrines of The Salvation
Army. One cadet remembers:

'Commissioner Catherine took Field Drill classes, which were
to help us with public speaking. She dealt with how to address
children's meetings and open-air services and evangelistic meetings too. There were groups for training in enunciation, for there
was no amplification system in those days. We were taught how to
deport ourselves as well as how to use illustration and descriptive
language. Commissioner also took us for Orders and Regulations,
which involved knowing what a Salvationist can do under certain
circumstances as well as how to handle your bands and choirs. We
also learned about the Salvation Army attitude to social evils and
the handling of social problems. There was a class, too, for how to
prepare notes for public speaking. We had to supply notes we had
prepared to the Education Department, demonstrating the use
of a particular text for different age groups and different types
of meeting.'

The Principal gave lectures and there were a number of visiting
lecturers too.

One cadet who had come 200 miles from her Yorkshire home to
train, remembers that the food was plentiful and good, although
not all cadets agreed:

'When I found that we had a two-course dinner in the middle of
the day, I wrote to my mother telling her to send the food parcels
that she had promised me to my brother, Bert, who was with the
British Army in France. You see, we'd heard that food was very
short in London. But we had plenty to eat and a good wholesome
diet. I had been brought up in an austere Salvation Army family

140

and had learned to take things in my stride. I suppose those of a different temperament or any who had been coddled might have found the way of life hard. There were two beds in each of the little cubicles, but I was fortunate in having the room to myself. At first we found it very strange that, for the first time in our lives, we had a half an hour every morning when we were not allowed to do anything but be quiet. They wanted us to spend it in prayer and personal Bible study and meditation. It was a new experience for many of us to have half an hour to be alone and speak to no one else.'

Catherine gave a great deal more to her students than useful examination material or even practical advice. She made it her business to get to know every one of her cadets as an individual. One cadet recollects her saying to them all, about one month into the session:

'When you first came and sat in the lecture hall, you were in the treacle stage—all your faces ran together; then came the turnip stage when every face was individual but alike; now you are all persons in your own right and we know you by your name.'

It was Catherine's responsibility to interview each cadet separately. If she suspected that she had an 'awkward one' on her hands, she would stoke up the fire and invite her to come for a talk in the evening, out of working hours. She would invite her for a chat, quite informally. She believed that it was absolutely necessary to win the cadet's confidence first. Once they would open their hearts to her she could help them. Very often they were fearful and shy. She felt able to help them out of the pain of her own experience. 'I had been a shy, shrinking child. I was a shy, shrinking adult, and the public work was a torture. But I had to face it. And then I'd say to the cadets: "so will you".'

Many of the cadets came from working-class homes where there had been little opportunity for reading and culture. One cadet in that 1915 session said:

'I owed her, next to my mother, so much for the development of my mental outlook and for widening my range of reading and interests. Her outlook had a depth and width that I had never known as a girl in Yorkshire, in a very narrow, confined area of mental adventure. I remember Christmas. I'd never seen a decorated table before. I'd been the eldest of four children living in a very austere way because there was very little money in our family. We had a white tablecloth and cups and saucers that we'd kept from being chipped or broken but they were either white or with a blue edge. We didn't have anything pretty for the table. And when we had tables decorated and titivated and little place names and all that kind of thing at the college, this was all new to me. The word "pretty" had only been used for flowers in the garden. Everything in our house had to be sensible. In the Sergeants' room, in particular, there was a more relaxed atmosphere. Major (Catherine) would read something deep. She introduced us to Edith Hamilton King and *The Disciples*—Garibaldi's disciples—and Hugo Bassey and *The Sermon in the Hospital*, with beautiful thoughts in rhyme. Yet, on the other hand, she'd bring a comical book, so that we had a range of reading that was beyond us and yet relaxed us as well. I owe a great deal to Major Catherine for those two years.'

As well as providing them with education and culture, Catherine saw that she gave her cadets fun. One of her sergeants from that time recalled:

'It was as a sergeant that I discovered her great sense of fun and enjoyment. Two experiences stand out in my memory. The first was when she took us all to Hadleigh Farm Colony for a couple of days. We had a sitting-room with French doors opening onto a sheltered patch of grass. The day had been hot, but the dew was very heavy on the long grass in the evening. At her suggestion we took off our shoes and stockings, lifted up our skirts, which were very long, and ran round and round chasing each other and screaming with laughter. Thereafter we always referred to it as the BFB—bare foot brigade.

'The other occasion was a happening in the sergeants' room, called the Red Room. One evening after tea we had a visit from a "little old lady" accompanied by a "young man" whom she introduced as "my son Jim". After a while we realized that the young man was none other than one of us sergeants—well disguised by stuffing her mouth with bread, thus changing her features, and dressed as a boy. Major Booth was tall but she had disguised herself as a little old lady by walking with bended knees and wearing a long skirt, with cape and cap.

'For some time we were all nonplussed but I can remember eventually searching her face for identity and as I looked at her eyes I exclaimed, ''It's Major!'' The game was up! She then proceeded to chase us all round the table with her stick.

'Later, I was surprised to find that many people, including officers of higher rank, found her ''standoffish'' and ''unapproachable''. It was a characteristic I never knew and I have ever been grateful for her great kindness and understanding.'

Catherine now lived in a house in Mayola Road, adjoining the College, called 'Home Lodge'. About eighteen girls at a time would spend a month at Home Lodge, where she had the chance to get to know them more intimately. 'We had breakfast with her and morning prayers, and a little more personal contact.' Another cadet of the time said:

'About twenty of us stayed at Commissioner's house for a month, for her to get to know us. I wasn't nervous, although I was very quiet in those days, but quite enjoyed it. There were five of us together and we vied with each other not to lose a mark. The food was very poor in those days—it was wartime. Someone said that we were supposed to live on sevenpence halfpenny a day, the war had been on two years then. We were vegetarians and didn't like the food so we decided we'd stay in our cubicles and study for the exams instead. We were discovered and interviewed. I remember going in to Major Catherine and she asked why we'd done it. She said, ''Don't be a fool! Don't do it any more.'' So we had to go down to lunch whether we ate anything or not.'

Catherine saw that uncongenial duties were performed too, as one remembered well:

'I remember I was put on dining-room duties (you changed duties every two or three months) which meant I organized the laying of tables. I said to the Major (Catherine), ''Really, you shouldn't put me on dining-room because I'm not a practical sort''—I was a bookworm and I was an office hand. So she said, ''Didn't you come here for training? We know the things you *are* good at. You've to be trained in the things you're *not* good at!'' '

That same cadet was one of fourteen chosen to stay on as a sergeant, after her preliminary training of nine months. She explained why that particular session was a special one:

'It was the only session in The Army when three of the Booth sisters were at the Training College together. Major Catherine was on the staff, Olive was the Sergeant Major of the session and Dora was a cadet. I think we saw quite a lot of Major Catherine because her sisters were among the students.'

Olive Booth has vivid memories of her arrival as a cadet at the previous session:

'I didn't go for training until I was twenty-three because darling Miriam was ill and I stayed at home to help nurse her. I had been a year in a chalet in Switzerland with her and a nurse. Catherine came over early in 1914 and took Miriam home and I stayed on and helped nurse children at one of the clinics. It did me a world of good to be on my own. I was due to start training in April and I had my tonsils out rather near the time of going. I wasn't at all well when I first arrived and everything got on my nerves terribly. So I went in to Catherine one morning and said, "I'm going home." She said, "But you can't go home now, darling. What's the matter?" So she talked to me and sent me to the sick cottage to ask nurse to give me a day's rest. Then she arranged for me to go home for a fortnight. I came back and was quite different.'

Excitement was provided for cadets by the college ghost, taken over with the College from the previous owners, The London Orphanage Asylum. This lady in grey, actually seen by some, had been a nurse who was murdered at the orphanage. One concerned member of staff decided to exorcize the ghost, but her eventual disappearance may have been due to the atmosphere of holy jollity that pervaded the place.

More excitement came in 1917 when German zeppelin raids began on London. Cadets were given strict instructions as to correct procedure once the warning maroon sounded. One of them recalls those days—and nights:

'The dining-room was in the basement and it was used for an air raid shelter too. When the air raid warnings came for the zeppelins at night, we had to put on a dressing-gown, wrap a blanket round us and come down the stairs with the sergeants, with a little oil lamp. We mustn't switch on any other kind of light. We'd see Catherine with just her slippers on and no time to put stockings on or to put pins in her hair. She had to come from Home Lodge to the Training College, so she had to hurry. We saw all the staff just as they'd come down in the emergency to keep us organized and get us cocoa, as it mostly was in those days. We had no fire extinguishers—there were fire buckets and with this mob of 300

*Catherine addresses a gathering in Hanbury St, September
1934 to mark the fiftieth anniversary of the Women's
Social Work (see page 205).*

ON THE
2ND JULY 1865
IN A TENT
ON THIS SITE
(FORMERLY A QUAKER BURIAL GROUND)
WILLIAM BOOTH
CONDUCTED A MEETING
WHICH BEGAN THE
WORLD WIDE WORK OF
THE SALVATION ARMY

Commissioner Catherine (Retired) unveils a sundial on the site of William Booth's first Salvation Army meeting in 1865.

In 1971 Catherine Bramwell-Booth was awarded the CBE (see page 223).

*Catherine in her home at North Court. The bust is of her
father, Bramwell Booth (see page 231).*

*The three sisters, Catherine, Olive and Dora (above) on
television with Russell Harty.
At London's City Temple (below): Catherine Bramwell-Booth
with Her Majesty, Queen Elizabeth the Queen Mother (see page 227).*

Catherine in October 1971, in front of the statue of her grandfather, General William Booth, outside the house in Notintone Place, Nottingham, where he was born.

A relaxed Catherine in the drawing-room at North Court.

20 May 1983—a centenary gathering at Finchampstead Village Hall: Catherine (centre, seated) with her sister Dora (right). Sister Olive stands behind, with her brother Bernard and his wife.

The one hundredth birthday: Catherine and Olive admire the cake (see page 234).

girls coming down to the dining-room, the officer would say, ''Sit down, girls, sit down!'' and you'd sometimes sit in a fire bucket! There were some exciting episodes!'

But what began as an exciting adventure one winter evening, early in 1917, turned into a grim and harrowing experience for Catherine and some of her trusted cadets, as one of them will never forget:

'It was in January, at about a quarter to seven one evening. I was kneeling in prayer in my room before going to a prayer session with my brigade when I was literally bounced off my knees. I thought it must be a bomb on the Congress Hall but it was an explosion at a TNT factory in Silvertown. When we went down to the sergeants' room and looked out of the window we could see a line of flame on the horizon. I don't know how far away it was as the crow flies—we were on the second floor looking over houses—but it was from East London, past Canning Town towards the Thames. The field training officer took a handful of us to Hackney Downs station and we followed the police. We didn't know where it was but we followed the police who were getting on the train and went wherever they went, to find out where the trouble was. The explosion at the factory had devastated a whole area including a lot of residential parts. At a quarter to seven some had been out at the shops and some of the children were still playing out while others had been in bed and been blown out. My first job was in the club room of a public house where they were bringing in the children that were wandering about. The parents who'd lost a child came to the club room to see if we had them.'

The evening's escapade turned into a sustained trial of Christian faith and nerve for these young and inexperienced cadets, as one of them reported:

'The next morning I went back to Silvertown and they said to me, ''You've got pretty good nerves, haven't you?'' So they put me on mortuary duty. When a woman whose husband or son, who worked in the factory, was missing, the police took her round the mortuary, but they had a woman Salvationist to accompany her. We had a kettle on and biscuits and tea so that if the women were distraught they could come and talk to us. Later we went to the inquests to help them when they had to report about it all. Because there were 300 of us—and no men—the Salvation Army girls became the nucleus of relief work in the area. Classes and College had to be kept going, so it was decided to put Major Catherine in charge of all the relief work for the Silvertown explosion. The Major organized us into groups for the different duties to be done. I've seen her sitting on a pile of rubble, in the bitter cold, giving out orders for the different kinds of activity. Some took drinks to the people doing salvage work in prohibited areas where there were chemicals and debris. It was thick in mud and only workers and servicemen were in this area, but Salvation Army girls took refreshments to them. Others supplied food two or three times a day for those whose homes had been devastated—soup, sandwiches and drinks. Many of their routine facilities had been destroyed when the houses had gone. Our girls made inventories of everything that was salvageable from the disaster—furnishings and so on, anything in reasonable condition that might be taken away and used for rehousing later. There were very few cars then, it was mostly carts and horses and, to save looting, every cart that took off the salvaged goods had a Salvation Army girl on it, with an inventory of the load and the name of the owners and their old addresses. No one could take anything away from the devastated area without a Salvation Army girl going with it.'

Silvertown made a deep impression on Catherine too, as a letter to a former cadet tells. She began by acknowledging the adventure element in the whole experience which is often present, at least at first, but tastefully suppressed by less honest people:

'You would have revelled in the opportunity we had recently at Silvertown. I do wish you could have been there. For one thing, you would have been pleased with the cadets. It did them a world of good, and many of them thoroughly forgot themselves. Anything which helps us to do that is a blessing. I truly believe nothing could have daunted some of them whilst they saw a chance of helping the people.'

Then she described the underlying shock and horror imprinted on their memories:

'Many things about our experiences on the scene of the disaster will never be forgotten. Danger, and death, and desolation, were seen in some of their most hideous forms, I suppose. No one could look on it all and not be stirred. Who could forget the flaming sky throwing into dark relief the ruined homes on all sides, the dumb despair of the people, the crushed and scorched bodies lying in the mortuaries.'

But Catherine's main purpose in writing was to ask the question that was tormenting her after the disaster had passed:

'Ever since those days I have been asking myself: ''What is the Army doing for those people and their like?'' . . . I was compelled to admit to myself that, but for the disaster that overtook them, the majority of those families would hardly have come in touch with a Salvationist.

'Surely, no such disaster should be necessary to discover to us, as this one did, the old man of seventy-odd who lived alone with his two cats, positively without a soul to care whether he was dead or alive. We found him sitting before the fire; one wall had fallen in, windows out, and wreckage all around. How he escaped with his life was a miracle. He was the last to leave that street, and sat in the midst of his ruined home three days and nights after the other people had left, a helpless heap of human misery. Poor old dear! But think if the Army could have found him *before*, and made him understand that there was still someone in the world to care, to whom he might send when the last enemy—death, drew near! To some of the forsaken ''old'', life is surely more lonely, more cold and more cruel than the grave!'

As Catherine went on to describe others widowed or made homeless through the disaster, the same question burned in her mind—*Why* hadn't The Salvation Army been there long before? If the Army was failing to reach such people, was she herself, Catherine wondered, failing to train new Army leaders in the right way? She was prepared to change her methods in any way so as to spur her officers on to the work of relieving distress and bringing the good news of salvation to the inner cities of the land.

But as Catherine's former cadets—now retired officers—confirm, she served them well. As their course drew to its close, they were bursting with ill-concealed excitement at the prospect of the work that lay ahead. Catherine looked at them all with varying emotions.

Outwardly they were all dressed impeccably in the uniform of the day. It consisted, one officer remembers, of 'skirts to ankle length—protected at the hem with brushbraid—a tunic with twenty-two buttons (awful if one came off!) and a brooch at the high collar in the form of a large ''shield'', which we dubbed a chest protector. There was a row of red braid round the collar—

two rows for a sergeant and a set of stripes. There were no wellington boots in those days, but in winter button boots were worn over thick stockings that called for much darning.'

Some cadets Catherine looked at with a mixture of hope and fear, doubting their strength to face the battles ahead. For all her students she exercised an 'insistent faith', so intense that it seemed to 'drink up even bodily strength', and for all she prayed with tears.

Her care and concern followed them once the solemn Covenant day and Commissioning day were over and they had left for their new posts. Many had problems and questions in the weeks and months that followed and wrote for her advice. Bramwell suggested to her that instead of sending individual replies, Catherine should answer the problem of the specific officer, but publish it in a current monthly Army magazine, called *The Officer*.[1] The letters began 'Dear D' or 'Dear O' but even initials were changed so that the true recipient should remain anonymous. The officer concerned was told that a letter intended for her would be published that month, but all officers benefited from Catherine's wise counsel. She dealt with such matters as how to organize the day, deal with finance, cope with criticism and keep alive a time for communion with God.

Her days of teaching were packed and she later admitted that these letters 'were often written during the small hours of the morning, when a swiftly passing silence fell upon the Clapton streets, and one could be sure of an uninterrupted spell, unless indeed the night watchman blundered in to put out the light. Some I wrote piecemeal in moments snatched from the overcrowded hours of those dear Training Garrison days. Those who know the glorious rush of our Salvation Army War will not expect to find in these pages the perfection which takes time, but will, I hope, recognize here and there the touch which love can give in the twinkling of an eye.'

In December 1917 Miriam, whose health had fluctuated over the past seven years, took a turn for the worse. Bramwell had written in his journal the previous year:

'I do not think that anyone, if even we ourselves, can know what

[1] These letters were later published in a book which has now been re-issued under the title: *Catherine Bramwell-Booth: Letters*.

a strain of heart and mind and body and nerves these years of anxiety with recurring hopes and despair have been to us.'

And on 8 December he wrote:

'At three o'clock I kissed her for the last time in this life and she smiled very sweetly. At 3.10 leaning on Cath and her mother she quietly ceased to breathe and was gone! . . . We have all suffered much. After all our expectings and fearings the end was much more rapid than anyone had thought probable. Only Mim herself seemed calm and fearless! Strength to die well is God given! It was given to her.'

Miriam's memorial meeting was held in the Congress Hall on 17 December. In spite of a blizzard, Bramwell reported that the place was full and it was a 'wonderful meeting'.

One fifteen-year-old girl who was there—and who was later to become a brigadier in the Army—attended as part of a guard of honour. It is Catherine's words that she remembers.

' "Is there anyone here" she said, "who will help to fill my sister's place?" and right away I said in my heart, "Yes, Lord, I will." I was only fifteen and had to wait several years for its fulfilment in 1924.'

A few days later, as the old year came to an end, Catherine was given a new post. She was sent to International Headquarters in Queen Victoria Street, to take charge of affairs in Europe, with the official title of Under Secretary for Europe.

CHAPTER 16

Love and Marriage

THE YEARS WHEN CATHERINE served on the staff of the Training College cover the period when she might have been expected to marry. She was twenty-four when she was appointed and thirty-four when she was given her new post as Under Secretary for Europe. Journalists who interviewed her in later years were not slow to ask why she remained single. Just before her one hundredth birthday *The Daily Express* carried as the headline of an interview with her: 'The Reason I never Married is No One Ever Asked Me.' The truth is a lot less simple.

'If I hadn't been a Salvation Army officer', she told Peter France on television in 1978, 'I should have liked to be married to a farmer and I should have wanted at least ten children and two sets of twins—and dogs and horses.'

She was probably speaking tongue in cheek, for the picture she paints sounds far more like a child's fantasy than a seriously considered adult approach to the subject. But the first part of what she says is very relevant—'If I hadn't been a Salvation Army officer.' When Catherine signed her covenant at the completion of her training, she vowed obedience to God and the Army and embraced poverty (considering Army salaries!). In effect, though chastity was not the third of her vows it came very near to being so in practice. She herself explained:

'We were born at the wrong time, because it was unthinkable to marry anyone outside the Army—you couldn't have done it. It would have been a betrayal of all that had gone before. Naturally we were amongst the earliest officers' children going for training . . . I think that has something to do with it. So there wasn't much choice, as it were, at the time when we were available . . . But I should have loved to have had children of my own!'

On another occasion she said to Peter France:

'I never met anyone whom I wanted to marry so it wasn't a sacrifice. You see, as far as that goes, we were too early in the

Army, among the very first. The Training College hadn't been going very long. When I went in, it was a new thing. There weren't many officers our age and it was unthinkable that you should leave the Army to get married. So it didn't matter.'

No officer was allowed to marry a non-officer and there were too few who were suitable by education or social background to marry into the Booth family. In another context Catherine remarked, 'The type of people coming forward for officer training were mostly . . . what we used to call (we dare not now, dare we?) working-class people.' Not only were Catherine and her sisters in a different social group from most of the men they would meet, but they were also members of the Booth family and as such a very special elite.

According to Salvation Army regulations an officer may marry only another officer, and a woman always takes her husband's rank, even when this is lower than her own. In Catherine's case this ruling even further diminished the possibility of marriage. Yet although in some cases an officer, once married, acted in a supportive role to her husband, it was then still possible, as Florence clearly demonstrated, for a wife to pursue an active Army career in her own right. Thanks to the Army Mother, the first Mrs Booth, woman's equality was never doubted. Catherine felt strongly on the subject, as she told *The Times* journalist in 1970, when her biography of her grandmother was published:

'Of course we were all staunchly for women for the vote . . . (No, we didn't help the Suffragettes. That would have been politics.) . . . We were all brought up to feel that some women were equal to any man. (All women aren't equal to all men, and neither are all men.) This is a characteristic of Christianity, that in Christ there is neither male nor female.'

A retired officer recalls:

'In 1926 my husband went to one of the three-week seminars at Sunbury and when he came back he told me that Commissioner Catherine had been talking about the ministry of women. The chief thing my husband remembered when he came to tell me about it was her admission, "Of course, men have their uses!"'

Catherine certainly felt strongly when some of her own staff decided to marry. One said:

'When I went in after I was married she just looked at my ring and said, "When I saw that ring I wondered what horror was that!'' And before as a cadet, when I had an interview with her and I was unofficially engaged, she said to me, ''Have you no ambition of your own?'' I think the fact that there weren't many suitable men at that level was the real reason (she didn't marry), especially as the war broke out.'

Perhaps one indication of her attitude was the fact that she continued to call her officers by their unmarried names to the end of their days. Yet she took an interest in their families. 'How many children have you?' she asked one former cadet. When the answer was given as 'three' she advised, 'Have six!'

Another officer—a man—said: 'I have a family of five and if ever there was sickness she was most careful to inquire and see whether we needed anything. I wouldn't hear a word against her . . . The Commissioner was very fond of my wife. When she heard of her promotion to Glory she phoned me and expressed her very deep prayerful sympathy. I said, ''Of course there was a lot of gold in my wife.'' The Commissioner said, ''She was pure gold!'' '

The very happiness of her own family life may have deterred Catherine from marriage. In Catherine's eyes her father was 'just perfect'. Rather fancifully, perhaps, she suggests, 'I feel sometimes that I should have been so much in love with my husband, as my mother was with my father, that perhaps God couldn't trust me with a husband. He would have taken the place of God in my life.' Bramwell had loved his own parents deeply too.

Letters that pass between members of the family in both generations are full of expressions of love that would hardly be possible in a post-Freudian age. Bramwell wrote to his father:

'Tomorrow will be your birthday. What can I say? That I love you is an old song and yet it is the best I have to sing. . . .' and later, 'I love you more than ever and the sight of you for an hour or two would have been a joy to me.'

To his sister, written on his honeymoon in reply to a letter from her:

'Darling, you are the only person in the world who could write such a letter as the one I received this morning . . . You are not to think that my love for you is touched or lessened by my love for one other . . . my love of you is a complete and perfect whole untouched by this or any changes that ever come or can come in this world or the next.' (*Bramwell Booth*)

Brought up in this atmosphere of easily expressed love,

Catherine could write to her mother when she was a cadet, for her birthday:

> My own dearest love,
> How can I tell you a quarter of all I feel about you? I do so love you and long to be more of a comfort to you. You will be happy, won't you? . . . My own darling, all that is of any good in me I owe to you and darling Papa. I often tremble when I think of what I should have been without you. You know how I can never say what I feel, but I do realize it every bit . . .
> Love, Love, Love—from my heart . . .

Sadly, in our society, love is always assumed to have sexual overtones. But the love which Bramwell saw as the necessary foundation in the upbringing of children was not allied to 'eros' but to the divine 'agape'. Writing to *The Times* in 1906 he said:

'Fundamental Christianity would surely involve a life of love. "Love is the fulfilling of the law." But love is an experience, a state of heart. How can you teach children to love God and to love each other, to love those who injure them—and injuries are often more keenly felt in youth than perhaps at any other time—and to love those who have rule over them, by any other way than by Jesus Christ's way of receiving His own love by direct personal union with Him? . . . The learning of a catechism . . . will not do it unless there is a person with a heart touched by love behind it all.'

Catherine wrote to her officers:

'Pray for love. It is a fire—feed it—fan it. Neglected, it will soon die out. Stir it up by exercise every day. See to it that love *is* the motive behind all you do *now*. Respond quickly to its promptings. Guard it, O guard it from the stifling atmosphere of selfishness. Self-seeking will extinguish it before you realize what has happened, and *then* you will be changed.' (*Letters*)

When she celebrated her one hundredth birthday, Catherine summed up her attitude to love and life in these words: 'Love is the secret of life. Someone who hasn't learned to love someone better than they love themselves, I say they haven't begun to live. That *is* life,' and she concluded triumphantly, 'and I've been rich in people to love.' She gave her love freely, above all to her family, but also to her colleagues and the officers and cadets in her care.

Her love was available to anyone in need who crossed her path, for, as Florence had taught the children, 'you can't run short of love, when God's love is mingled with yours.' God's love in Christ was the mainspring of her love.

For most of her life, Catherine expressed her deepest feelings and experiences in her verses. When she wrote them, she poured out her true feelings—often kept hidden from others, even the closest members of the family, if she thought that sharing them might hurt them. One of these verses sums up her life of loving in a prayer:

> *O loving Lord,*
> *Let love to Thee*
> *The crown of all my loving be,*
> *That every love of mine*
> *May be transfigured and made Thine,*
> *And I love naught*
> *Save as I ought*
> *In Thee.*

CHAPTER 17

In War-torn Europe

WHEN BRITAIN DECLARED WAR on Germany on 4 August 1914, The Salvation Army, like the British army, mobilized its forces. On 15 August General Bramwell sent a woman colonel—Mary Murray—to reconnoitre the war front. She had been in charge of the Army's work among British troops during the South African war in 1899. By September he had decided that help must be sent to the suffering in Belgium and despatched a Swiss commissioner to be in charge of relief operations there. His own daughter Mary was one of the many officers sent to France to work among British troops and Bramwell organized help for soliders in home camps too.

Catherine quotes the reminiscences of one lady, a friend of the Army, who wrote:

'Early in the Great War I wrote to him describing the soldiers' plight when waiting for trains at the termini. The same night he sent his Major Greenwood, a helper and bedding into an apartment by Liverpool Street station. Within a few weeks Salvation Army hostels were in working order, and thousands of men supping and sleeping in safe comfort.' (*Bramwell Booth*)

But Bramwell's objectives were still unashamedly spiritual. He wrote to one of his officers working overseas:

'I am not blind to the many difficulties which must be in your way . . . pioneering a new branch of Army labour. Amidst the whirlwind of varying emotions and excitements which surround you, keep steadily before you that your business is with eternal things . . . Be careful, therefore, to turn *every energy* into the direction of the men's eternal interests.'

Unfortunately the Army met with widespread criticism and misunderstanding on many sides. Pacifists complained that Salvationists were helping the war effort, yet both the War Office and the Red Cross had misgivings about accepting that help because of the 'religious' nature of the Army. Bramwell reported that the Red Cross hesitated to accept the first ambulance unit donated by The Salvation Army, but concluded, 'Red Cross people very nice. Some hesitation on the part of Secretary about our religion, but the President, Hon. A. Stanley, brushed it away— says of course the SA will have religion!' (*Bramwell Booth*)

The Salvation Army donated thirty ambulances in all. But Bramwell reported, 'We are not wanted, and, as Sir Reginald Braid, the Secretary of the War Office said . . . "Well, you see— you are so religious!" It is, as ever, the offence of the Cross at which men stumble.'

What damaged the Army's image most seriously was the attitude of love and tolerance towards national enemies, exemplified by Bramwell. Seventy years after that war and forty after the Second World War, it is hard to imagine or understand the depth and bitterness of the ordinary person's hatred of the enemy. To be forgiving and compassionate was regarded as unpatriotic and a shameful betrayal of those whose lives were being laid down for their country. But Christians have always recognized that the bonds of unity between them are too strong to be broken by any temporary hostility between nations. The Christian ethic also precludes hatred and vengeance towards enemies of any race. The Salvation Army practised as well as preached these virtues. The bond between Salvationists in Germany and Britain was strong because many were known to each other personally. In 1915 General Bramwell's Christmas message to the worldwide Salvation Army included the words, 'Every land is my fatherland, for all lands are my Father's.'

The Archbishop of York had deplored vulgar attacks on the Kaiser in certain newspapers and Bramwell supported him. He also wrote in *The War Cry* about the sorrow in German homes and of a German mother who had lost seven sons. But even some Salvationists thought that he was going too far and Bramwell grew concerned about the spread of what he called 'the war spirit' among his own ranks. He wrote:

'I have been much exercised about the war spirit. Higgins wrote me a letter much affrighted in its tones as to the danger of being thought too friendly to Germany. I have told him in reply that unless we can love our enemies and forgive their injuries—we are lost. Christianity has never been *really* hurt by war unless the war spirit has got into the Christians themselves.' (*Bramwell Booth*)

It was the beginning of 1918 when Catherine took up her responsibilities for Europe and even then, before the war had ended, Bramwell had begun to set in motion plans for post-war relief work. Dora explained:

'He saw that they (Germans) were starving, so during the war he arranged with his Swiss officers—a neutral country—to collect tins of Nestlé's milk and store them ready on the border with Germany so that the instant the armistice was signed and the borders opened he could get it into Germany.'

When peace came in November, The Salvation Army—and Catherine—were in the thick of celebrations in London. *The War Cry* for 16 November carried a report:

'Almost immediately the joyous announcement that the Armistice had been signed was made in London, immense crowds thronged the city streets. It was a happy inspiration that the International Staff Band should assist the spirit of praise and thankfulness, taking up a position at the entrance to International Headquarters, where it led the great host in the singing of the doxology and suitable songs. Then Major Catherine Booth stood on a chair and prayed in earnest tones of gratitude.

'Shortly afterwards, in response to a message from the Lord Mayor, the Staff Band . . . made its way to the Mansion House. Commissioner Kitching and a number of the leading officers of International and National Headquarters and an imposing procession of officers of the various Departments followed. It was a procession of rejoicing into which the general public entered with utmost enthusiasm.

'The scene at the Mansion House defies description. There was only room for a strictly limited number of officers of the Staff, in addition to the Band, on the front of the historic building. Stretching as far as the eye could see were faces and flags representing all the nations of the Great Alliance. Once more the solemn notes of the Doxology rang out. Then came hundreds of salvoes of cheers, not cheers for war but cheers for peace. The National Anthems of the several countries were greeted with acclamation, but amid all the thunder of patriotic fervour was the religious note of joyful thanksgiving.

'The appearance of the Lord Mayor, Sir Horace Marshall, was the signal for a fresh outburst of cheering. His Lordship expressed to Commissioner Kitching, with whom were Major Catherine

Booth and Ensign Bernard Booth, his warm thanks for the presence and assistance of The Salvation Army.

'The return march via Cheapside and Queen Street to Queen Victoria Street was a stirring and memorable event. To the delight of the Officers and other comrades in the procession, and not less to the great crowd of citizens who surged about the entrance to IHQ, it was seen that the General, who had just arrived at his office, was at the window. He received a great ovation and after the Staff Band had again sent forth its message of thanksgiving, there was a cry from the people for the General to address them. Need it be said that the General's words were clear and true, in very essence to the vital principles of worldwide Salvationism? They reminded us again that the supreme need of all men is THE SALVATION OF GOD!'

The worst fears about conditions in Germany were realized. Thousands of children were dying as a result of the blockade imposed by the victorious Allies on the defeated nations. The Red Cross carried reports of the suffering which urged another woman, Eglantyne Jebb, into action. She possessed only ten pounds but she used that money to have hand bills printed telling the story of the suffering in Berlin. They were the precursors of the posters and bills that have become a familiar part of the work of famine relief organizations. It is hard to believe now that anti-German feeling ran so high in Britain that Miss Jebb was branded a traitor and charged with distributing handbills without the permission of the censors. But the trial and prosecution that followed served to bring her the publicity she needed. Donations began to flood in and the Save the Children Fund was set up. No records exist to document the exact course of events, but it seems that Catherine joined with both the Red Cross and the newly-formed Save the Children Fund to cross to Germany with much-needed relief supplies. The Salvation Army had the expertise that the new organization lacked and had the added advantage of national members on the spot in Hamburg, Essen and Berlin. Wherever she went she was met by fellow Salvationists. Florence gives an account:

'In 1918 the General appointed our eldest daughter Catherine to work at the Headquarters, London, in our Overseas Department as Under Secretary for European affairs. She was the first officer from London (apart from Colonel Brain, who superintended the milk distribution) to visit Berlin. Later she went as the Salvation Army representative on Lord Weardale's Save the Children committee to Geneva.'

Dora told the story from first-hand experience, some sixty-five years after the event:

'It was just after the war that Catherine did a tour as International Secretary and I went with her as a sort of aide-de-camp, a travelling secretary. I looked after the money. (On the way back I looked into my big purse and I had five different currencies and I wondered how I was going to make them tally!) We went to Belgium first—I don't remember anything about that—and then to Berlin where we had an officers' meeting. There were a few German Salvation Army officers who had not been taken into the forces and were still in position. My father had hurriedly rushed in a Swede to be in command just before the war began. He was neutral so the Germans couldn't touch him. I remember I sat on the platform with Catherine during this meeting. There were about eight German officers who had married English wives and they had been in Germany, separated from their own country all through the war, hearing only the German news and propaganda. I think it had the most terrific effect to hear the English language because they sat in the front row beaming at her. Then when she talked they began to weep—tears ran down their cheeks—but they didn't stop looking at her.

'Catherine can speak German but she didn't reckon she was familiar enough with it to do an address. She could use it in conversation but didn't like to risk mutilating it when she was talking about something serious to a crowd. So she had a translator for the evening meeting.

'At night we went to stay with the Swedish officer and his wife. They'd starved terribly during the war and Catherine and I guessed that they had saved and scrounged to give us a meal. It seemed almost sacrilege to me to eat it. But then (it's the stupid little things in life you remember, isn't it? Not the important things) they gave us sweet soup. Never in my life had I tasted anything so revolting, but what could we do? To them it was something most special. If we hadn't eaten it we should have wounded them. Catherine gave me a look as much as to say, "You get on with that, or . . ." So I did!

'Then we saw what a wonderful thing my father had done,

arranging with his Swiss officers to collect the tins of Nestlé's milk ready at the border and get them in straight away to the nucleus of German officers still remaining. They didn't have to look for a hall or somebody to organize the relief work. The German Salvation Army was there ready to do it. The rule was that a child had to bring back the empty tin if she was to be allowed a new one, because they had discovered that some of the mothers were so desperate for money that they were selling the tins on the black market and the children weren't getting any. I remember the faces of the children. Children don't often *look* starving—their cheeks are not sunken in like a starving woman's—but they look bedraggled and eager and there is a look in their eye. They came in a single line, the mothers often with them, and it was their attitude, the way they handed over the empty tin, then clutched the new one and went out another door. We visited several depots one morning.

'It came to my sister's ears when she was there that the German authorities were at a committee arguing about what they could do for the state of the country. There was inflation, the currency had gone. There was a miserable argument, then one of them went to the window. It was near one of our depots and he looked out, then turned back and said, ''What fools we are! There's The Salvation Army doing it now!'' So they stopped squabbling and began to organize something themselves.

'After the Swedish officer left, my father sent our sister Mary to take charge in Berlin. He felt that being a Booth and a woman would help.'

Catherine spoke to Mary Parkinson in 1983 about additional aspects of the work in Germany:

'We were in Hamburg and we were in Essen and we were in Berlin and in each place there was a store for distributing the food and clothing. The government had a sort of market where all the societies went to buy food, according to how much they could pay.'

Florence wrote in her *Sunday Circle* reminiscences that the German Salvation Army officers had said, 'Tell the General that we have done our best.' She also told readers that The Salvation Army had been commended for their efficiency in using a cross-checking system that prevented duplication of supplies. The empty milk tins that had been returned had been sold by the

Army and one journalist commented that only The Salvation Army would be as practical as that. As each child was handed a tin of milk, he was also given a dose of cod-liver oil and a home check by a Salvation Army officer was arranged for him.

In 1920 Catherine returned to Germany to help look for new property to meet the Army's needs. She met Commissioner Ögrim, for seven years in charge of The Salvation Army in Sweden and now appointed by Bramwell to the leadership of the Army in Germany. Together they looked over various buildings, including one that seemed ideal for their purposes. It had originally been built as an exhibition hall for machinery, and was the premises of an engineering firm. It resembled a small edition of the Albert Hall, domed and with a gallery all round. It seemed impossible to secure but Catherine and Commissioner Ögrim 'stood and prayed on the kerb opposite, that this magnificent building might come into Salvation Army hands; this it eventually did.'

The Salvation Army magazine *All The World*, which reported on overseas news, carried two photographs with captions identifying Lt. Colonel Catherine Booth (International Secretary) and Captain Dora Booth, on their way to a remote Army centre at Faeto, in southern Italy, on mules. Dora clearly remembers the visit:

'We went to Italy and stopped at a great number of places and one of them was Rome. The Salvation Army doesn't organize any time for sightseeing—you rush from one meeting to another, have a meal, catch a train and go on to the next. But when we got to Rome the Colonel who accompanied us said that he was very sorry but we couldn't get out of Rome because everyone was on strike. Meetings would have to be cancelled. He didn't know how long it would last. He said, ''I don't know what you'd like to do, would you like to see the Coliseum, and St Peter's?'' Catherine and I were all agog.

'There was a going Salvation Army corps at this little village of Faeto, right up in the hills. There was no real road to it, just a track and most of the traffic went by pack mule. I hadn't ridden a mule before and we had no proper riding clothes. We rode side-saddle because our skirts were long in those days. We had breakfast but I heard afterwards that the mule I rode hadn't had any, so it was a torment to ride because every bit of green grass we came to the poor thing wanted to tip me off its back. When we reached the village top the whole village was there, out to greet us, and we felt dirty and bedraggled and wretched after a whole day in the saddle.

'That night (Catherine) developed the vilest cold—I don't know where she'd caught it. She was streaming and she couldn't speak and the officer who was with us thought it very serious. (I think he had visions of no meeting.) He made her go under a towel and inhale from a jug of boiling water and eucalyptus and Catherine snorted and coughed and carried on—''Let me out!''—but he was adamant. Then we had a meal and all the officers were at the party. I began to eat with gusto, but it was ruined for me because everything on the plate was covered with grated sheep's cheese. I tried to scrape it off but I couldn't and I had to eat the meal. Then came the pièce de résistance, the sweet, which was a huge dish of yellow custard (enough for ten of us round the table) with ''Welcome'' written in chocolate custard. All made with sheep's milk.

'Catherine said, ''Go on, eat it—it's quite nice.'' Then she was given a glass of hot milk and we went to rest. And that was sheep's milk. But her cold was so bad that she couldn't taste it. Next morning, when she *could* taste, she declined milk with her coffee or tea—said she drank it black. I don't remember much about the meetings—but she got through because of this wonderful treatment of the night before.'

Catherine admitted that travelling was 'an absolute terror'. More than once she had to be carried off a channel steamer on a stretcher. Later she was to find flying a great relief. Wherever she went she was expected to speak, both to local officers and soldiers and at large evangelistic gatherings.

'My public work was a tremendous burden because I never felt equal to it. But I had such wonderful opportunities to lead congresses and speak at important occasions. They really were a torture to me because I didn't feel equal to it and I used to remember Grandpa's words: ''Do your best but count on God to help because your best isn't enough.''

'I could preach in French and a few words in Swedish and German . . . and I got to know Swedish fairly well; I can read it now. To say a few words brought you nearer the congregation, but otherwise I had a translator and learned to speak for a translation to be made. Don't leave sentences hanging in the air. That's the great mistake people make.' (*Commissioner Catherine*)

Catherine recalled one occasion when she was preaching in Helsinki and her address was translated into three different languages. As she spoke each paragraph it was translated into Finnish, Swedish and then Russian, because there were many Russians at the meeting who had come across from St Petersburg. She found the main difficulty was remembering what she was going to say next, after so long a pause between each paragraph.

Such a large, international meeting was a far cry from the first occasion when the Army used a translator when Bramwell visited Germany as a young man. The sisters, Olive and Dora, recalled the occasion as it had been described to them:

'Father was a young man. He had been very poorly and a friend invited him to go with him to Sweden, where he was building a railway. They put in to Hamburg where there was a wonderful little mission and there was quite a crowd there. Father got excited but couldn't speak a word of German. So he got up and said, "Is there anyone here who can speak English?" And a man got up and said, "I can, but I'm not a Christian." Bramwell said, "That doesn't matter—come with me and tell the people what I'm saying." And that was the first time the Army had done it, sentence by sentence.'

Catherine, in her book about her father, gives her own account of the incident:

'They stayed a night at Hamburg where, after dinner, Mr Billups invited his guest to go with him to a mission for English sailors. Bramwell was asked to speak. After a few words it occurred to him that if someone could translate for him the Germans present would be enabled to follow. He paused to enquire, found that the English missioner-in-charge spoke German, engaged his help on the spot, then continued the address, waiting after each sentence for the translation. Thus, from the desire that his message should reach a handful of German seamen, Bramwell Booth inaugurated a system of communication which was to give Salvationists ready access to congregations of whose language they had no knowledge. And, what was more important to the unity of the Army, it provided for an intimate interchange of thought between Salvationists of all nations and their leaders. For this method, which made the interpreter an echo, in another tongue, of the speaker, was in its effect far removed from the formality which is the result of reading at stated intervals a translation from shorthand notes of the address.' (The 'Hamburg experiment' was used in Sweden, where 'unsaved' railway men often acted as translators for Bramwell.)

But much of Catherine's time was spent back in London at International Headquarters in an administrative role. A qualified shorthand typist, who was her private secretary at the time, has happy memories of working with her:

'She was charming to work with, she was very considerate. Sometimes she was very busy all day and she'd say to me at about five o'clock, ''Can you stay on, then we can get down to some work?'' And she would dictate about eighty letters. She was the best dictator of letters that I've ever had to take down from. She knew what she wanted to say and she said it. She seldom asked me to read it through or anything like that because she knew what she'd said. I don't think she had made notes, it was just there in her head. Then she'd meet me next day and if I'd got through them she was so amazed. Once she said, ''You know, it's like the verse in the Bible—'Before he calls, I will answer.' '' ''

In the autumn of 1922 Catherine accompanied her father, the General, to Holland. No doubt she silently suffered her usual forebodings about the journey, but she can have had no idea of the event that was so soon to change her whole life. It was late at night when the two parted. Bramwell was escorted to his 'billet' and Catherine set off for hers under the care of Brigadier Bertha Smith.

Bertha Smith was a Dutch nursing matron when she first came into contact with The Salvation Army in Holland. She felt that theirs was the work that God was calling her to, and she threw in her lot with the Army. Her family was so angry that they disowned her. They never forgave her and were never willing to have her home again. But this meeting with Catherine was to lead to a lifelong friendship with the Booth family, who made her part of their own home circle until her death many years later.

Bertha Smith took Catherine to The Salvation Army home where she was to stay that night, but herself prepared to leave a little later. Catherine took a bath and it was then that she experienced a sudden and extremely severe haemorrhage from both lungs.

Fortunately Bertha had not yet left and she immediately took control. She sent at once for a doctor and did all that was possible herself. Olive and Dora are convinced that but for Bertha's swift action, Catherine would not have lived through that first critical night, when she was at death's door. Even when the crisis was passed, Catherine was desperately ill and Bertha stayed with her, giving her every possible nursing care. That care was to last for the next three to four years, during which Catherine made the long and difficult climb back to health. She talked to Ted Harrison of her own doubts and despair at the time:

'I remember the illness; it made a great impression on me spiritually because the fear of having to give up my work was a great grief. And I had to keep calm. All the doctors agreed I was not to excite myself or I would bring on another haemorrhage. . . .

'I had been a very active person and as I lay in bed I felt I'd followed God's call; in a sense, it sounds a horrible thing to say, but I felt it was God's fault. It wasn't my fault: I'd done what I'd been called to do and been prompted to do and I had broken down . . .

'I don't know what God's purpose was in allowing me to fall ill. You never know God's purpose. He never explains. That is what in my old age I have come to accept. Don't expect the Almighty to explain his doings to me or to you or to anybody. You see, God gives his commands and says, "Trust me—be obedient children, love the Lord thy God with all thy heart and thy neighbour as thyself. Live that kind of life and I'll help you." But he doesn't explain why sorrows come. It's one of the great stumbling blocks in people's lives. Why should this happen to me—why should I lose such and such a one? It's very difficult to comfort them.

'These thoughts went through my head as I lay ill. I felt it was very strange. I thought I'd come to the end, but I hadn't. I went through some very dark passages at the time.' (*Commissioner Catherine*)

As well as blaming God for her illness, Catherine felt a deep sense of her own lack of worth, perhaps partly the effect of extreme physical weakness and also the result of the high demands that she had always made upon herself and that had been made upon her since her earliest days as the eldest child in the family.

Catherine may not have been able to understand the purposes of the God she had followed and obeyed, but she was conscious of his presence with her during her illness, as one of her verses shows:

> *When sickness comes and all my plans lie shattered,*
> *When praying seems to be of no avail,*
> *When to get well, I felt, was all that mattered,*
> *When even love no longer could prevail:*
> *Then,*
> *Jesus I see!*
> *And He speaks to me,*
> *He tells me His love is the same*
> *In sickness or health,*
> *Privation or wealth,*
> *He loves me! He knows me by name!*

At first Catherine had to lie completely still. Bertha did everything for her. 'She couldn't even wash her own face,' Olive remembers, 'and at one time she was not allowed to eat toast because the extra effort would move the muscles of her chest. She was not allowed to read or knit, and having someone like Bertha with her made all the difference.'

Bertha too had an active and well-educated mind and she devised numerous ways of keeping Catherine occupied mentally. Olive explained:

'Bertha used to read endless books to her and they had very interesting discussions together. Then they would play little games to keep Catherine's mind occupied. In one of them Catherine would think of an English proverb and Bertha would have to think of a kindred one in Dutch. Then she would give a Dutch one and Catherine would have to think of an English proverb to match. Those sort of games were possible when Catherine was allowed to do nothing but talk quietly.'

When Catherine was beginning to recover, Bertha took her into the country among the pine woods in Holland. Then the Army gave Bertha leave so that she could accompany Catherine first to France and then to spend a winter in Switzerland.

Against all earlier expectations, Catherine began to regain full health. She was able, once more, to 'take a deep breath' and, as she put it, 'to shout as well as ever I could'—a necessary accomplishment in Army work. But her doctor warned her that continued care would be needed and he advised her to find a place among pine trees, where she could at any time get right away and rest. Catherine consulted an estate agent and he recommended the surrounds of Wokingham in Berkshire as fitting the doctor's prescription and being comfortably near to London. She found and bought a little cottage near Finchampstead.

In May 1926, over three-and-a-half years after the onset of her illness, Catherine was fit enough to go back to work. Even then, Bertha Smith used to go with her up to headquarters by car in the early months of her return. Her appointment was a fresh one and she went to it with zest. At her welcome meeting she took as her text, 'This is the day that the Lord has made, let us rejoice and be glad in it.' That summed up her feelings.

CHAPTER 18

The Women's Social Work

CATHERINE WAS A YEAR OLD when her mother carried her through the mean Whitechapel streets to the small terraced house where she was to begin the 'rescue' work for women and girls. At first Florence worked almost single-handed, her baby in a clothes basket beside her. By the following year she had four officers to help her in larger premises, and three years later the number of staff had leapt incredibly to seventy. For the next twenty-eight years Florence Booth was leader of what came to be known as the Women's Social Work. The Booth children visited the Homes on special occasions, learned to pray for 'Mama's other girls' and at six years old Catherine was hemming gowns or pinafores for 'Mama's poor little babies', as Florence recorded in *The Deliverer*. She certainly grew to womanhood fully familiar with the many aspects of the work which her mother had developed.

Now, in May 1926, forty years after its beginning, Catherine was appointed as full Colonel to the post her mother had held as leader of the Women's Social Work. Eighteen months later she was promoted to Commissioner, the highest rank in The Salvation Army below General.

When Catherine took command she had up to 600 officers under her charge, as well as a vast band of workers and helpers in the various institutions. The headquarters of the work was at Mare Street, Hackney, but its scope covered the length and breadth of the British Isles. The work had diversified enormously too. The original rescue—or 'midnight'—work was still carried on among runaway girls and prostitutes in the big cities but that was only one part of a network of care for women and girls of all ages and at all stages of life. There were homes for unmarried mothers and their babies, maternity hospitals and district maternity care. There was a home for those suffering from sexually transmitted diseases and homes for small children in need of protection, as well as crèches and day centres. Salvation Army officers attended the police courts and took into care teenage girls in trouble with the law. Women prisoners were cared for too. There were night shelters for women vagrants and eventide homes for the elderly.

To run such a varied and extensive organization called for a variety of skills. Catherine had them. She needed to be able to make overall judgements and decisions and pay attention to detail too. She must inspire and lead her officers, many of whom were working in incredibly tough situations. She had to be able to speak publicly, both at Army functions and fund-raising events and she had to have skill amounting to wizardry in the field of finance.

Catherine believed that it was of great importance to visit the homes and hospitals regularly. 'There weren't many weeks when she didn't visit quite a few homes,' one officer at headquarters recalled. Her personal secretary of the time recalled that Bertha Smith went with them on the longer journeys to the provinces. It must have required considerable courage on Catherine's part to set out on visits to Scotland, Wales and across to Ireland, when she had barely recovered from such a long illness. Cars were open-topped and she seems to have managed the journeys without too much discomfort, in spite of being such a poor traveller. They would ride bare-headed, hastily tidying up and putting on their bonnets before arriving at their destination, especially if a civic reception was part of the programme, as it sometimes was.

In spite of being on official business Catherine found time to enjoy the countryside, especially when they stopped, as their custom was, for a picnic. Once, after their lunch, she heard a bird singing and insisted on following the sound into the nearby wood, taking her secretary with her to track down the source of the song. Another time she caught sight of a flock of birds flying overhead and sought out a local countryman in order to discover what they were. She was delighted to find that she had seen a skein of geese.

In and around London, Catherine enjoyed introducing a surprise element into her visits. Sometimes she would announce that she would take breakfast in a home and would sit with the girls or women, talking to them about spiritual as well as practical matters. When she visited the children's homes, she used all the skills she had acquired when she looked after her own sisters and brothers.

'One of her great points was her wonderful way with children,' one of her officers said. 'I have not only seen her with

''Nestlings''[1] but with children at Whitechapel in the East End of London and she was so lovely with them. That is one of my choice memories of her.'

Catherine wrote about a visit to a night shelter in Hanbury Street in London, where some 'old darlings' had been 'night dwellers' for up to twenty years. For sixpence a night, they were provided with hot bath, bedding, bed and the freedom to cook food and wash and dry clothes. If they wished to buy food, every item on the menu cost them a one-penny ticket, whether it was a pint of tea, a slab of cake, a portion of currant duff or a cheese and rice savoury. Those too poor to pay were provided beforehand with eight food tickets free, so that the servers would not know who had free meals.

Catherine was a great advocate of mixed eventide homes. She believed that women took more care of their appearance and men were more considerate and polite when they were together. She horrified the officers at one of these homes, when she visited them, by conducting the inmates in some rousing singing of 'Daisy, Daisy, give me your answer do!'

When she visited a children's home in Wales for boys on probation, she took a meeting with them. She preached on the verse, 'God so loved the world that he gave his only begotten Son', and invited any boys who wanted to give their lives to Christ to come forward. She was deeply moved when one lad of sixteen cried openly, telling her that he had never before understood that Christ died for him.

Catherine cared deeply about her officers and wherever possible, eased the conditions under which they worked. One who was in a girls' home in Liverpool said:

'As a very young officer I can recall my feelings about coming face to face with a Commissioner—particularly the General's (Bramwell's) daughter. Her cheery smile and friendly words very quickly put me at ease and I was for ever grateful for some changes she made in our home routine. One was an order that no officer should rise before 6 a.m. for early morning duty. Previously, officers who were what we called ''on whistle''—which meant getting kitchen fires going and preparing breakfast for fifty people

[1] Inmates of The Nest, a home for 'child victims of immorality' which later received any ill-treated or neglected child.

170

—were rising no later than 5 a.m., with two girls to help them.'

Catherine was a shrewd assessor of character and gift and she took considerable care to place her officers in the job that was right for them. She did not approve of square pegs in round holes. One officer remembers an incident when Catherine returned after a long absence and found her doing an administrative job at Mare Street:

'She sent for me and I was very nervous because her leadership was absolute. I sat there and thought, ''What have I done?'' Then suddenly she bolted out, ''What are you doing here? I don't want you here, I want you with people.'' I said, ''I didn't ask to come, Commissioner.'' But it so happened that at that time my mother really needed me and if I hadn't been able to travel up and down from home I would probably not have been able to work at all. So I told her what was happening at home.' Catherine immediately recognized a higher authority than her own at work, for, the officer continued, 'her eyes sparkled and she said, ''Then you'll never doubt God's leading again!'' '

A senior officer, who worked with her at Social Work headquarters, said:

'Personally, I never had an unkind word from her. We didn't always agree and I'd sometimes say, ''Well, I'm sure you know what I really think about this, Commissioner'', and when I'd finished outlining my idea, she would possibly say, ''Well, I think I'd rather have it *my* way, if you don't mind.'' And of course I would accept that. There was no matter of principle, just the methods involved.'

Officers held her in wholesome awe. 'I've heard of one dear officer who used to salute even over the telephone!—''Yes, Commissioner''—''No Commissioner''! '

But for Catherine, as another retired officer emphasized, 'everything to do with officers was *very* confidential. She was terrifically particular—anything to do with an officer was sacred and you knew it. I had to go in when she was holding a conference about forthcoming changes and take a junior part, with papers and so on. Before I went in she said, ''Everything that goes on in this office is private.'' I knew that, because I'd had similar work before. Sometimes there would be senior officers sitting round the table and she'd say something about an officer who hadn't fitted in very well

171

and was on the list for a change. Then she'd look straight at me as if to say, ''Forget it!'' and you knew she hadn't meant to say that in front of a junior officer.'

'How we loved her!' a one-time nursery officer exclaimed. 'I had been a nursery officer for some time. I loved babies and usually had eight in the nursery. One day I was called to the office and asked if I could take on a married couple's baby. The mother was very ill with TB and was dying, they thought—made worse by her anxiety over her baby being in what was then known as a work-house nursery. I gladly accepted the baby, and the father and seven-year-old brother came to visit her every week and reported to Mum how happy she was. The baby was loved and cared for for three months and then I was appointed to a larger nursery in Manchester. But by then the mother had recovered and was home and so was baby Barbara. The parents wrote to Commissioner say-ing how grateful they were and especially mentioning my love and care. This could have been the end as far as I was concerned, but not with our Commissioner. She took the trouble to write to me, enclosing the parents' letter for me to see. Such were our treasured rewards in those awful days of the slump.'

An important aspect of Catherine's leadership was the financing of the multitudinous projects. She had seen her father pray, work and scheme to find the funds needed to turn ideals into practical realities. She must do the same. She began by improving the use of such slender resources as they possessed. Her sisters explained one method she introduced:

'She organized central buying of all materials for curtains, bed-covers and so on from Tootal (the manufacturers). Previously, every home had ordered separately at far greater cost. Catherine arranged for large discounts because of the size of the purchase. The initial choice was made at headquarters, the materials bought wholesale and costs paid centrally. Then every home was sent patterns from which to choose, within the given range. This scheme covered the whole of Women's Social Work in this country and set the trend for other departments in the Army to follow.'

Every home bought day-to-day supplies at the best rate. One officer in London remembered five years of travelling by tram 'at four o'clock in the morning to go to Covent Garden and collect vegetables'. Sometimes the officers had to undertake the even more unpleasant task of 'begging' gifts from nearby market stall-holders or from those who grew their own vegetables on allotments. 'It was a sore trial to me,' one of these officers confessed, 'as I felt that in the Thirties people could hardly afford to feed themselves.'

Catherine used her skill in public speaking to gain support for the work. In *The Sunday Circle* Florence described the report Catherine gave at an annual meeting of the Women's Social Work held at London's Hyde Park Hotel. Instead of presenting an uninteresting collection of facts and figures, Catherine told them a story that blended pathos with humour. She first told her audience that 800 people had applied for places in eventide homes, yet only 200 had been accepted because of lack of space. One old lady had applied whose doctor said that she was quite unfit to live alone. She had twice almost asphyxiated herself by turning on the gas tap and forgetting to light the gas, and her landlady could no longer be responsible for her. When she applied to the Army she was told that there was no vacancy but was given a form to fill in and assured that an officer would call to see her. When the officer arrived, she discovered the old lady waiting patiently, seated on her two carefully corded boxes. She had misunderstood the letter and was expecting to be taken straight to an Army home. Catherine assured her listeners that the old lady had been lodged in temporary accommodation to await, like many others, a permanent place in a home.

Catherine had a flair for inventing novel ways of raising money that made giving *fun* instead of *duty*. Imaginative appeals to give in kind were likely to bring better results than asking for pounds, shillings and pence. It gave those with very little money the opportunity to share in the pleasure of giving too. One year, during Easter-week, Catherine appealed for gifts of ordinary eggs. As a result, 17,508 eggs were handed in. A stock of new dustbins was bought and the eggs put into them, preserved in isinglass. The bins were distributed to the various institutions with instructions that once the eggs had been used, the bins could be used as they were originally intended.

In December 1928 Catherine wrote, 'Please look out for a poster with indigo camels and a pink sky!' It was a poster depicting the wise men, with the caption, 'The wise men brought their gifts to Bethlehem. Will you give for the needy under our care in— ' (A space was left for name of institution.) The poster, Catherine explained, was to announce an appeal for gifts in kind:

'My ambition for the Christmas Appeal is that each Home should receive a sufficient supply of goods to supply its needs for six months. This is not nearly as formidable as it looks. Indeed, if all our friends, when ordering their own supplies during December were to make a *very* modest addition for the nearest Home, my ambition would be more than fulfilled. Rice, raisins, rashers, sugar, soap, sago, tea, tapioca, or turnips, if you choose one of them a pound at a time, could not be called a burdensome gift, yet if we only have a sufficient number of such gifts, the maintenance bills which are so heavy when one looks at the monthly totals, could be more than met . . .

'Last year we had the jolliest gifts . . . from the errand boy who brought a pound of salt to the servant girl who brought a pound of pence. I think the bulkiest gift was a ton of coke (what a welcome gift it was!) and perhaps the largest in value, the giving of breakfast which included bacon and egg, to all the women in the White-chapel Shelter. We do not want our Christmas Appeal to worry anyone. If it cannot be part of the happiness of Christmas to you, then please do not think about it any more.'

Catherine knew how to disarm, as well as to persuade.

One retired officer recalls taking part in a Christmas drive:

'We had no help from the government, it was absolutely volun-tary in those days and Commissioner had a Christmas drive. We had to go out all over London with our boxes, collecting for Christmas cheer. She appointed a captain and lieutenant and one or two little teams. I was quite young but I was made a captain. We had a little tea at 280 (Mare Street) just to set us off. I wasn't sitting next to Commissioner—I was two or three places down, next to Brigadier Bertha Smith. She said in a very quiet voice, "How is your faith, Captain?" and in a meek voice I answered "High!" Commissioner bounced round and said, "You'd be afraid to say if it wasn't, wouldn't you?" and I knew that was true. I thought, "Why has she chosen me for the job?" Then I thought, "I'm sure I can do it!" That was her—she knew you and it was wonderful!'

In January 1927 a sales depot had been set up in aid of women's and children's work. Goods were produced or packaged at the homes, including 'Women's Social Tea', recommended as 'delicious'. In addition, useful articles such as roller towels were for sale, as well as beautiful lingerie made and embroidered by unmarried mothers. One retired officer from a maternity home explained: 'We would have them for three months before the baby was due and then as long as three months after.' Another officer remembered that the ten mothers they had whose average age would be fifteen, often stayed a total of nine months. They were taught how to care for their babies and do general domestic work but they also made articles to sell that would help to finance the home. Nightdresses in fine nun's veiling, beautifully worked, were in demand by wealthier supporters. Catherine herself used to speak at drawing-room or garden meetings organized by some well-to-do and sometimes titled lady, who invited a circle of friends and neighbours to hear about the work. Florence had done the same kind of thing during her leadership and Olive remembers the awesome experience, as a girl, of accompanying her mother on such visits.

The homes held their own sales of work. One retired officer recalled such an occasion in 1932:

'Commissioner Catherine was to open the sale. She always liked a local nonconformist minister to pray at this occasion and one was duly secured. I, being the most junior officer, was detailed to the kitchen for the opening ceremony, to watch preparations and have tea ready to serve. One over eager young mother collected china from upstairs during the minister's prayer, dropped a plate down the wooden stairs and, not content with the noise already made, swept the pieces into a tin dustpan.

'As soon as the ceremony was over I expected trouble, but Commissioner Catherine was first out, calling me, the new Lieutenant, by name, to my surprise. She asked, with a smile, what the damages were, and continued on her way. I would add that there were some 600 officers under her command at that time, yet she knew me. Commissioner knew her officers.'

Catherine herself referred to her officers as 'heroines' and longed to find enough money to provide for them too. She wanted to open a home of rest for officers and appealed for donations. An ideal property came on the market but only one-third of its cost was available, so when another property came up for sale, less suitable but at a price they could afford, Catherine began to think that they should negotiate for it. But before the sale could be completed, the property was unaccountably withdrawn from the market. With a gleam in her eye, surely, Catherine asked, 'Is the Lord preparing some heart to give us the money to make possible the purchase of our first love, which, as I write, is still for sale?'

Catherine had an ideal tool ready to hand for communicating with the public. In 1889 a monthly magazine called *The Deliverer* had first been published as the organ of the Women's Social Work. Each month Florence contributed her own 'Personal Notes'. But in 1923 the magazine ceased publication. Then, in 1928, *The Deliverer* reappeared, complete with a 'Greeting from Mrs Bramwell Booth', who wrote: 'I am very glad to know that the General has spoken the word and that *The Deliverer* again comes into being . . . I congratulate daughter Catherine on this beginning again of the magazine.' Was Catherine directly responsible?

Catherine's 'Personal Notes' in this first April issue take her back to her childhood:

'My earliest recollection of *The Deliverer* 'Personal Notes' are not happy! . . . How often I see myself leading the hopeful group from the nursery or school-room in happy expectation of an evening with our beloved Mother, to be gently rebuffed with, ''Not this evening, darling, I must do the 'Personal Notes'.'''

But the 'Personal Notes' became the ideal showroom for the Women's Social Work. Catherine used her considerable writing skill to paint a picture of the various homes and institutions and to bring alive the statistics of social work. She told real-life stories of those desperately in need of help:

'Did you notice what I said in last month's notes of my desire to establish a Children's Lodge in London to afford shelter for children in temporary need? Yesterday I had a letter imploring me to receive a family of eight children. All had been turned into the street, desperate efforts had been made by a distracted mother and father to find a house or rooms. All to no avail. They needed *time*. The man had work and there had never been anything against them. The appeal to me was backed up by the superintendent of the Sunday School where all the children except the youngest (an infant) attend. *But I have no children's shelter, and all our beds are full*. I had to refuse. *This* morning I have another urgent appeal. Man, wife, and four children turned out of furnished room; could The Salvation Army help temporarily while the parents searched for accommodation? No, we could not, but if I had my children's shelter I could have said "yes" instead of "no".'

Sometimes readers were encouraged by 'The Happy Sequel to a Sad Story'. Help given to a young expectant mother had resulted in marriage, a Christian home and the grateful testimonial, 'We shall never forget what The Army did for us.'

To furnish a practical outlet for readers' compassion a scheme was outlined in a coupon appearing in the magazine: 'Please enrol me as a member of The Women's Social Auxiliary Force. I undertake to contribute 2s 6d yearly with two useful articles.' Readers were reminded that, with proper thrift, the coupon could be sent for ½d if the envelope were left unsealed.

In one year alone, the 'Personal Notes' carried articles about: the 'midnight work' and the need for a midnight centre, where street girls could be taken; Darby and Joan homes—another was urgently needed in addition to the twelve that already existed; the Mother's Hospital—badly in need of extensions; homes for girls, who would otherwise be sent to prison (Catherine wanted one with a garden, so that the girls could get some fun and exercise); homes for young girls; night shelters; and the home of rest for officers.

As well as informative facts and appeals for money, the 'Personal Notes' were full of titbits of Salvation Army news. Catherine writes about being present at the stone-laying ceremony for a new Training Garrison at Demark Hill (where the College still stands), a meeting of the Home League (The Salvation Army's women's meeting organization) at the Crystal Palace and an 'at home' held for branch secretaries of the Women's Social Auxiliary Force—those ladies who contributed two shillings and sixpence yearly, along with 'two useful articles'.

The needs of the readers themselves were not forgotten. Every issue of *The Deliverer* carried a small boxed advertisement which ran: 'Are you anxious about any one dear to you? Or about yourself? Then write to Commissioner Catherine Booth, 280, Mare Street, Hackney, London.' There is no mention anywhere of the additional work and correspondence that being an 'agony aunt' must have created.

Catherine never forgot the circumstances which had led to the establishing of the Women's Social Work, the need which had been the cause of such pain and heartache to both her father and mother when she was a baby in her cradle. Writing about the 'midnight work', and the need, as usual, for more funds, she said:

'You see, this side of our work is difficult to speak of; the tragedy lies hidden away, it is part of the very help itself that all is done, as it were, in secret . . . If I give you a few extracts from the monthly report of one of my Midnight Officers, surely some who read will feel as I do, that this work *must* go on, regardless of cost. Not that the cost is very high. But when one's exchequer is empty even small extras are big problems.'

Several case histories follow and statistics which Catherine modestly says will prove 'more eloquent than any remarks of mine are likely to be'. In 1927:

Numbers of appeals to women in the streets	3,854
Appealed to in public-houses	711
Girls brought to Salvation Army Homes	95
Sent to situations, returned to friends or otherwise assisted	532

She concludes:

'I value this work highly, not alone for the actual results . . . but because I believe the presence of our Officers amongst the sinners who congregate on the streets of our great cities, is a constant invitation to "cease to do evil". No woman sees them but is reminded that if she be willing the Army Sister will help her to leave her evil life and begin afresh; no man with an evil purpose in mind but is reminded of better things and in some degree reproved by the sight of the Army uniform. I believe many of whom we never hear are deterred from evil, but it is not an uncommon thing for a man to thank our Officers for their word of warning, coupling the thanks with a promise to finish with such doings . . . Salvationists on the streets at night are there to help men as well as women.'

For her officers, the highlight of the year was the officers' council held each autumn at Swanwick conference centre in Derbyshire. There were two sessions because it was not practicable for all officers to be away from the homes at one time. Certain leaders and clerical staff attended both conferences but other officers attended one or the other. It was usually left to the Home to decide who to send to each session, though occasionally a special meeting might be called for wardens, or house mothers, for example, and they would all be summoned to the appropriate session.

'We would arrive Monday morning and be back Thursday. There was a welcome meeting, two whole days, and the next morning we came back on the coach or train. The Commissioner was in charge but often the General would come on the second day and in between our leaders would have all sorts of special meetings. I had to go to both sessions to do business in the office and although I was doing work in between, I loved even the second session. I was longing to hear the Commissioner again.'

Memories of past Swanwick Councils remained vivid many years later:

'She was at her best at officers' councils. Had she been an actress she would, I am sure, have made a fortune. I'm only sorry that these councils were confined to officers in Women's Social Work. What a wealth of inspiration and blessing she was! She knew the hardness of those days, the misery of getting up at 4 a.m. in turn to clear the flues of an old kitchen range, get a fire going, make babies' feeds and get breakfast for everyone. We depended on this old range for everything—cooking, hot water, warmth. There was no gas or electric lighting—not even an electric kettle. Yet she inspired us all to go back to it with a zest and love that now seems unbelievable.'

'The women there were captivated and charmed. She would always say solemn and straight things with grace and acceptability. That's my feeling about her.'

'In her councils at Swanwick she was a wonderful speaker. One minute you would be laughing and the next you would be crying. In her prayer meetings I seemed to lose all sense of being on earth, she was so uplifted.'

'Her councils at Swanwick were really something to impress. It was an uplift to hear her expounding the Scriptures, but she was very straight in her dealings. She made me realize once again that God had called me to work in this great Army of ours and whatever work I was given must be done well . . . I think of the crowd of young officers who had become discouraged and down-hearted but found themselves down at the mercy seat, renewing consecration, then returning to our appointments with spiritual renewal and determination to do our best for God and our Army and lost souls.'

One officer summed up her feelings for the Commissioner by saying, 'I loved all the leaders I worked closely with through my years at headquarters, but she was different. She was a genius.'

CHAPTER 19

'The Cross . . . the Pain'

'Prepare thee for thy Calvary,'
Whispered a still small voice to me . . .
And often if my heart were gay,
If joy and beauty filled a day,
The shadow of that thought would creep
Across my soul, or mar my sleep.
I cried to God and prayed that He
Would fit me for my Calvary . . .
It came;
The cross, the cries, the pain, the shame;
But 'twas not I
Whom they led forth to die:
It was the one I loved!

Catherine Bramwell-Booth

The love between all the members of the Booth family at The Homestead was unusually strong and deep, but Catherine's love for her father was of special intensity. He was the love of her life and brief but glorious hours spent with him were bright points of childhood and adult life. Holidays were rare but 'When they were older', she wrote, 'it was sometimes arranged that one or other of his sons or daughters should spend part of the holiday with him. And then, what walks! What talks! By the sea, or all about Dartmoor, talking, walking and worshipping, for though topics were as varied as life itself, God, and the spiritualities always came in. And another delight was to be read to by him . . . On one of the last holidays I spent with him, I remember he read aloud Quiller-Couch on Job; some, to me, unknown poems of George Herbert (he had lately obtained a complete set of Herbert's works); and, as only he could, or so it seemed to me, favourite passages from his beloved Milton.'

181

In March 1926 the family were all together to celebrate Bramwell's seventieth birthday. It was just before Catherine took up her duties at the Women's Social Work headquarters. There was a huge meeting at the Albert Hall, to which King George V sent a birthday message, and a luncheon at the Connaught Rooms, chaired by Lloyd George. As usual with the family, the occasion was used to boost Army efforts and funds. General Bramwell Booth noted in his journal that at the Albert Hall 'Birthday Demonstration' the gifts of money amounted to £164,000. A 'Birthday Seventy' officers were dedicated as missionaries from Britain to Europe. In April he and Florence left for a campaign in the United States (their only long tour together). When they arrived back at Southampton in May Bramwell noted,'Cath here to meet us; looks well. We are very thankful.' No doubt her health was still a cause of some concern to her parents, following the serious illness of previous years.

There was no thought of Bramwell taking it easy and certainly none of possible retirement from active service. General Coutts, Army historian, wrote:

'On March 8th, 1926, Bramwell Booth celebrated his seventieth birthday. There was then no retiring age for a General and his forward-looking spirit still sighed for fresh worlds to conquer for his Lord and Master . . .

'There was only one shadow over this. No leader could live for ever. Who was to be the General's successor and how was he (or she) to be appointed?

'Such a question never arose when, on August 21st, 1912, the sealed envelope was opened which contained William Booth's nomination of his successor. The mantle of William fell automatically on Bramwell. But on whom was it now to fall?'

Bramwell himself saw no cause for doubts or questionings. Following his father's precedent, he too had exercised the General's stated prerogative of nominating his successor, by writing down the name of the one chosen and putting the paper into a sealed envelope, to be kept by the Army's solicitor and opened only after his death. But others saw the situation in a different light, as General Coutts explains:

'As far back as 1886 the Orders and Regulations for Field Officers had laid down that "the General must and will appoint his successor" but "the succession to the position of General is not in any shape or form hereditary, nor is it ever intended to be so.''

'It was on this last point that concern—justified or unjustified—had begun to be felt, and this increased as illness overtook the General.' (*No Discharge in This War*)

1927 was to be Bramwell's last complete year of Army service. It was as packed as any that lay in the past. But a visit from his sister Eva in October presaged conflict and suffering ahead. She presented him with a memorandum which declared:

'The time has arrived when some change must take place in the Constitution of the Army, particularly with respect to the appointment of its General.

'It could never have been in the minds of the few Evangelists who consented to the proposal to invest the Founder as Sole Trustee for all temporalities of the Army, and give him such absolute power, that it would grow to such huge proportions.

'While the Officers were content during the Founder's life to entrust him with all authority, including the appointment of his successor, it must be apparent that with the changing conditions some alteration in the Deed Poll must be brought about . . .

'Surely the methods adopted to create the Deed Poll can again be adopted to amend it. The legal aspect therefore may be set aside, for if other religious bodies can change their constitution it must be clear that The Salvation Army can.'

Bramwell was adamant that nothing would induce him to renege on his father's wishes. He wrote later to his wife, 'You know as far as I am concerned the General's decision, whatever it is—will be law for me.'

In his written reply to the memorandum he stated the impossibility of any General seeking to change the constitution and reiterated his conviction that, 'As to the appointment of a succeeding General, your suggestion aims at cancelling the General's most urgent duty—his duty to discern and name his successor.'

Catherine wrote of him:

'He was the one person in The Salvation Army who could *not* act in opposition to William Booth. Even a modicum of imagination might have spared untold sorrow and suffering to one who deserved some consideration and whose views could not be said to arise from any lack of experience or knowledge, either of the

Army's history and needs, or of the wishes and opinion of its Founder . . . None about him ought to have been able to conceive the possibility that he would depart from what had been enjoined by the Army's first General.'

General Bramwell was still in the thick of Army business when in January 1928 a disastrous high tide at Westminster left ten people drowned and hundreds homeless. He was taking meetings at Leicester at the time but immediately telegraphed instructions for Army help with relief work and within a day or two was on the scene himself. A few days later he was speaking at Blackfriars and Catherine went to meet him:

'I, having been engaged elsewhere, was called for on that Wednesday night, that I might steal the joy of the journey home with him. The crowd, determined to catch sight of him as he left the building surged about the entrance to the hall and round the car. The hall was packed to suffocation: it was after 10 p.m.: traffic had diminished and the waiting "shut outs" were excited and eager. Men and women peered into the car, and spying me, greeted me first from one side and then from the other: "It's one of the family," "It's Catherine," and one and another shouted to me, "We're waiting to see the General," "We love him!" "He belongs to us as much as to you!" "I'm going to have a look at 'im!" "You give 'im my love!" There was something almost brutal in their fervour; these were not Salvationists, though distinctly of those whom sixty years ago and more William Booth had described to his son as "our people". I felt unaccountably saddened.

'These, and crowds like them, had claimed and as it were devoured the gracious presence who was my father; for *me* there had been only brief moments, as was to be this drive home. Always between us, his own, and him, had come the claims of the people —"the Army". "He's ours as much as yours!" came the hoarse voice. I felt almost resentment, and thought: when he is really old *we* shall have him for a little.' (*Bramwell Booth*)

But that expected time was no more than a few months of unutterable sadness and pain to be endured in the very near future. General Bramwell did not return to his office at International Headquarters after 12 April 1928. In spite of being far from well he insisted on fulfilling an engagement in Sheffield, where 'snow, driven by bitter blasts,' contrasted with the stifling atmosphere in the packed hall. Bramwell caught a chill on his way home and failed to regain full strength.

'His health now caused grave anxiety. A specialist whom he consulted said, after a thorough examination, that the physical condition was good, but that he was nervously overdone and required some months' complete freedom for worry and work.' (*Bramwell Booth*) By September Catherine was writing in *The Deliverer*'s 'Personal Notes', 'As I write there is every evidence that he is climbing steadily towards a complete restoration of health.'

But towards the end of October 'the General grew worse; he was now virtually without natural sleep, and during the second week of November his condition was serious. The Chief (of Staff) came down on Tuesday, November 13th, but as the General was sleeping under the influence of a narcotic he only went into the bedroom for a few moments and did not speak to him. During this visit the Chief told Mrs Booth that he feared an effort was being made to call the High Council, that while he hoped it might be averted for a time the position was very uncertain . . . On his return to Headquarters that same Tuesday night, however, activities were set in motion for the immediate requisitioning of the High Council.' (*Bramwell Booth*)

William Booth had made provision for a decision-making body of The Salvation Army that could be called together to take action should the General be unfit to do so. It was to be called the High Council and would consist of the Chief of Staff, all active commissioners, and colonels of two years' standing who held territorial commands. As a commissioner, Catherine herself would be a member of this body which, however, had never up to this point been assembled to act on the Army's behalf.

General Coutts recorded:

'In the previous October Commander Evangeline Booth, the General's younger sister, had presented him with a reasoned memorandum urging that "it would be wise statesmanship for the General to abolish the present system of appointing his successor and establish a method for his election." This, for reasons that seemed good to him, the General was unwilling to do. He could not waive the right, he declared, of nominating his successor. The tension heightened as by mid-November it was known that "his condition was serious". A national newspaper even announced that he was dying. So it was that under the provisions of the supplementary deed of July 26th, 1904, seven Commissioners . . . addressed a requisition to the Chief of the Staff . . . asking that a High Council be summoned. Whether their action be judged wise or unwise, right or wrong, they felt this step to be necessary lest the General's nomination of his successor should extend the hereditary character of that office.'

In the December issue of *The Deliverer* Catherine, back from a visit to Scotland for meetings, wrote:

'A gloom was cast over the cheer of the Scottish meetings by the news that my beloved father and General was not so well. There had been a period of acute sleeplessness, and I found him very weary. He was interested in my account of the meetings, and especially in hearing of an old friend I met in Edinburgh, and he enjoyed a share in a little fun we had by the way. (Colonel Cameron accompanied me on this tour, and when she and I are together we usually find some fun.) How I long for some great good news to cheer him; this sickness is a terrible trial to one who has always been in the thick of the fray as the General has. Will those who love him pray that God will restore him the much-needed physical strength? His recovery would indeed mean a happy Christmas to us and to thousands who love him.'

For the time being Bramwell was told nothing about the calling of the High Council, and Catherine did not visit him. She explained: 'The General was told the doctors had enjoined greater quiet, and for the same reason he was told I must not see him until he was stronger, for it would have been impossible to prevent his discussing Army affairs with me . . .

'At the end of December the doctors pronounced him well enough to bear the shock of hearing what action had been taken. It was decided I should tell him. I travelled down from Headquarters for this purpose. The journey no sooner begun than ended, for hours fly to meet those who crave even a moment's respite. I felt that the words I must speak would be his death. How then could I speak them? It was New Year's day, 1929, and in the evening, soon after my arrival, my mother and I went into his room, our hearts steadied to the task. I kissed him and he spoke cheerily, told me he was ''on the mend'': he had not seen me for some time; then, looking steadfastly into my eyes, he said, ''They have called the High Council.'' His words struck me like a blow: so God had told him! I could not speak, I nodded . . . Then question followed question . . . And the position was fully talked over. After some time my mother left us, and my father at once said to me, ''If I die, Catherine, remember, there must be no bitterness. I forgive; you and the others must forgive too. They want to change the General's plan, they must know I shall never agree.'' '

Catherine wrote nothing for the January issue of *The Deliverer*, but in February:

'It was a matter of regret to me that I was unable to give *The Deliverer* its usual pages last month. The date for writing them came just at the time when my beloved Father suffered a sudden and unexpected relapse, and for some days we experienced the gravest anxiety on his account. The doctors are satisfied he is now making steady improvement though it is evident it will be some time yet before he recovers his usual strength.'

General Coutts wrote:

'The High Council met at Sunbury Court on January 8th, 1929. Some days of discussion ensued. A proposal was made that the General ''should retire from office retaining his title, and continuing to enjoy the honours and dignities of the same''.'

A deputation visited General Bramwell and, Catherine recorded, 'he spoke to each of the seven, personal words applicable to them, enquired after wife or friend', and prayed with them.

But in his written reply to their proposal he stated:

'The wisdom of our Founder decided that The Salvation Army should always be under the oversight, direction and control of some one person. It has pleased God to call me to that position.

'Now I am asked to relinquish a sacred trust, which, in the sight of God, I solemnly accepted; I should not be justified in laying down that trust unless I believed that I were no longer able to carry out its responsibilities.

'I have therefore thought it my duty to turn to those medical advisers who have attended me throughout my illness, to ascertain from them whether, in their opinion, I am likely to regain my health and strength. I am advised by them that, in all human probability and subject to God's Providence, I shall, in a few months, be fully recovered. Having this medical report and bearing in mind my deep obligations to the Founder and to the Army, I am bound to ask myself whether I am justified in laying down the Trust committed to me.

'Such a question answers itself. I cannot do so . . .'

General Coutts summarizes what was a long and complicated matter:

'When he (Bramwell) declined this suggestion (to retire) the High Council then decided by a secret ballot of fifty-five votes to eight that his term of office as General should now end. These proceedings were arrested however when, on an application to the High Court of Justice, Mr Justice Eve ruled that the High Council resolution was out of order because the General (or his accredited representative) had not been given the opportunity of stating his case. Obedient to this ruling, the High Council met again on February 13th when the General was represented by Mr William Jowitt KC. Medical evidence was heard, as was the testimony of two ex-officers who spoke in his favour. Again by secret ballot the High Council confirmed its earlier decision, by fifty-two votes to five. The five dissentients were Mrs Bramwell Booth, Commissioner Catherine Booth, Colonel Mary Booth, Mrs Commissioner Booth-Hellberg (Bramwell's sister, Lucy) and Commissioner J. Allister Smith. Immediately thereafter two names were submitted for the vacant office of General, and Commissioner Higgins was elected by forty-two votes to the seventeen cast for Commander Evangeline Booth.' (*No Discharge in This War*)

The Times carried a lengthy article about the meetings of the High Council. After commenting on the dignity and courtesy observed during all the proceedings, it concluded:

'The late General and the members of his family about him have at least this to comfort them: the present differences are fortunately due to no disagreement over the mission in the world which The Salvation Army lives to fulfil; it is no case of that *odium theologicum* which has so often wrecked religious bodies. It is a matter entirely of business efficiency, of the ways and means by which The Army may be extricated from existing embarrassments and set free to run as smoothly as organization can ensure. Also, fundamentally the crisis has arisen from circumstances which . . . are due in some measure to the very success of The Salvation Army itself. Its founder and his dynastic successor have built better than they know, and to the world at large, as also to the Army, the reputation of General Bramwell Booth as the faithful guardian and zealous enlarger of his father's inheritance is secure.

The present year will soon bring about the celebration of the centenary of the births of William and Catherine Booth. As their successors recall, as they will, the humble beginnings of so great an adventure, and give thanks for the manner in which it has prospered, they will certainly feel nothing but gratitude for the guidance which the founder's son gave them as long as his health permitted.'

Whatever agony of soul Catherine was passing through, she outwardly maintained a calm and resolute manner. Those who were with her at those fateful meetings of the High Council could find nothing but admiration for her dignity and restraint. She continued to discharge her responsibilities at 280, Mare Street with nothing more noticeable than a slight impatience to be done with the business of each day. During the Swanwick Council of 1928, when events were moving to their crisis, those who listened to her 'were just as fervent in their applause, just as careful to listen and just as much rewarded'. Those working closely with her, but who held opposite views, were still able to state that there was never any personal bitterness.

But the hurt went deep and a sense of betrayal wounded every member of the family at The Homestead. The wound for Bramwell, they believed, was mortal and brought about his death. Catherine's narrative continued:

'On April 29th he received the Prime Minister's letter announcing that the King had appointed him a member of the Order of Companions of Honour. He said, ''It is kind of the King. It will be good for the Army.''

'The doctors did not anticipate any sudden change. The anxiety now appeared to be that the shock of all he had passed through would result in an extended period of invalidism . . .

'On June 7th I went away for a short rest. He knew I was to go, and the evening before I left we talked together. He spoke . . . of many things, of the sorrow of the past months, and then, resting his eyes with infinite love on mine, he spoke to me about accepting God's will. ''My darling girl, we must trust him. You must trust him.'' I did not know I should not hear his voice again.' (*Bramwell Booth*)

On 16 June the family was summoned to his death-bed and that Sunday evening he was, in Army terms, promoted to Glory.

CHAPTER 20

Aftermath

FOR THE FRIDAY AND SATURDAY following his death, Bramwell Booth's body lay in state at the Army's Congress Hall. *The Deliverer*, in an article headed 'Our Late General, His Passing, and some Tributes of Love,' described the thanksgiving and funeral services:

'On Sunday evening ten thousand Salvationists and friends filled the Royal Albert Hall to bid farewell to our promoted Leader; a representative procession accompanied the entry of the coffin, which was followed by his family. Mrs Booth, her daughters and daughters-in-law, wore broad white sashes, each bearing a large cross and crown in red. One of the songs he had written was sung . . .

'Among the many messages of condolence received by Mrs Booth was the following from His Majesty the King:

' ''The Queen and I have heard with great regret of the death of General Bramwell Booth, and we offer you our sincere sympathy in your bereavement. With his father he will always be gratefully remembered as the promoter of the widespread and beneficent activities of The Salvation Army.'' '

A message was read out from Commander Evangeline Booth, who was unable to be present in London due to the effects of a motor accident. In the context of all that had happened her comments, however honestly intended, may have held undesirable overtones for Catherine. Evangeline wrote:

'We loved him, we valued him beyond words to express; we fain would have kept him with us, relieved from the innumerable and exacting claims of the Generalship, in a position for influence and service to the peoples of the world unparalleled in all history. No other can ever fill it as he could have done. But his warfare was finished . . . How sorrow-stricken I am . . . I shall for ever more be lonely.'

The Deliverer account continued:

'Two chief speakers at that great gathering were, naturally, Mrs Booth and Commissioner Catherine . . .

'Commissioner Catherine Booth, speaking for herself and her brothers and sisters, paid tribute to her beloved Father and General, both at Albert Hall on Sunday evening and at Abney Park next afternoon. We quote from her words at Albert Hall:

' "We thank God for him! Our grief is the price of our love. If we had not had the joy of his love we should not be grieving as we are tonight." '

Next day:

'As for his father, the traffic of London was halted as the funeral procession moved from Queen Victoria Street to Abney Park with the coffin bearing the motto of the Order of the Companions of Honour: "In action faithful, in honour clear." ' (*No Discharge in This War*)

In her funeral oration Catherine had spoken passionately of her father's compassion and love, for his family, for any in need and distress and for animals too. She had made an earnest appeal to the thousands present to let God do for them what he had done for her father and to let 'his silent testimony be his message to you'. But it had never been her way to wear her heart on her sleeve. Even the emotion she showed was controlled and suitable for public display. It was in her private verses that she poured out her inner anguish and sorrow. One she called 'Public Behaviour':

> *Oh, heart's anguish never need be known;*
> *Never need be known*
> *Save to God alone*
> *That the heart's not turned to stone,*
> *If you smile and smile,*
> *Keep smiling all the while. . . .*

Even her own family must not see her grief displayed:

> *Oh! When shall I weep for my Beloved,*
> *When shall I weep?*
> *When thou art alone; then weep for him,*
> *Hiding from those who love him too thine anguish . . .*
> *   alone, at dawn,*
> *Then thou shalt weep for thy Beloved,*
> *Weep long.*

One practical course of action, to show her loyalty and love, was to link his name with her own. Florence wrote:

'After my dear one's death, under the sorrowful circumstances of 1929, Catherine, then over 40 years of age, changed her name by Deed Poll, taking her father's name in addition—Catherine Bramwell Booth.'

The legal aftermath of the changes brought about by the High Council, with regard to election and terms of office of the General, dragged on for another two years. During that time Catherine addressed committees of the House of Commons and the House of Lords and spoke in the High Court. Meanwhile, she began to feel a strong compulsion to write her father's biography. In her preface to the book she wrote:

'I only dared attempt a task for which I knew myself unqualified because circumstances combined with conviction to make me see it to be a duty. And having recognized a duty there remains but to do it; results are not our concern.'

Accordingly she was granted working furlough from the Army from March 1930 until 1932 to prepare and write the portrait of her father in words. The book, simply entitled *Bramwell Booth*, was first published in May 1933. Her aim, Catherine wrote, was 'to manifest the man, who is my father, rather than to recount his doings . . . I have refrained from any expression of my own opinion about the events at his life's close, and have recorded them only as they appeared to him. The histories of those happenings will doubtless be written and will throw further light on their causes and upon the motives of the chief actors, but these pages are only concerned with their effect on the life of Bramwell Booth.'

Catherine drew upon journals and letters to provide a meticulous account of her father's life. But the book is far more than an accurate compilation of facts. It comes to life because of her deep love and understanding of the man she wrote about and her intense desire to show the world what manner of man he was. For all its control and factual detail it is an impassioned eulogy of the person she loved with all her heart. When she was over 100, she recommended a reading and rereading of her book about her father as the key to understanding her own personality. Certainly, one of her comments about him may come close to the mark in describing her own nature and temperament:

'Temperamentally, Bramwell Booth was a mystic. A little less energy; opportunity, in the shape of congenial surroundings: and instead of a man of action, earth would have counted one more dreamer among her sons . . . As it was, necessity drove him on to a battle-field, and the mystic was almost lost in the soldier. Almost, but not quite, for the two can survive side by side . . .

'This strain in him was at variance with the man of affairs he was obliged to be. He hungered for the wilderness when duty kept him in the market-place.'

It was duty too that took Catherine back again to the market-place of the Women's Social Work headquarters in Mare Street in 1932, to resume her hectic round of institutional visits, administration and personal care of the officers and people in her charge. Those who looked on saw the same indomitable personality and sparkling wit. One retired officer recalled the first time that she attended an officers' council at Clapton Congress Hall, where the Commissioner was in charge:

'Standing tall and erect, her long cloak flowing around, I see her now introducing us to the verse . . . "Wherever he may guide me, no want shall turn me back," to a lively tune, which she announced as "When the cats get up in the morning." I saw then a twinkle in her eye which spoke volumes to me.'

Three years later this same officer faced the disappointment of having failed her midwifery examination, 'with the very slim possibility of a resit, other authority deeming it not possible for me to do so. Because of my questioning, Commissioner was approached and she decided I should have a second chance.' The result was success and the opportunity fully to pursue her chosen career as an officer.

In a letter marked 'personal' Catherine wrote to a newly-fledged officer beginning her first post at Women's Social Work. It is remarkable that she found time to write such a letter, to enter imaginatively into the young officer's feelings and to encourage her confidences:

My dear Lieutenant,
This letter will find you at work with your first responsibility as an Officer. I send this line to tell you that I have prayed and shall pray that you will be blessed and used of God. I

believe, and I hope you do too, that He over-rules for His children and that it is by his guidance you are where you are . . .

I shall always be pleased to hear from you, especially about your own spiritual progress, you may write me at any time and if you mark your letter 'Personal' it comes to my hand unopened . . .

One other letter to the same officer, three years later, charts her progress:

My dear Captain,
It is always important to answer every 'Call' the Holy Spirit makes, and I feel glad you have written to tell me what you feel about Missionary Work. An official record shall be made, which means that when next we are asked to supply Officers for the Mission Field, you will be considered . . .

At the end of the typewritten letter, a handwritten paragraph brims over with feeling: 'Dear child—be *wholly Christ's*—His presence is the only anointing for the service of winning souls—at home or abroad. I believe he has chosen you and if you follow your Lord He will fit you, Catherine Bramwell Booth.'

In 1934, two years after Catherine had taken up the reins again in Mare Street, the Women's Social Work celebrated its golden jubilee. Florence, the first leader of the work, had an important part to play in the celebrations, as well as the Commissioner, her daughter. *The Deliverer* carried an account of events, which included a pilgrimage to the place in Hanbury Street where the work began:

' "The only word to express it" ', said a veteran Social Officer concerning the Jubilee Pilgrimage, ' "is *wonderful*!" '

'More than one of the noble army of "Retireds" echoed her words in their hearts. "Hope Town", the hostel for 300 homeless women, where they and others assembled, was in itself a witness to the fact that the work commenced "round the corner" fifty years ago *had* gloriously succeeded, in spite of all the fears of the pioneers.

' "Hope Town" was agog with excitement. "Hope Town" was swept and garnished, bright with sunflowers and Michaelmas daisies, and with the Army Colours. Helpers in their neat print frocks and spotless aprons, and officers of the Women's Social Work, gathered together for the pilgrimage.

'Then Mrs Bramwell Booth arrived with Commissioner Catherine Bramwell-Booth. The pioneers and their followers marched away down the back streets of Whitechapel singing as they went the old songs, "Marching on in the Light of God", and "Bright Crowns There Are". There was no Band, only the music of concertinas played by Staff-Captain Dora Booth and two Army lasses; the only banner was the Flag they had pledged themselves to follow.

'Mrs Booth and the Commissioner led the way. . . They marched to the spot in Hanbury Street dear to the hearts of many, where fifty years ago Mrs Booth first began the Women's Social Work in a little six-roomed cottage. There they held a little Open-Air meeting while men and women from the tall, unlovely tenement houses, with little children clinging to them, gathered around and joined in.

' "Salvation! Oh, the joyful sound!" was sung, before the Commissioner and Mrs Booth addressed the gathering . . .

'Back in "Hope Town" Mrs Booth received the Officers and entertained them to tea. Then followed a happy gathering . . . Adjutant Lamb, warden of "Hope Town", said for the younger officers, "We want to be what you were when you were in the Women's Social Work." '

The war clouds were gathering over Europe, yet Catherine seems not to have noticed them. It is not surprising that she was not 'in touch with the politics of the thing', as she put in later, because she was far too busy keeping the wheels of her enormous social enterprise turning. 'I was concerned with the people who were drinking or stealing or the young folks who were unmanageable and the war didn't impinge on it much—until it broke out, and upset everything,' she explained. It is noteworthy that the *people*, rather than the administration, were still her chief concern, even in retrospect.

For the duration of the war Catherine lived at her Finchampstead cottage, travelling up to Mare Street for the first twelve months. But in August 1940 she was given a new posting and a special 'farewell gathering' was held for her at headquarters. *The War Cry* reported it briefly:

'The farewell gathering of Commissioner Catherine Bramwell-Booth from the leadership of the Women's Social Services, of which she had been in charge for eleven-and-a-half years, had to adjourn to the public shelter beneath the headquarters.'

The Deliverer gave a more colourful account, thoroughly in character with their colourful leader:

'On a raid warning sounding during the London gathering, the officers adjourned to the public shelter beneath the Mare Street headquarters, where, with the folk who came in from their shopping in the high road, the Commissioner led the community singing, assisted by the fiddles and concertinas of the Women's Social orchestra.'

Catherine's new appointment was to the International Training College. She would have faced conditions similar in many ways to her first period on the staff, when most men had been called up and a strong hand was needed to plan and control. But the premises were different. In 1928 Catherine had written in her 'Personal Notes' for *The Deliverer*, 'On May 10th I hope to be present at the stone-laying ceremony for the Training Garrison now being built at Denmark Hill.' That ceremony was to be Bramwell's last public meeting. He did not live to see the International (William Booth Memorial) Training College completed. But it was here, not at the old premises in Clapton, that Catherine took up her post in August 1940.

In September, however, she became ill and never returned to that work. It was not until the end of 1946 that she was plunged fully into Army affairs once more, when the newly elected General Orsborn appointed her International Secretary for Europe with additional responsibility for European relief. Again, history seemed to be repeating itself.

The bi-monthly journal of overseas Army work, *All the World*, noted in January 1947 that 'Commissioner Catherine Bramwell-Booth . . . has just visited German corps and relief teams'. The article went on to refer to the extreme cold which had caused canals to freeze and resulted in coal shortages which made the distribution of meagre supplies even more difficult.

Olive and Dora remember the journey which took Catherine from Sweden to Finland, when the ice-breaker that went in front of her boat broke down:

'The captain of the boat said, "I'm sorry, we're stuck," and

Catherine asked how long it would be before they could move. He said it might be hours as they had to wait for another ice-breaker to arrive. She said, ''I must get a telegram off,'' but he said that he couldn't help as they had no radio. But there was a mass of little islands and the captain said, ''There is a post office on that little island.'' So she said, ''How can I get there?'' and he answered, ''Walk.'' So she and her officer climbed out of the boat onto the frozen sea and walked to the little island over the ice. She sent her telegram and they walked back to the ship. That was quite an experience. Later on, when she was speaking to officers, she talked about Peter walking on the water and she said, ''I did that, didn't I, Colonel?'' and she looked round at an officer who had been with her at the time. The Commissioner was laughing, but I don't think the Colonel thought it very funny.'

In 1948 Catherine had an accident and then was taken into hospital for an operation for removal of the gall bladder. She was not yet back in her office when the month of July arrived, the official time at which she was due to retire from active service. Like the rest of her family, Catherine did not agree with the idea of compulsory retirement at sixty-five. 'I should never have retired,' she said later, 'but the Army rules retired me at sixty-five', and again, 'I should have liked to go on longer, but there you are, the powers that were decreed, and you have to make the best of it.'

A letter from the Chief of Staff, circulated in that same month, indicates that she was at least given six months' grace. He wrote:

'My dear Comrade, I feel I should send this special notification to you regarding the pending retirement of Commissioner Catherine Bramwell-Booth. The Commissioner is due to retire this month, but the General asked her to remain on active service until 20th October, to which she has agreed, to better enable us to make the necessary adjustments which her retirement occasions.'

A résumé of her Army career follows, then:

'In the retirement of Commissioner Bramwell-Booth there will pass from Active Service the senior Commissioner of the Army, whose knowledge of and love for the Movement, as well as her clear and keen analysis of situations and individuals, has been most helpful to the General and myself during these past two years. It is a source of gratification, however, to know that the General has asked the Commissioner after her retirement to continue as a member of his Advisory Council.

'The Commissioner has not been too well recently. Not long ago she had a rather bad accident, which might have been fatal, and recently was suddenly stricken and taken to hospital for a serious operation; she has not yet entirely recovered, but is gradually improving and we are all hoping that she will be back in the office within a week or two.

'I am sure you will join me in praying that God's blessing shall be upon the Commissioner, who for over forty-five years has carried with distinction the honoured badge of Army Officership.'

It seemed like the beginning of the end, and so, for any ordinary person, it might have been. But a bright new chapter in life lay ahead, still in the distant future.

CHAPTER 21

Retirement

WHEN CATHERINE RETIRED from active service in the Army at the age of sixty-five, she could look back, as the Chief of Staff had written, on forty-five years as an officer on active service for God and the Army. William Booth once warned new officer cadets that he was condeming them to a life of hard labour and most Salvation Army officers can vouch for the truth of his words.

Catherine's hard labour began as a field officer, first in Bath and then at Walthamstow, and continued during her ten years on the staff of the Training Garrison. She spent herself in teaching and also counselling individual cadets and worked far into the night to write the letters that would help her past students through their first difficult months in the field. After both the First and the Second World Wars she superintended relief work in Europe, travelling personally to areas of need and encouraging Salvation Army corps all over the continent, as well as preaching at huge public gatherings. After suffering an illness severe enough to warrant her taking it easy for the rest of her days, she undertook the enormous task of leading the Women's Social Work for fourteen years. In the midst of these major appointments she suffered the sorrow and distress, never fully healed, of the circumstances that surrounded her father's illness and death, taking time from active service to write his full-length biography.

Now she had good reason to relish the prospect of sitting back to enjoy some well-earned leisure. However, few energetic and gifted women or men look on retirement in that light and Catherine certainly did not want to retire. But she bowed to the inevitable with a good grace and, in spite of any feelings of frustration or despondency she may have suffered, does not seem to have confided them to the rest of the family. When she was much younger she had warned young officers that 'the blues are catching' and she always saw to it that she kept her own blues to herself.

One major decision about the future was soon made. The family would move away from Hadley Wood. By that time Mrs Florence Booth was eighty-seven, but she had retained her zest for life and entered into the spirit of adventure about the planned move, in spite of muttered comments from some outsiders that it was wrong to make her leave The Homestead. Southwold, the East coast resort with many happy family memories, was considered as a possible place, but rejected on the grounds that the seaside can be cold and that it was too far from London.

Deciding to move was one thing, but finding a suitable place and house was quite a different matter in the post-war world of property shortage. Olive and Dora remember the search, which lasted for eighteen months. In the end they did not choose an area to settle but simply went where the right kind of house was advertised. There were certain stipulations: there were to be no attics—the house must be on two floors only—and it must be private. At Hadley Wood it was only too common to have to brave waiting Salvationists before going out of the front-gate to take a walk. As well as being secluded, the house should have a good view and the soil must be light.

The house which they eventually bought, which is still the family home, is at Finchampstead, not far from Catherine's cottage among the pines. Olive explained:

'After we had searched and searched, Catherine saw this house advertised in the local press. She said to Mama, ''We'll go and see it,'' so they got a taxi and went off to the agent. We knew the area and had often passed the gate but had never been inside. The RAF was there all through the war so there had always been a policeman stationed at the gate and it had all been deadly secret. It hadn't been inhabited since the RAF moved out. Someone had bought it and begun renovations and then decided to resell in a great hurry.'

The property included two cottages as well as the main house and was set in a large acreage of land which included woodlands. They bought it at a bargain price, entirely from their own resources, helped by assets from the sale of Catherine's cottage and the little house at Southwold. Mrs Florence Booth was living with Catherine at the Finchampstead cottage beforehand, so the move from there to the new home was as smooth and painless as possible.

The extended family group that moved into North Court in 1949 numbered eleven, with three kitchen staff and a gardener to help. Mary, the second daughter, had also been retired from active service in the Army, as Catherine explained:

'In charge of the Army's work in Belgium when the Second World War broke out, Mary might have escaped to safety but felt that she could not leave the small band of officers who, under her charge, were caring for refugees in the most awful conditions. The suffering and anguish she saw in those dreadful days lived in her heart all her life afterwards. It was in Brussels that she was arrested and tried as a spy, released for want of evidence and, with her faithful helper Lieut.-Colonel Eva Smith, arrested a second time. They were taken from prison to prison, suffering privations, and witnessing horrors of cruelty that affected dear Eva Smith's mind, before they finally reached an internment camp.

'Retirement on her return home came as a deep disappointment. Mary so longed, as she put it, to make up on active service the years lost in prison. As it was, she set out, often alone, to lead week-end campaigns in the United Kingdom, and also held enthusiastic meetings in Paris and Berlin, where she was able to greet some of her many German friends.'

Dora, the youngest sister, was already living at home, working only part-time, in order to take care of her mother. Olive, who was doing relief work in Germany, working together with the Red Cross, was home for week-ends, so that there were four daughters and their mother living in the new home as well as a cousin and an uncle—Florence's brother—which made an extended family of seven. But the Booths had opened their home to others too, and drawn them into the family circle.

Mary's colleague, Eva Smith, had been in prison while her father lay dying. Florence promised him, 'I'll take Eva as another of my daughters, so don't worry about her.' She kept her word in spite of the fact that Eva's mind had been permanently deranged by her war-time experiences and the burden upon them all was heavy.

Bertha Smith, whose family had turned her out when she became a Salvationist, had been told many years earlier that her home would always be with them. She had cared for Catherine during her long illness and also nursed Bramwell before his death. Bertha brought with her another retired officer, and an officer colleague of Olive's, of some fifty years' standing, completed the household of eleven.

Catherine had retained her life-long passion for gardening and for creating gardens and she channelled all her creative and physical energies into transforming the grounds at North Court into something beautiful. During the war the RAF had kept lawns and ground under control, but no more. They had cultivated a vegetable garden, which was now managed by the gardener who had come with them from Hadley Wood. Catherine, with Dora's enthusiastic help, took over the rest. She had created a garden at Southwold and then at her little cottage at Finchampstead, where she had planted hundreds of daffodil bulbs (Olive remembers being dragooned into helping in the operation). But the grounds at North Court were on a far larger scale. She made a lawn for her mother to walk on every day and, as she remembered, 'I had the thrill of creating the pathways in the grounds, which had hardly been touched since the war; they all have special names—Popinjay's Parlour is one.' She and Dora cleared the woods, replanting saplings to more suitable sites. A larch that she planted when she first came is now a large and beautiful tree. Catherine also planned and planted a huge bank of azaleas, rose gardens and, again, hundreds of spring bulbs. She would begin work in the garden before breakfast, suitably dressed in a tweed suit, poke bonnet and sturdy boots bought for ten shillings at a jumble sale. Florence, when she could no longer walk or stand easily, would be brought in a special chair to sit where the sisters were working and be with them.

Catherine loved natural beauty as well as ordered gardens and when she was over 100 she claimed, 'They say our house has the best view in the village, we overlook such beautiful woods and fields. I'm very fond of trees and nature is still very important to me; to keep a few trees going that might otherwise be cut down is a great joy.' In spite of the log fires which burn cheerily in the drawing-room grate, it is the sisters' proud boast that they have never cut down a tree. The wood they use comes from natural wastage.

One compensation of retirement was the chance for the family to be together again. Dora explained:

'Our work took us all away from each other. We have all been frightfully busy in the Army most of our lives and didn't see much of each other. I don't think we wrote. It was a seven-day week and you went at it from when you woke in the morning until you fell into bed. We didn't have time for hobnobbing, except for our three weeks' holiday.'

They had always enjoyed one another's company enormously. Catherine wrote of it as one of life's chief hapinesses:

'We grew up and went forth to our work as officers of The Salvation Army. Nothing could exceed the happiness of meeting after separation! . . . The delight of meeting, the telling of old jokes, often against the teller, the delight of recounting new adventures, successes and problems of our work, the pandemonium as two or more told of new experiences. Singing together, praying together and feeling afresh our love for one another all combined to fill my heart with happiness!'

They were as uninhibited in their expressions of love as Bramwell and his generation had been. Letters written when one of them was away from home, or to mark birthdays and anniversaries, are as tender and private as love letters.

To Olive, on her birthday, when she was away from home, Catherine wrote:

'Darling, tenderest love, let us rejoice that you are spared to us. God gives different gifts and is not one of the *most* precious that we have each other? I feel so . . . Life is ours so long as God gives it and what he gives is full of joy and blessing. He means us to be happy.'

Later, when Wycliffe, the youngest of the family, retired from active service, the sisters helped him and his wife to choose a house not far from from their own. He shared Catherine's love of gardening and together they would discuss the planning of his own garden as well as that at North Court. 'He used to pop up to see us in the car,' his sister Olive remembered, although tours on behalf of the Army still took him overseas. Sadly, the onset of Parkinson's disease limited his unfailing vigour and a fall at a friend's funeral hastened his death in 1975. Bernard, the older brother, who lived to be ninety-five, retired to Aylesbury, near enough to come to North Court for special occasions.

There were other lesser loves that Catherine could now enjoy. One was her love of animals. 'One of the joys of being retired,' she wrote, 'was for me to own once again a small, affectionate self-willed Yorkshire terrier. Her name was Fancy. She loved me enough to refuse food if I were absent and on my return would dance in ecstasy uttering small sounds of welcome before rushing to devour the contents of her little bowl of food.'

Fancy had some verses written specially for her which seem to explain the choice of her name, because they begin:

> *Oh, shall I indulge my fancy*
> *And buy me a little dog?*

The answer was yes, and Fancy was bought at what Catherine considered an exorbitant cost.

'She was only about eight inches long, a darling little thing and such a character. If I was talking and she didn't approve she used to nip me at the back of my heel. Then one day I was able to catch her, I nipped her back and she never tried to bite me again! She began by being jealous of the robin who used to come and sing to me, oh so beautifully, when I was in my bedroom or digging in the garden. The dog took to chasing it away, but sometimes I wouldn't let her out with me because I wanted the robin instead. We've always been very fond of animals.' To Olive she once wrote: 'Fancy is sound asleep on my lap. I really am too fond of her.'

Catherine herself complained that even in retirement she found no time for reading, but her sisters recall her joining a 'literary guild' where, 'every month they gave you a list of books to choose from at reduced prices. She bought many more—it was one of her luxuries.' In spite of Bramwell's warning 'mind, no fiction', faithfully observed except during furloughs, Catherine found mental relief in some escapist reading. Dora said, 'She read mostly at night. The detective novel occupied her mind on quite another layer from that taken up by the anxieties of the Army or the household. Dorothy Sayers and Agatha Christie were two of her favourites—there's a whole bookshelf of her paperbacks.'

Now that they had a bigger house it was easier to accommodate visitors. Fellow Salvationists came to stay and one commissioner's wife remembers that however early their morning hour of departure, Catherine was always up to have breakfast with them and see them off. On one occasion she slipped away just as they were getting into the car, returning with a bunch of wild flowers picked in the wood near the house. She pressed them into her guest's hands 'with a wonderful prayer of farewell'. At Christmas time fifty or more people from the village would gather in the large drawing-room for a carol service.

Florence was still the centre of the sisters' adult lives, as she had been when they were children. They all adored her and thought her the most beautiful woman they had ever seen. Dora looked back on her influence from their earliest years:

'She was not from an Army home and was determined that we should taste all we could of the beautiful things. We were given the opportunity to learn to swim and to learn to ride. She gave us music lessons and helped us to read and to want to know. There was no restriction. She didn't allow any undesirable books in the house—of course not—but we were allowed a full range otherwise —comic, biography, and were especially encouraged to read history. We were much nearer to the deliverance of the slaves and the Civil War in America and I remember the best life of Lincoln was put within our reach and *Uncle Tom's Cabin*.

'All our lives our mother was what I call a reader-aloud. There was always a book on the go, usually being read to Catherine. She read aloud Churchill's *History of the First World War* and a strange book by Walter de la Mare. We'd come into the house and after tea Mother would get out her knitting—she could knit without looking—and her book. Catherine would be doing embroidery or making a rug. I often didn't stay long enough to hear the whole book but when I came home from my corps it was much better rest than everlasting Army talk. But that was before, when Mother was younger.'

Many years earlier Catherine had written in 'Personal Notes' for *The Deliverer*:

'September is a beloved month for us because it encompasses within it our mother's birthday.'

A few days after Florence's ninety-third birthday in 1954, Catherine wrote a letter to a friend:

This note is to thank you on my mother's behalf for your sweet letter on her birthday. We have now persuaded her to take breakfast in bed, and yours was one of the birthday greetings I gave her at breakfast. I read your letter through and we spoke of you together.

We had a happy day. Colonel Bernard and his wife were able to be with us, and our dear one lead (*sic*) us at Family

Prayers. It was lovely to hear her dear voice reading the Scriptures.

I hope you are keeping well yourself (here the typewritten portion ends and, as she often did, she appends a more personal, handwritten note) and *proving* the Saviour's presence is the spring of life.

Yours affectionately,
Catherine Bramwell-Booth

1956 was the centenary of Bramwell Booth's birth and to mark the occasion Catherine was interviewed on television by Malcolm Muggeridge, who was to become a devoted admirer, although at that time he did not share her faith. There seems to have been little sign at that time of the popular television success that she would achieve some twenty years later. She referred to the occasion in an interview with Harriet Chare for *The Times* in 1970:

'He asked me if there was anything for The Salvation Army to do now that the Welfare State was so well organized. I told him . . . ''You see, the whole point is to preach the gospel, to say there is a power in the world to change bad people into good people. Anything that comes short of putting man in touch with that power will come to nothing. Warm people, feed them, but never leave out the reason for warming and feeding them. My grandfather said unless you change a man's heart you won't change him . . . I said to Malcolm Muggeridge, as long as there are sinners in the world, The Salvation Army will be needed with its message of salvation.'

Death brought changes to the household at North Court. Bertha Smith died and the funeral service was held in the large drawing-room, before her burial in the country churchyard at Finchampstead. Two officers who knew her from the days of Women's Social Work travelled down for the occasion. One of them remembered it well:

'I got down there and the Commissioner said, ''You've got to speak.'' The service was not in a church but in the big lounge— the flag and the drum were there. And I said to the colonel I had come with, ''Oh, what *am* I going to do?'' and she said, ''I know how you feel—but you'll have to do it!'' And *I* knew I would have to do as she said. I did speak, but I can't tell you what I said. Then we went to the cemetery. It was a beautiful day and we stood there

—I can remember all the lovely trees and I thought, ''This is like the gates of heaven!'' Afterwards the family served us tea. You saw a different side to them when you were there. They were very sweet.'

Florence enjoyed seven happy years at North Court. Her daughters installed a special lift to get her up the stairs, so that in spite of failing health she was not confined to her own room until the last six months before her death in 1957. For her family she will always be the most beautiful woman they have ever known and she remains at the centre of their thoughts, because all that they value and treasure is the result of her influence on their lives.

The funeral service was held at the old Congress Hall and it was, as Olive put it, 'a proper Salvation Army funeral'. Catherine spoke to the large congregation and during the long prayer meeting moved among the crowds. At the end of the service several came forward to the 'mercy seat'. The burial took place on the next day, 16 June, by a strange chance the same date on which Bramwell had died twenty-eight years before. It was also the wedding anniversary of William and Catherine. The day was very hot. Catherine led the service in Abney Park cemetery, with all the sisters taking some part. Then Florence was buried in Bramwell's grave.

CHAPTER 22

Into the Limelight

AS THE HOUSEHOLD DWINDLED, the financial upkeep of the large house and grounds brought problems. Dora explained how they managed:

'We had to have paying guests so that we could remain here. That was better than giving up the house. And it was very good for us—it kept us on our toes. We couldn't come down to dinner looking like anything on earth because the ''PG'' was there, looking very nice, in her evening wear. We had some very nice people. Another thing, we couldn't talk shop, which was good for us. It broadened our interests. There wasn't much for them to do —they couldn't get to the cinema or theatre or anything, so to keep the place from getting dull, Catherine used to arrange things. She made much of every birthday in the house. We used to have a little ''hullabaloo'' so that it was a party. She invented extra days (to celebrate). I remember we had a terrific party for Leap Year and we used to have a party on 21 December, too, to celebrate the passing of the longest night. One time she came in as a little old lady—very short. She had dressed herself up. It must have been a tremendous strain on her legs because she walked with her knees bent. She had a voluminous pillow strapped to her and a skirt over the top. One year I was dressed up as her grandson. I had my uncle's trousers on—that was something unusual in those days. I wore a top hat, which I couldn't take off because I'd tucked my hair inside. She came in and greeted all the guests. She carried a little basket with a special small gift for everybody—a box of chocolates or a bottle of chutney—and she offered them all round. There were shrieks of laughter and the evening went, as they say, with a bang!'

It was some forty years earlier that she had entertained her cadets in a similar fashion—though the accompanying boy had then been her 'son'.

Catherine now settled in earnest to the task of writing a

biography of her grandmother, the first Catherine and 'Army Mother'. She said later:

'I can't say how long it took me to write the book. When I retired in 1949 I settled down to begin in earnest. Then darling mother was with us and I didn't want to rob us of our time together.'

But Florence had helped with some preliminary study of letters and papers, whose spidery handwriting had to be deciphered. By 1957 Olive had retired and was ready and willing to help:

'She read enormously for the book. She would mark the bits she wanted and I would type them out—I loved it!' But she admitted to calling a halt when it came to 9.30 in the evening, although Catherine was still at work. She immersed herself in her subject. A portrait of her grandmother hung where she could look at it constantly. In the preface she wrote:

'During the years of preliminary study I have lived in her thoughts, searched out her motives, become familiar with her idiosyncrasies; felt my pulse quicken as I have been drawn along by her zeals; experienced a longing to be young again, that I might better emulate her example. And from that useless longing came another hope . . . that my version of Catherine's story might be an inspiration . . . to venture all, as she did, in faith's certainty that "God is enough for us".'

In 1969 Mary died. Catherine described her sister as 'by nature a pleasure-loving, artistic, vital creature. To be an Army officer meant, in a literal sense, *daily denying herself*.' But her last years had been very happy.

'Mary enjoyed retirement very much,' Olive said. 'She was again able to sculpt and took up oil painting. At nineteen she had sculpted a bust of William Booth, copies of which are still being sold in the Army. She did a new bust of him, which is now in the USA.' Before she died, 'she was taken to hospital but as no more could be done they wanted to send her home. But there was an ambulance strike. Through the services of two friends an ambulance was finally arranged to bring her back. She lived only three days but was content to be at home.' She was not buried at Abney Park, as her parents and grandparents had been, but in the country churchyard at Finchampstead.

Catherine's definitive life of Catherine Booth was published in 1970 and received with acclaim. It resulted in a profile of the

author for the women's feature page of *The Times* and another
television interview, this time with Magnus Magnusson. One
viewer commented:

'She had that thing that eludes prime ministers and party
leaders, and great churchmen, and the heads of industry and the
trade unions, the perfect TV manner, simply because after the first
few seconds she was perfectly unconscious of being on TV at all.'
That is as it may be. What made the deepest impression was 'the
memory of her happiness . . . I never saw so contented a human
face. Yet how little had she enjoyed in her eighty-seven years all
the things that most of us, including you and I, have thought we
needed to cushion ourself against the thorns of life! No cigarettes,
no alcohol, no fine clothes, no luxuries of any sort. Hers has been a
long, sparse life of simple service to her kind, spent mostly among
degraded slaves of sin and pitiable victims of poverty, daily seeing
things that would turn most of us into cynics, but which to her
have been only splendid challenges to be met in the Power of her
Lord.'

A year later, in 1971, Catherine was accorded the CBE and
travelled with Olive and her brother Bernard to Buckingham
Palace to receive it. Olive remembers some amusement afforded to
Catherine by the over-zealous attentions of an official who had
been told that her sight was poor. He led her with great care,
warning her of steps and directing her when to sit down.

One Salvationist who turned out to see the Commissioner
described the scene afterwards:

'It had been announced that the Commissioner was to receive
the CBE from Her Majesty the Queen. I thought that it would
be a fine experience to see the Commissioner on this occasion,
and so on the 9th of February, 1971, I made my way . . . to
Buckingham Palace. I took with me a copy of the Commissioner's book . . . *Catherine Booth*, with the idea that there
might just be the chance of being close enough to ask her to
autograph it . . .

'Over an hour and a half went by, the guests began to leave, but
there was no sign of the Commissioner in the cars that came out.
Then, I just glanced back towards the archway in the forecourt of
the Palace and saw what seemed to be a picture of one hundred
years ago, for there she was *walking*, with her sister Colonel Olive
and her brother Colonel Bernard . . . the two sisters in their long

skirts and lovely bonnets and Colonel Bernard with his white beard. They were walking out together, without any fuss, and so I ventured over to ask if the Commissioner would kindly sign my book. She did this, leaning on the shoulder of Olive to steady her writing. She said, ''I hope the book will be a great blessing to you.''. . . By this time the national press had crowded round the Commissioner, asking her to pose and so on. She said, ''What good publicity for my book!'' '

At home there was a dinner party to celebrate. One of the guests wrote:

'It was a wonderful privilege . . . to be invited to join the family party last Tuesday . . . The memory of the beautifully decorated table will stay with us. I feel that a loving message of thanks should go to Dora, who no doubt was responsible. The pheasant was a wonderful idea. I hadn't eaten any for years.

'It was such a happy and delightful evening, thank you again for giving so much pleasure, and for twenty-one years of unfailing kindness.'

The following year Catherine took up her pen again, this time to write a strong complaint to *The Times*:

Sir:
Finding the expression of their thoughts by my fellow human beings of intense interest I have recently been 'sitting in' with Mr Parkinson and his guests on television. On Saturday I was one of millions who received various impressions of Mr Peter O'Toole.

The interview included glimpses of Mr O'Toole acting in several famous films. The last of these portrayed him impersonating my Lord and Saviour Jesus Christ: giving a burlesque of the Cross, blasphemously misquoting His words and engaging in revolting antics with a group of old women.

Is there, sir, no power in all the land able to prevent the instrusion into any programme of such a beastly travesty of Him whom I hold most holy, most worthy to be worshipped, most truly 'my Lord and my God'? . . .

There is a growing tendency to acknowledge the good in other great religions. Would the BBC tolerate the mockery of Buddha or Mahommet? . . .

What can be done to protect me and masses like me from such a wound to the spirit and such bitter shame as I suffered last night?

Catherine Bramwell-Booth

In reply, Mr Bill Cotton, BBC Head of Light Entertainment, stated that the person portrayed by Peter O'Toole was in fact a paranoid schizophrenic who *imagined* he was Jesus Christ. But he regretted the distress caused to Miss Bramwell-Booth. *The War Cry* commented truly that 'Not all Salvationists could express themselves in such eloquent terms or with such forthright challenge,' but added that 'few would not agree with her'.

In 1973 Catherine was ninety and suitable tributes arrived from Salvationists everywhere and Christians in other fields. The American evangelist, Billy Graham, sent a telegram beginning, a little archly, 'Word came to me that you will be 90 years young on July 20,' and continuing, 'You have a great heritage as well as effective leadership in your own right. May God give you many more birthdays to serve him.' His prayer was to be answered.

Catherine's own pleasure in the occasion came chiefly from a reprinting of a book she had compiled from her father's writings:

'Let me thank all my comrades who sent a greeting for my 90th birthday,' she wrote. 'The chief surprise, bringing me *intense* joy, was that the Publishers Hodder and Stoughton, to celebrate my 90th birthday, have reprinted a new edition of the selections made of my beloved father's words for every day.'

Olive explained that the book she spoke about had first been published by the Army under the title *Bramwell Booth Speaks*. 'She compiled this book at the time of her illness. It's a book of daily readings with a quotation from one of his writings, a Scripture passage and text and a verse from one of his hymns— they're all in the Army song book.' The book was given the new main title, *Trumpets of the Lord*.

Once the ripples of excitement had died down, Catherine entered a period of depression. She talked of it often in later interviews:

'I hadn't the physical strength I used to have to travel. I was always a bad traveller, but still I used to get through—travel and preach and stay in a strange house, then travel home. I can't do it any more, so I began to think I was no good. I stood on that door (step) you can see over there and said, ''Lord, help me to be reconciled to old age. Old age is thy ordinance—I didn't decide to grow old—you decided it for me''. . .

'The next morning the telephone rang. It was the BBC wanting to come down here and interview me. So they came with their lights and their cameras, and after a ten-minute interview, I became known to millions of people.'

It was 1976 when Peter France arrived at North Court for an in-depth interview with Catherine. The viewing public had their first glimpse of the entrance hall with its full-size Army flag, huge drum and life-sized bust of Bramwell. They gazed too as Catherine talked about the family portraits hanging on the walls of the large dining-room. Later the two sat and talked. Catherine told a *War Cry* reporter:

'Peter France helped me in that he just let me talk. He would say, ''It's all right. It's just what we want. Remember you are talking to millions.''

'He thought he was encouraging me, but in fact I was trembling from head to foot. He was frightening me. He made me feel I could sink through the floor. I prayed: ''O Lord, have mercy on me! Millions! Do help me to say the right things!'' . . .

'That was the interview that caused all the sensation and made me almost a Punch and Judy. You know what I mean: come and see this old woman!'

One unexpected and amusing result of the publicity she received and the quality of the interview she gave was that she received the Best Speaker of the Year award for 1977, presented by the Guild of Professional Toastmasters. In March 1978 *The Daily Telegraph*'s Ann Morrow wrote:

'Sitting bolt upright and wearing her black bonnet, Commissioner Catherine Bramwell-Booth . . . was still treating her Best Speaker of the Year award as a huge joke yesterday. ''You see, I did not make a single speech last year,'' she said with a light smile . . .

'While The Salvation Army is opposed to after dinner delights like smoking and drinking, the award, a rosewood gavel on a silver stand, is being presented to Miss Bramwell-Booth because of a recent television appearance.

' ''In twenty years I had never heard anything like it'', said Mr Ivor Spencer, President of the Guild, who has heard most good speakers in his time. The rules were altered and this remarkable lady with the sprightliest of minds was honoured.'

When the time came Catherine made full use of her opportunity to speak. She said afterwards:

'The room was jammed with television, BBC, press people . . . as I looked at them I thought, surely it is the Lord's will. They're here and they can't get away . . . So I preached to them and I don't think many of them liked it . . .

'At the end a man wanted to ask a question . . . He asked, ''Commissioner Catherine Bramwell-Booth, do you know you have the gift of the gab?'' So I said, ''Oh yes I do, all the Booths have it.'' '

In 1981, when she was ninety-seven, Catherine was presented with the Humanitarian Award for the year by the Variety Clubs International at their annual convention. To overcome any difficulties that might arise from the juxtaposition of Christian mission and show business, the programme was divided into two parts. After the first half, which included the award presentation itself and a colourful pageant of The Salvation Army—from its nineteenth-century beginnings to a projected future mission to the moon—Variety Club members 'will quietly depart for the Humanitarian Award Banquet,' Mr Eric Morley explained in the glossy programme. They would first be treated to a pre-banquet cocktail party sponsored by John Haig and company, whisky distillers. Catherine and her fellow Salvationists would remain at the Albert Hall, for what was billed as the 'first ever Salvation Army Promenade Festival!'

During the first part of the programme Catherine delighted the crowds by apologizing to HRH The Duke of Kent, who presented her with the award, for not being 'well up in etiquette where royalty is concerned', then asking him to convey her greetings to 'his princess' who had recently given birth to a daughter. 'May God bless you and your family,' she concluded. Then she turned to the crowd and, in characteristic fashion, used the golden opportunity to talk to them about Jesus Christ, her Saviour and Master.

The Commissioner had also encountered royalty the year before, when she had been invited to speak at a gathering of the National Free Church Women's Council in the presence of Her Majesty Queen Elizabeth, the Queen Mother. The venue was London's City Temple, memorable for Catherine because it was the place where, ninety-two years earlier, her grandmother had preached for the last time before her death. Both guests of honour had recently been ill, but both were well enough to be present, and the Queen Mother sat chatting with Catherine for some while.

Catherine became a well-known figure above all through her appearance on the Michael Parkinson and Russell Harty shows. Millions watched her, appreciated her wit and relished her ability to upstage her seasoned hosts. Both men have views on the reason for her success.

Michael Parkinson, who interviewed her twice, commented on her 'sublime ability to spread good will and humour wherever she goes. She was a wonderful television personality. She was totally natural, exceedingly articulate and her timing was equalled in my experience only by the very best actors and/or comedians. She knew exactly about the meaning of centre stage and projection and she had the greatest facility for up-staging the interviewer, as I know to my cost. The moment during our first interview when I carelessly said: "My money is on you reaching a hundred", and she retorted: "I hope that doesn't mean to say that you're a gambling man", remains for me the classic irretrievable situation. She is one of the rare people whose interview carries not just the sense of her philosophy but . . . the flavour of her personality.'

Catherine made a similar, innocent-seeming reply to Russell Harty when he asked her if she had let some 'rude or naughty word escape' her lips, when she was thrown out of a pub many years before by an irate publican. 'No, certainly not,' she replied, adding, 'I don't know any.'

Harty summed up her special television appeal:

'Whatever she says she is a performer—that means she knows how to look and where to look. She is used to platforms. She is also a highly intelligent woman, which means that she quickly learned the new tricks of television. She is also honest—television quickly gives away anything less than honesty. She needs no make-up—and make-up anyway cannot disguise pretence.

'Her humour is robust. When I asked her if she had ever suffered for her faith she agreed that she had but said that it was her own fault because she had been foolish. She did not speak sadly and convictingly against her enemies but took the responsibility herself.

'She is a woman of great nature, great guts. It is impossible to know how she will answer any given question. Sparks are always flying during conversation and there is an acerbic note. You can't squeeze her into any mould—it would limit her. She is too great to be contained in any single definition.'

Popular television appearances led to a flood of mail. From the time of the Peter France interview letters had been pouring in and Catherine found that a new kind of work had opened up for her to do. Some correspondents told of past family links with The Salvation Army; others poured out their sorrows over a bereavement or personal tragedy. 'It made me long for them,' Catherine said.

Many wrote telling her of the help and inspiration she had given them. Some asked for autographs or signed photographs, while others gave donations or a copy of their own verses. There were those who were sure that she would remember them from a single meeting long before. One asked her to contribute to a book and another to advise on a thesis on Shaw's *Major Barbara*. Some Catherine must have found specially moving or significant. A former editor of a London newspaper, since retired, wrote saying that he had 'a marvellous collection of (Salvation Army) memorabilia, dating from the 1920s, including my late mother's Bible which she was given, and used in family prayers, when as a young girl in her teens, she was in the employ of our dear old General Bramwell at their home in Barnet'.

Another Salvationist wrote from Devon where her eighty-eight-year-old mother was 'just sitting peacefully in an Eventide Home —often not recognizing even myself . . . Can you imagine what happened when I described as fully as possible your actual appearance on the screen? . . . My mother cried out, ''Commissioner Catherine! Oh, she was lovely—we worshipped her—Is she here? Bring her in!'' ' And later, ' ''Give Catherine my dearest love and thanks for her example.'' '

No doubt Catherine remembered her former cadet. She still recognized even the handwriting on the envelope of those who had served under her many years before. She wrote to them too. To one recently widowed she wrote—still addressing her by her maiden name:

'You have often been in my thoughts lately. Are you really settling to live alone. Somehow I can't think this is good for you.

'Don't bother to write unless you feel inclined to but I should like to hear if you are attempting anything in the writing line yourself. I think it would be good for you. I am sure you could write verse or how about a song? I remember how successfully you coped when in the Training College and we already have you in the song book! If we could meet and talk I should beg you to take this seriously. I am sure we ought not to neglect doing what we can do just because we are old.'

Another said, 'Commissioner has been wonderful these last years. When she speaks on television she speaks just like she is. The corps officer here in the over-sixties club had staged a *This is Your Life* and, to my horror, I was the victim. He's written to the Commissioner and this was her letter:

If I were to be with you on this happy occasion I should say, 'How lovely it is to see you!' and you would smile as you so often did in the midst of the rush of work at 280 (Women's Social Work headquarters). Looking back to the days when we served together I realize how your cheerful willingness to run the extra mile became something your comrades could count on, and your kindness and conscientiousness was a continuing testimony to the Lord's presence with you. Now that we are both retired and have not the vigour we once enjoyed, we cannot do all that we should choose to help in the fight for God and souls but we can go on loving and praying and the Lord is still able to work miracles and use the crumbs we have to offer to feed some hungry heart. May you have this joy! Do you ever sing to yourself? I do—and one of my favourite choruses is 'Keep on believing, Jesus is near. Keep on believing, there's nothing to fear.'

May the Lord bless you and keep you till we reach the end of our journey . . . Hallelujah! which means, Praise be to God!

No letters must go unanswered but the task was more than Catherine could manage on her own. The Salvation Army arranged for an officer who could type to come across and deal with the correspondence. Even then, until neuritis in her arm made rest imperative, Catherine would take up the pen, in her own long-accustomed manner, and add a few choice words at the end of the typescript.

Visitors as well as letters arrived at North Court. An endless trek of journalists arrived at the door of this woman who so late in life had captured the public imagination and heart. Interest was enhanced when it seemed that she would live to celebrate her hundredth birthday, still in peak form. Articles about her proliferated in newspapers, Sunday supplements and women's magazines. A succession of journalists described the authentic Salvation Army flavour of the hall at North Court with its drum, flag and bust of Bramwell. They wrote about the large dining-room table (the very same chosen by the first Catherine for her daughter-in-law, over a hundred years before), the row of family portraits and the large drawing-room, hung with the curtains that once belonged to Florence's parents and with the pictures painted by members of the family.

Journalists were usually invited to coffee. Strict protocol was observed. The two younger sisters received the visitor and it was only later, when the scene was set, that Catherine made her entrance, dressed in full Salvation Army uniform, which she referred to as her war-paint. Sometimes the journalist would be taken into a room where she was waiting for him. On one such visit a slight hitch occurred. Coffee and talk with Olive and Dora had gone on longer than the prescribed time and Catherine herself appeared in the doorway.

'What is happening?' she asked. 'I have been left like a pelican in the desert.'

During the inverviews Catherine told them about her idyllically happy childhood, when they ran barefoot through the countryside, of the pets they kept and of her love for the younger children. She decribed her 'perfect' father and adored mother and the importance of the 'Concern'—the Army that was to absorb every energy and faculty for the rest of their lives. She described the 'old General' in slightly more realistic terms than she had allowed herself to do as an Army officer in the pages of *The Deliverer*. She recalled the 'platform voice' which struck terror into her heart and the stern manner that made it hard for a child to recognize the affectionate nature which lay beneath it. She talked of her heartbreak at leaving home and the tiny cadet's cubicle, where only the moon linked her with home. She described her days as an officer and came at last to the fresh opportunities to talk about the gospel which had come to her when she had supposed that her useful life was over.

Catherine did not talk only about herself. She had discovered, from constant personal inquiry, that journalists are not often 'believers'. She still saw her prime task as one of bringing the good news of Jesus Christ to all with whom she came in contact and she used every opportunity to question her interviewer about his own spiritual beliefs. For, as she had written to young officers some sixty years before, 'the great fact remains that, unless we are saving sinners, our very existence as an Army is not justified,' adding incredulously, 'A Salvation Army that does not save!'

CHAPTER 23

One Hundred Years

THE AMERICAN EDITION of *The War Cry* for June 1983 carried an article by Major John Bate of International Headquarters:

'I recently motored down to the beautiful English county of Berkshire on a brisk, sunny morning to visit Commissioner Catherine Bramwell-Booth who will celebrate her 100th birthday on July 20. My visit had been arranged so that I could interview her for the American *War Cry*. The commissioner has often spoken of her regret that she did not have the privilege of visiting the United States, and so welcomed this opportunity to speak with American Salvationists from coast to coast.'

'If I live for that hundredth birthday meeting,' Catherine said in the course of the interview, 'I intend to have a song sheet and I intend to sing again and again the chorus for my own life, "Give to Jesus glory".'

Before that day arrived, there was a further flurry of reporters and photographers arriving at North Court and meticulous preparations were made, both at home and at Salvation Army headquarters, for the birthday celebrations. Captain Rob Garrad, Director of Information Services, was kept particularly busy ferrying journalists to and from North Court and stagemanaging the whole occasion. His press release for 20 July stated:

'The Commissioner will celebrate this special occasion by travelling from Berkshire where she lives with sisters Lt. Colonel Olive Booth (91) and Sen. Major Dora Booth (89) to London to attend a private reception at the Cumberland Hotel and then to attend a public meeting at the Salvation Army Regent Hall, 275 Oxford Street W1 at 7.00 p.m.'

Olive was extremely concerned that the day should not prove too demanding for her sister. She refused to have any photographers at the house other than one local one and, after persuasion from Captain Garrad, one from The Salvation Army. All the Commissioner's energy must be conserved for the evening meeting at Regent Hall, still affectionately referred to by Salvationists as 'The Rink'—a reference to its original use before being bought by William and Bramwell Booth in 1882.

An invitation to Catherine to take tea with the General was refused by Olive ('Catherine would talk instead of eat'). But, because of her diabetes, it was important for her to have some food before going to Regent Hall. A light tea at the Cumberland Hotel was decided upon, imagined at first as a quiet little affair. Catherine was persuaded to stay in bed for the morning, rising after lunch in time to greet the Lord Lieutenant of the county, who was due to arrive at 4 o'clock. He presented her with a message from the Queen. Then followed a surprise visit from the Parish Council, who came to give a speech of congratulation. The photographs were taken and the little party set out for London.

As soon as the car stopped at the hotel and Catherine started to alight, she was received and greeted by the Mayor of Westminster. Inside the hotel, the manager was waiting to make a speech and when he had finished his chef came in, wearing his tall hat, to present Catherine with a huge birthday cake, decorated with the Salvation Army badge. Olive asked him how he had managed to represent it so accurately and was deeply touched to learn that he had gone to International Headquarters in Queen Victoria Street to check on every detail. The press had gathered and must be seen and it was only with difficulty that Catherine was prised away from the most persistent and shepherded off to take tea in peace. Meanwhile Olive asked what was to be done with the cake. When she was assured that it was for Catherine, she made arrangements to take it home afterwards, so that it could have pride of place at the family party later that week.

At Regent Hall, Catherine sat on the platform flanked by her two sisters and supported too by her brother Bernard. True to her word, her first request, after thanking the huge crowd for coming, was to ask that they should all sing 'Give to Jesus Glory'. She resisted Olive's tug at her sleeve and went on to say, 'The whole of our experience and service is in that short chorus (I'll sit down in a minute, Olive). By being his witness and speaking our testimony, wherever we happen to be, we're giving to Jesus glory . . . Now I'll sit down.'

A birthday cake with 100 candles was wheeled to the front and later cut for everyone present to have a slice. (One officer saved two slices to take to a Salvation Army women's meeting that she was to address the following day. They were cut into small pieces for everyone to taste.)

The Queen's message was read out while all stood to attention: 'I am much interested to hear that you are celebrating your 100th birthday and send you my warm congratulations and good wishes. Elizabeth R.'

There was a special greeting from the Queen Mother too: 'I am delighted to send my congratulations and warmest good wishes to Commissioner Catherine Bramwell-Booth on the occasion of her 100th birthday.

'Through her dedication and high Christian ideals, Commissioner Catherine has been an inspiration to members of The Salvation Army at home and in countries throughout the world who will, I feel certain, be wishing her every happiness on this important anniversary. Elizabeth R, Queen Mother.'

The Scripture reading was given by Colonel Bernard Booth. He began in leisurely fashion:

'How lovely to be in ''The Rink'' once more—It's a long, long time—' But at this point Catherine, who did not allow others the privilege of talking at length, interrupted with: 'The one hundredth psalm for my one hundredth birthday.' Her brother, more in sorrow than anger, commented, 'Well, now the Commissioner has gone away with my introduction. That's what I was going to say!'

The General of The Salvation Army, Jarl Wahlström, made a suitable tribute to Catherine's many achievements and admitted her to the Order of the Founder, the highest Salvation Army award, instituted by Bramwell in 1917 to mark distinguished service. When the General cited her achievements and included her 'personal magnetism and literary skill, which would especially have commended her to the attention of our beloved Founder,' Catherine murmured, 'I hope so!' remembering, perhaps, the forbidding figure who had been her grandfather.

When it was Catherine's turn to speak, she said nothing of her own life work but made an impassioned plea for the Army to be faithful to its original mission to seek out and save men and women who had wandered away from God.

On a more personal level she dwelt on the passing of time: 'It's a very strange experience I'm called to go through now, living so near to death', she said. But Christians must use the present 'to stand up for the Saviour in whatever compay they may be.'

Mrs Commissioner Genevieve Cachelin, a daughter of Wycliffe and niece of Catherine, made the speech of thanks on behalf of the Booth family. For her, as for other nieces and nephews stationed overseas, North Court had been 'home' in England over many years and the 'Aunts' loved and valued confidantes.

'We want to "give to Jesus glory",' she said, echoing Catherine's quotation, 'for all that he has done in your life, Aunt Catherine . . . We thank Jesus because knowing you we have seen what Jesus can do in the life that is open to his Spirit and touched by his love.'

Before the meeting ended, Catherine asked for the Army flag to be brought to the platform. She looked back in time some eighty-five years to the day when she had been sworn in as a soldier in the Barnet corps. 'When I was sworn in under the flag we sang, "I'll be true, Lord, to thee." I want to sing it again on my hundredth birthday.'

Two books were published to mark Catherine's centenary. One was a collection of her verses, *Fighting for the King*, which she had written over the space of many years for her own private comfort and relief during the joys and griefs of her life. Major Jenty Fairbank helped her to select the verses and write the biographical preface. As Catherine checked each for publication she relived the particular situations that had caused them to be written. In the preface she explained:

'At night when I cannot sleep I often turn a thought into a line. As I lie awake a thought possesses the mind in a rhythm that governs following lines. Sometimes a group of lines make a verse. They come as a message to my own heart or as fitting for one I love, never with any thought of publication. But when it was suggested that they might be of help to others if published, I was delighted and felt it was almost too good to be true.'

The second book published for her birthday was *Commissioner Catherine*, by BBC journalist, Ted Harrison. He had been so impressed by a first interview with Catherine that he had asked to see her on a number of occasions in order to put together many of her memories of life and of The Salvation Army.

The Regent Hall meeting had been on Wednesday and it was decided that the family party should be on Saturday 'so that Catherine should have two days' rest in between,' Olive explained. With her customary personal and Army trained efficiency, Olive had written to key family members asking them to round up all the relatives they were in contact with and invite them to the Booth gathering. It was decided that uniform would not be worn, so that those who did not belong to The Salvation Army would not feel out of place. For some months beforehand Olive and Dora considered the best way to cater for the occasion. Sample sausage rolls bought from various bakers did not come up to standard, so in the end different friends contributed all that was needed, Madge, their cook, making the 'fancy cakes'. Not all those contacted had replied giving numbers that would attend and Dora admitted to being in 'a blue funk' that there would not be enough food to go round. At four o'clock on the day, a total of seventy-eight members of the Booth family converged on North Court. And there were enough sandwiches, sausage rolls, jam tarts and fancy cakes for all.

With the invitations to the party had gone the suggestion that gifts should take the form of contributions to a family cheque. This was presented by Bernard as everyone gathered in the drawing-room. One member of the family had made a beautifully illuminated scroll bearing all the family names as a lasting memento for Catherine after the cheque had been spent. (The first thing that she bought was a colour television set, which she thought that Olive and Dora would enjoy.)

A short Bible reading and prayer taken by Catherine completed the indoor ceremony and the guests spilled out into the grounds to enjoy the beautiful summer afternoon. Olive was amused to hear snatches of conversation between younger relatives which began, 'Who was *your* grandmother?' Everyone wanted to take photographs of their particular branch of the family and all wanted the three aunts to be included in them.

One niece, working for The Salvation Army in Geneva, wrote a few days later to her aunts:

'Thank you for having so many of us to the grand party, it was fun to get acquainted with some of the cousins once or twice removed . . . it was a special joy for our family to get together and this would not have happened but for the special celebrations . . .

As things return to normal for you all I hope you will enjoy a beautiful and peaceful summer's end.'

In August *The War Cry* reported a motion passed by Members of Parliament on 26 July, to which many signatures had been appended:

'That this House congratulates Commissioner Catherine Bramwell-Booth on attaining her hundredth birthday; places on record its admiration that her entire life has been spent in practical Christian witness which acts as a reminder of the untiring work which The Salvation Army has done for over a century in helping the homeless and unfortunate; and hopes that the ideals which have motivated her throughout her life, will be an inspiration to present-day legislators and politicians and that she will continue to enjoy life for many years to come.'

CHAPTER 24

The Last Enemy

TO ATTEMPT TO EVALUATE Catherine Bramwell-Booth's success in terms of wealth, fame or achievement is to use the wrong yardsticks. In her long life she certainly found both happiness and fame, and the list of her achievements is considerable. But these assets were not the goals she set out to reach; they were secondary spin-offs. Her life was set in a quite different direction.

Catherine's grandfather, William Booth, officiating at her dedication ceremony in the packed Congress Hall at Clapton, began his address with these words, 'It is the principle of The Salvation Army that everything we have or possess belongs to God.' That 'everything' included the new baby, so he turned to the young parents, asking them, 'Are you willing that this dear child of yours should be thus consecrated to God, and will you engage to train it for his service?'

When Bramwell and Florence made their responses they were not merely going through a form of words. What they had promised publicly they fully intended to put into practice in their home. On Catherine's sixth birthday Florence wrote, 'I called my loved one (Catherine) in to pray before coming down this morning. My heart was very full as I gave her again to the Lord. We mingled our tears.' It is impossible to calculate the effect of such an experience on a sensitive child but it is certain that Catherine grew up from her earliest days with the clear understanding that to please her parents she must learn to please the God they loved and served. That was their ambition for her, rather than success in any other field. How fortunate that the atmosphere of the home was one of love and happiness, so that belonging to God and pleasing him was as attractive and desirable as belonging to her own parents.

Once Catherine had embarked on her officer training, Florence admitted in *The Deliverer* that it had been her dearest wish that

Catherine should give herself to God in this way. For the Booths, commitment to God and total commitment to the Army went hand in hand. In spite of her protestations that no pressure was brought to bear upon her, Catherine must have been fully aware that a full-time career in the Army would be the obvious fulfilment of her parents' dedication pledge. It is not surprising that as a girl in her teens she recalled a growing sense of 'oughtness', as she put it, about the decision to become an officer, for she longed above all things to please the parents she adored and who, in her eyes, represented Christ himself. But she was far too definite a personality in her own right to accept at second hand the ambitions of others for her life. She had to battle until she had made the borrowed sense of 'oughtness' a personal response of duty and of love. Once she had decided that it was her own desire to give herself to God, she made a commitment that was total. Writing in her thirties to young officers whom she had trained, she said:

'When I gave myself to God, I gave all I was; and since that time what I do, I do unto Him. I do not consider I work for payment. Whatever I may receive in the way of money is God's, to be used in the wisest way, whether for my own needs or for the needs of others . . . Further, when I gave myself to God I decided He would know how to overrule so that I might be placed where He willed. I made no reserves; and while some kinds of work would not be so congenial to me as others, I can truly say that that willingness for anything is still part of my consecration.' (*Letters*)

The deliberate decision to forego all choice of personal gain or self-satisfaction is so costly that few make it. Many men and women have listened to the teaching of Jesus that 'whoever wants to save his own life will lose it; but whoever loses his life for my sake and the gospel will save it', but very few have believed it sufficiently to put it into practice. Catherine did.

She did not consider that her chosen life-style impoverished her, for she also wrote, 'the joy, the wonder, the heaven of being able to dedicate my bit of life, actually in everyday sayings and doings to the service of God, grows continually more real. Not that it costs less . . . but the truth is, I love it more and more; and when you serve because you love, lots of things do not count.' (*Letters*)

Catherine is not unique. Tucked away in eventide homes there are many Salvation Army officers of her generation whose radiant faces and satisfied old age flow from similar self-giving. Few see or know of them for they are not likely to compete for attention in the world's market-place. Catherine's case was different. Her connection with the Booth family, her exceptional abilities and her attainment of great age combined to bring her before the public gaze in a welter of newspaper articles and television interviews. She was a star performer. Her audiences loved her humour and quickwittedness, the way she so often got the better of seasoned interviewers. They enjoyed her as a raconteur. But they were struck most of all by her rich involvement in the human lot and her zest for life. This woman, who had utterly forsworn all usual pleasures and ambition, was more full of life and happiness at 100 than most successful human beings are in their prime. Here was no life-denying, spiritual mystic but, as Russell Harty put it, 'a woman of great nature and great guts'. She was a living testimony to the truth of Christ's paradoxical teaching. She had lost her life for his sake and the gospel's and had found it in abundance.

At 100 Catherine's feet were still planted firmly on earth and she still enjoyed living. She frequently said, 'I'm in love with living', 'I want to stay alive.' She showed that love of the familiar and those misgivings about the unknown that are the experience of every human being. 'It's a strange experience living so near to death,' she admitted. 'I don't like it at all. I don't think God's vexed with me because he made me as I am and that's how I feel.'

Malcolm Muggeridge spent a day at North Court in conversation with Catherine for a television programme to mark her centenary.

'I got a dressing down from her,' he said, 'because I said that I was looking forward to departing and she wouldn't have that at any price. She said that was a ridiculous thing to do, that life was good and wonderful and she herself hoped that although she was now 100 she would continue. She was pulling my leg a little, I think.' She was probably not, because a few years earlier, when Peter France had asked if she agreed that death, as well as life, might be a thrilling experience, she replied:

'Oh no, I think death is awful. I've sat with many dying people and helped them to die—I remember the very first— and I've also sat with those who were dear to me. No, I think death is the last enemy, the negation of everything that man is.'

But Catherine's hope of resurrection is sure and certain. The Marchioness of Lothian worked with her in the interdenominational movement of the Order of Christian Unity, which aims to study the words of Jesus Christ and put them into practice. One Easter, when Lady Lothian had a house full of young grandchildren, she talked to Catherine on the telephone. 'Give the children this message,' she said. 'Keep him to his promise, we *will* rise again!' The crowd of children ran around, singing the words like a hymn.

Catherine was confident that there is something better to follow death, in spite of the admission that 'the actual dying is a trial'. 'I do believe in heaven and a hereafter,' she affirmed. 'I think it is part of the revelation God has given. If you don't believe in it you've wiped out the whole wonderful scheme of God's purposes for making you alive . . . I don't know what heaven is like, and perhaps it's a good thing we don't because if we really could know, we shouldn't be content with earth, should we? . . . I think that if God has made this little short spell of life so beautiful, so full of wonders, what will it be like where he has prepared a place for us?'

Catherine also endeared herself to her public as being thoroughly human in her honest admission of doubt. She frankly admitted that for a while doubt had made faith in God hard for her to maintain. But she learned to use her doubts as vantage points to strengthen her own determination to serve God and to help others who shared her problem. The only way out of the fog of doubt, she wrote to her young officers, 'is to cease chasing the unsolved problems that surround you. Do not for a moment imagine that any doubting inquiry of yours can reveal or explain what God has chosen to veil and withhold'. In her personal life she learned to go on trusting and obeying God however she *felt*, but she never pretended that it was possible to know the answers to the great human mysteries of suffering and concluded that in this life God does not choose to explain himself.

Members of the family are usually better able to see the human weakness of a public figure than those who watch from a distance, but in Catherine's case her sisters think her perfect. All three are bound together by the strongest possible ties of passionate love and loyalty. While Florence Booth lived, she occupied the centre of the family's affection and care. At her death, Catherine stood in her place, as she had so often done for the younger ones when they were children. She commanded and received the respect of the other two. In a hundredth birthday article for *The Times* Shirley Lowe wrote, 'The Colonel (Olive) and the senior major (Dora) exist for their commanding officer. They . . . type out her manuscripts and speeches, fetch her knitting, keep her uniform pressed and mended, her flower-bowls filled and worry about her.' Dora herself explained, 'When we were children Cath took our parents' place and if she said ''no'' that was it.' But the price of leadership is responsibility. 'Catherine has been a wonderful tower,' Dora continued, 'when anybody was in trouble, sick or anxious, she was always there . . . It was always, ''Ask Catherine''. There is nobody left for her to turn to herself. But she carries her own burden; her great idea is to spare us.' That had always been Catherine's great idea.

Catherine's own estimate of her life and experience would be very different. She constantly referred to herself as having been 'so shy'—'so fearful'—'such a wobbler'. She admitted that 'I felt my nature was against what the Army was asking me to do.' But such statements were followed by the joyful assertion, 'When I look back now I feel—''Oh, Lord, thank you for the miracles you've worked in my life''.' When she was ninety she wrote to one of her retired officers, 'Now that we are retired and have not the vigour we once enjoyed, we cannot do all that we should choose to help in the fight for God and souls but we can go on loving and praying and the Lord is still able to work miracles and use the crumbs we offer to feed some hungry heart!' She shared with any other penitent, at the Salvationist mercy seat, a sense of her own inadequacy and of God's grace and power to do the impossible in a life given to him.

God was never in the wings but always centre stage in Catherine's life. His immanence was always acknowledged. She could not look at her beloved trees, smell the first violets in spring, listen to the birds or to a piece of music, without recognizing the handiwork of God. God was most surely present too in the family she loved so dearly. 'God gives different gifts,' she wrote to Olive, 'and is not one of the *most* precious that we have each other?'

God's personal presence in her life was real too. In one of her verses she had prayed:

> *Lord! let me walk*
> *In Thy dear company;*
> *For I would walk*
> *With Thee.*
> *Hear with a listening ear,*
> *Through all life's changing way*
> *All Thou wouldst say*
> *To me.*

There was no doubt as to God's nearness. 'God is near thee', was a favourite comment. God is close to every man, woman or child, whatever their condition or knowledge of him. The only matter in doubt is their response—whether, like Catherine herself, they would choose to look, to listen and to go, in trust and obedience, in the way God would choose.

'God be with you,' she said, at the end of a television interview, including the millions who watched. Then she added with utter conviction, 'And he will, whether you want him to or not.'

REFERENCE

LIST OF BOOKS AND JOURNALS
quoted in the text,
by kind permission of the copyright holders.

Bramwell Booth A biography of her father by Catherine Bramwell-Booth, published by Rich and Cowan, 1933.

Booth's Boots By Major Jenty Fairbank, The Salvation Army, 1983.

Catherine Booth A biography of her grandmother by Catherine Bramwell-Booth, published by Hodder and Stoughton, 1978.

Commissioner Catherine Catherine Bramwell-Booth with Ted Harrison, published by Darton, Longman and Todd, 1983.

The Deliverer Official organ of The Women's Social Work of The Salvation Army, first published in 1889, discontinued in 1923 and issued again from April 1928.

Fighting for the King Verses by Catherine Bramwell-Booth, published by Hodder and Stoughton, 1983.

Letters By Catherine Bramwell-Booth, first published in book form in 1921 under the title *Messages to the Messengers*; republished by Lion Publishing, 1986.

No Discharge in This War A short history of The Salvation Army by the late General Frederick Coutts, Army historian, published by Hodder and Stoughton, 1975.

The War Cry Official organ of The Salvation Army, first published in 1880 bi-weekly, later a weekly newspaper.

GLOSSARY OF SALVATION ARMY TERMS

Articles of War The statement of beliefs and promises which every intending soldier is required to sign before being sworn in.

'Blood and Fire' The Army's motto; refers to the blood of Jesus Christ and the fire of the Holy Spirit.

Cadet A Salvationist in training for officership.

Chief of the Staff An officer second in command of the Army throughout the world.

Citadel A hall used for worship and as a base for corps operations.

Colours The tricolour flag of the Army. Its colours symbolize: the blood of Jesus Christ (red), the fire of the Holy Spirit (yellow) and purity (blue).

Corps A Salvation Army unit established for the propagation of the gospel; generally with its central meeting-place and under the leadership of one or more officers.

Dedication Service The public presentation of infants to the Lord differing from christening or infant baptism in that the main emphasis is upon specific vows made by the parents concerning the child's upbringing.

International Headquarters (IHQ) The offices in which the business connected with the command of the world-wide Army is transacted.

Junior Soldier A boy or girl who, having professed conversion and signed the junior soldier's promise, becomes a Salvationist.

Officer A Salvationist who has left ordinary employment and, having been trained and commissioned, is (until retirement) engaged in full-time Salvation Army service.

Penitent Form or Mercy Seat A bench (usually in front of the platform in an Army hall) at which persons anxious about their spiritual condition are invited to seek salvation or sanctification or make a special consecration to God's will and service.

CATHERINE BRAMWELL-BOOTH

Promotion to Glory The Army's description of the death of Salvationists.

Ranks of Officers lieutenant, captain, major, lieut-colonel, colonel, commissioner.

Soldier A converted person at least fourteen years of age who has, with the approval of the census board, been sworn-in as a member of The Salvation Army after signing articles of war.

Swearing-in Public enrolment of Salvation Army soldiers.

From *The Salvation Army Yearbook*, 1985

INDEX

INDEX

INDEX

Parkinson, Michael 13, 38, 117, 211, 215
Parties, tea-parties 80, 81–82, 208, 211, 223–224
Prayer(s) 45, 85, 100–101
Prostitutes/prostitution 33, 34–35, 38–42, 61, 122, 168, 177–178
Public houses 90, 117, 128–129, 130
Punch 22, 57

Q

Queen Elizabeth II 210, 221, 222
Queen Elizabeth, the Queen Mother 214, 215, 222
Queen Victoria 41, 47, 57, 60, 78
Queen Victoria Street 31, 60, 138, 158, 191, 221

R

Railton, George Scott 67, 106, 135
Red Cross, the 155–156, 158
Regent Hall ('The Rink') 31, 220, 221, 222
Rookstone (William Booth's home at Hadley Wood) 73, 79, 131, 135
Russia 139, 163

S

Salvation Army—throughout, but particularly:
  Antagonism to 19–24, 35, 43
  Beliefs/regulations/practices 48–49, 59–61, 91–92, 93, 101–102, 121, 151, 182–183
  Dedication Services 16–18, 32, 46, 47, 126, 226
  Founding 26–27, 77
  High Barnet Corps 80, 88, 89–94, 223
  High Council 185–188, 192
  Homes 62–63, 95, 169, 170, 175, 176–177, 194–195
  Open Air meetings 89, 112, 113
Save the Children Fund 158, 159
Silvertown disaster 145–147
Smedley, Dr 67
Smith, Bertha 164–166, 167, 169, 174, 201, 206

Smith, Eva 201
Soper, Dr (father of Florence Booth) 19, 21–23, 24, 28, 29, 51, 66, 73–74
Soper, Florence—*see* Booth, Florence
Stead, W.T. 41–43, 56
Stitt, (Wm) Samuel 24, 78
Southwold 136, 200, 202
Sunday 89, 90–91
Sunday Circle 62, 108–109, 160–161, 173
Sunday Times, The 83, 130, 135
Sweden 162, 163, 164, 196
Switzerland 113, 136, 144, 157, 159, 160, 166, 224

T

Temperance cause 52, 93
Testimonies 49, 99, 126
Times, The 42, 119, 151, 153, 188–189, 206, 210, 211, 229
Training Garrison 68, 106–120, 128, 134–135, 139, 140–148, 151, 177, 196
Trumpets of the Lord 212

U

Uniform 147–148
USA 106, 133, 182
US *War Cry* 98, 220

V

Variety Clubs International 214

W

Wahlstrom, Jarl 222
War Cry, The, extracts from 15, 16, 32, 54, 55, 56, 60, 61, 80, 89, 91, 94, 103, 104, 106, 119, 122, 125, 129, 156, 157–158, 195–196, 212, 213, 225
War Office, the 155, 156
Women's rights 15, 52, 151
World War, First 139, 140, 145–147, 155–157
World War, Second 195–197

Z

Zeppelin raids 144–145